BELIEVE

A Memoir in Stories

CHRISTINA
H.
WILSON

BELIEVE

A Memoir in Stories

Believe: A Memoir in Stories

All rights are reserved. No part of this book may be used or reproduced in any manner whatsoever without the written permission of the copyright owner except for the use of quotations in book reviews.

Copyright © 2024 Christina H. Wilson

ISBN: 978-1-959811-56-5 (Hardcover)
ISBN: 978-1-959811-47-3 (e-book)

Library of Congress Control Number: 2024904339

Cover Designer: Okomato
Interior Design: Amit Dey
Photographs: Christina H. Wilson
Author Photo: Michelle Cibene
Editor: Winsome Hudson

Published by Wordeee in the United States, Beacon, New York 2024

Website: www.wordeee.com
X Formerly Twitter: wordeeeupdates
Facebook: facebook.com/wordeee/
e-mail: contact@wordeee.com

AUTHOR'S NOTE

This memoir is a composition of my memories and perception of stories that impacted my life. My recollection of events is derived from what I know of the facts. While there are always different perceptions based on what others may know, I have written these stories from my knowledge and remembrance. Except for my family and a few select friends, names have been changed out of respect for the remaining cast of characters, all actual individuals.

ADVANCE PRAISE

For as gentle and kind as Christina is, there is also a strength and courage within her to find a deeper and greater meaning in life circumstances. What she goes through, she grows through. It has been my privilege to help her along the way.

—Tisha Hallett, HT, NLP, EFT

I have had the pleasure of calling Christina the sister I never had. I consider her and the kids family. I have seen all the challenges and rewards that she has faced and never once did she waver in her belief, that everything happens for a reason. She is first and foremost a superpower Mom and the most generous, kind, loving person you could ever want in your corner.

This book is all about unconditional love for her family, friends, and for all seeking a path to self-acceptance. In her powerful memoir, *Believe: A Memoir in Stories* she reminds us that life is not about regrets, but about embracing every experience as a stepping-stone to becoming who we truly are.

—Gina Ford
Sister first, Friend second, and
CEO of Prime Sports Marketing last.

Advance Praise

From a seemingly fairytale life to a life-altering tragedy, Christina's journey is one of resilience, self-discovery, and unwavering faith. *Believe: A Memoir in Stories* explores themes of unconditional love, family, and the power of self-discovery. Embracing the belief that everything happens for a reason, she navigates life's unexpected turns, finding meaning in each experience.

—M. Gary Neuman,
NY Times best-selling author
Host of Better and Better Psychology Podcast

DEDICATION

**This book is dedicated to my mother, Anna L. Hom.
Without her, I would not be.**

A mother is she who can take the place of all others but whose place no one else can take."

—*Cardinal Meymillod*

There is no influence so powerful as that of the mother."

—*Sara Josepha Hale*

TABLE OF CONTENT

Foreword	xi
Introduction	xiii
Believe: Preface	xvi
Story One: Growing Up In A Big Family	1
Story Two: Befriending a Serial Killer	16
Story Three: Overcoming Betrayal	24
Story Four: Living a Trader's Life	31
Story Five: Unconventional Ways	47
Story Six: Lessons from an Angel on Earth	53
Story Seven: Some Amazing and Horrible Firsts	58
Story Eight: I'm Out	66
Story Nine: Welcome Baby #2	70
Story Ten: And Finally, Marriage	73
Story Eleven: I Wanna Be Rich	78
Story Twelve: Life With a Whale	85
Story Thirteen: The Highs and Lows	89
Story Fourteen: With a Litte Help, Changes Can Happen	99
Story Fifteen: Golden Era	108
Story Sixteen: Meeting with the President	114

Story Seventeen: Eerie Fulfillment. 143
Story Eighteen: Next Stop Houston 168
Story Nineteen: One Year to the Date 171
Story Twenty: Til Death Do Us Part. 180
Story Twenty-One: A Last Goodbye. 185
Story Twenty-two: Home. 189
Story Twenty-three: Always Around 194
Story Twenty-four: Blue Jay. 198
Story Twenty-five: I'm Here, Believe It or Not 202
Story Twenty-Six: The Wolf in Sheep's Clothing. 208
Story Twenty-seven: Here I Go Again. 217
Story Twenty-eight: Daddy's Girl 221
Story Twenty-nine: The "C" Diagnosis 224
Story Thirty: Things Happen in Threes 230
Story Thirty-one: Fool Me Once, Shame on You;
                Fool Me Twice, Shame on Me 235
Story Thirty-two: At Last, My Prince Charming 257
Story Thirty-three: Life with My Blended Family 264
Story Thirty-four: Signs, Signs, Everywhere There Are Signs 269
Story Thirty-five: I Do, I Do 273
Story Thirty-six: A Decade and More of Wedded Bliss 277
Story Thirty-seven: Hindsight is Twenty-Twenty 281
Acknowledgements: 288

FOREWORD

From the moment I saw Christina Wilson walking around the pool in The Bahamas in kitten heels, carrying a little human almost half her size, I knew she was someone special. Though she looked like a powerhouse, dressed in Chanel from head to toe, Christina's vibe was warm and welcoming.

When Christina shared that she was writing her book *Believe*, I was immediately drawn to the title and the concept of belief. Belief is a powerful force that can shape our lives, guide our actions, and illuminate our paths during the darkest of times.

Many of us have faced life's difficulties, emerging stronger and more determined. Christina's story is one of remarkable resilience. Her analogy of diamonds formed under pressure resonated deeply. In reading *Believe*, I was struck by the imagery of diamonds formed deep within the earth's core under immense pressure and heat. The transformation of carbon into these coveted gems mirrors the journey of our own lives—forged through challenges, struggles, and moments of intense pressure.

As a woman proud of her Chinese heritage, Christina embodies resilience, strength, and beauty even in the face of adversity. Like many women, emerging stronger and more determined than before has been shaped by the fires of life, and today is more radiant than before.

Christina's book, *Believe*, delves into the transformative power of belief. Belief, as Christina argues, acts as a guiding light, propelling us forward even in moments of uncertainty. Just as diamonds emerge beautiful and strong, so too can we transform lives of trials. Christina's story serves as a testament to the strength we all possess within.

May the beautiful words of my special friend, Christina Wilson, inspire you to reflect on your own journey, embrace your inner diamond, shine brightly in the face of adversity, and believe in the infinite potential within you.

Thank you, Christina, for sharing your story with the world. May *Believe: A Memoir in Stories* serve as a beacon of hope and inspiration for all who read it. I encourage you to embark on this journey of self-discovery with Christina as your guide.

With belief and gratitude,

Tracy Wilson Morning

Introduction

BELIEVE

Diamonds are revered and unique among all gemstones. Unlike all other stones formed in the earth's crust, diamonds are formed deep within the earth's dense, super-heated core under great pressure and at lava-level temperatures. Before becoming diamonds, however, the carbon has to melt into the earth's mantle under precise conditions. Without this process, in its exact order, we could never behold these coveted dazzling stones.

I have lived my life as a diamond. Deep, lithe, under pressure, with the ability to withstand, and I hope, with grace and beauty. Being Chinese, I would say that I am a yellow diamond with inclusions.

And, like everyone and everything else on earth, I didn't get a pass on the tumult and trials of life. I, however, got an advantage being from a Chinese family as family is valued above everything else in life in China. Cleaving to that belief I stayed the course with my family when many felt I should have abdicated.

From the start, my life has not been easy. There were things, some remarkable and some destructive, that tempered me into the person I am today. It is through my lens for thinking and processing the world, and my own compass of a direction suitable for me that I have navigated the hills and valleys of life.

Many will and have questioned my choices, but I believe circumstances do not identify who we are, or our character. How we tackle and move past those circumstances, good or bad, is what I believe truly defines the character and the maturity level of our souls.

If I could sum up all I wish to share in this book in one simple word—just one word that might help through the adverse circumstances that will inevitably impact our life's journey—it would be *Believe*. Believe wholeheartedly that your steps are ordered, and in the possibility of universal truth, you are yet to understand. When you believe, you are likely to receive the life you are meant to live.

What is it that I believe in?

I'm not sure when I started to think of life the way I do, but I have organized my life around these five beliefs.

First: Everything happens for a reason. Sometimes we don't understand why until much later, but the answer is always presented. As it is said, "Hindsight is twenty-twenty."

Second: What goes around comes around, so be aware and careful of your actions.

Third: Believe in who you are. Believe you are on earth for your purpose, no one else's. Though you may float through life without a clear understanding of what your purpose is, you will live your life with the drive to reach your potential if you believe that you have a purpose. You will be driven to pursue it and reach that goal.

Fourth: Believe in love. Love is all around and delivered to us all the time in often subtle ways. If you believe in the love you have for yourself and understand the love language of others around you, you will feel love all the time. Don't forget that you get back whatever you invest into it. Love and watch more of it flow around you. You just need to listen to your heart and let it reign.

Fifth: My most impactful belief is that someone, somewhere, (might be God, guardian angels, or both) is always watching out over you and guiding your steps. This doesn't necessarily have to be in the Christian, Jewish, Muslim, Buddhist, or Hindu contexts, but in whatever or whomever you hold omnipotent. Just hold close to the omnipotent power you believe in. This will in turn provide you with the security and strength to live each day. The omnipotent power hears our prayers. We are never alone; we have guardian angels who listen to our prayers and protect us. We must learn to recognize the signs and messages which confirm that we are being protected. Whether it's instinct or what you might call a gut feeling, I believe we are presented with signs all the time to guide us in the right direction, give us hope, or let us know that our prayers and voices are being heard. If you recognize and believe in the signs, they will lead you to where you are destined.

My life up to now has been a testament to all my beliefs. They have provided me with the faith, hope, and strength to get through everything that life has thrown at me. My wish in sharing my story and experiences is that I may provide others with hope or the ability to find it. My stories reflect my beliefs and my resounding truth: no matter how tragic life may be, there is a reason for what you're going through. If you believe everything will work out as intended, they will. I've embraced life not knowing what it held for me. My ability to let go and allow fate to happen, illuminated my path which became clear simply because I Believed.

Christina H. Wilson

PREFACE

Life was a whirlwind. We were young, we were in love and we were rich. Life with Jeffrey, a man who lived on his own terms, was the path to my purpose. The morning of September 11, 2000, at six a.m. when the phone rang, the news on the other end of the call would change our lives forever. It was not the beginning or the end of my story but it was a cataclysmic moment that joined the past to the present and to the future. In this whirlwind I called our life, I couldn't breathe long enough to know how I got there. To understand why fate had led me here, I had to look back.

Story One

GROWING UP IN A BIG FAMILY

I was born in 1964 and raised in Philadelphia. I am one hundred percent Chinese, first generation U.S. citizen, or, in slang, ABC—American-Born Chinese. I have often been called by the three names that have mirrored the stages of my life: Tina as a child, Chris in college, and Christina in my professional life. I have been given other monikers as well, which I chose to ignore.

Nothing in the way we lived as kids suggested we were not one hundred percent Americans. I'm more just plain vanilla American than exotic Chinese. Still, my roots are embedded in China and regardless of where shrubs get transplanted, the tree bears branches nurtured from its roots. My roots hailed from South China and were replanted in the U.S. when my great-grandfather first came to America to help build the railroad out West. After his assignment, he returned home to his family in China. My paternal grandfather, Song K. Hom, and my paternal grandmother, Sue Fong Hom, were both born and raised in the South of China. Song K., like his father, would later come to the U.S. joining the U.S. Army. He'd travel back and forth to Canton to see my grandmother. After their third child was born, Grandpop was sent off to fight in WWII. Taking advantage of the repealed Chinese Exclusion

Act of 1943, like many, Grandpop, post the war, took advantage of his military service to become a naturalized U.S. citizen.

Grandpop then went back to China and brought his wife and their three children, the second oldest being my father, to Philadelphia where he was stationed.

My father, Ben Lim Hom, and his older and younger sisters had spent their early childhood on the Pearl River in Canton, China. Now a sprawling capital city called Guangdong in Southern China, back in the 18th and 19th centuries, it was an important port on the Silk Road and known for its potent opium. Canton was the administrative center of trading for over one thousand years before Westerners arrived. In 1936, the year my father was born in a small farming village in Guangzhou, there was uproar as culture wars raged on. The city was subjugated to Japanese control but in 1949 China's communist party was victorious and the city fell to their control. Today Guangzhou is considered a financial center and boasts the famed double pebble, Zaha Hadid's avant-garde Guangzhou Opera House.

Dad would remember life in his farming Canton village, Toisan (Cantonese) as challenging, having to walk miles upon miles to get to school. When he came to the United States he was around eleven or twelve years old and Philadelphia was quite a city to behold. His father lived in the Northwest Philly neighborhood called Germantown and from his savings over the years as a military man, had opened a laundry and a Chinese restaurant, typical businesses for Chinese in America. Dad, who did not speak any English upon his arrival was remediated, to kindergarten at eleven years old. By the third grade, however, he had been mainstreamed and showed an inclination for the arts. Dad was doing great all around and because his father's business was also doing well, he had the opportunity to be the first in his generation and family lineage to go to college at the Philadelphia Academy of Fine Arts.

A brilliant artist and a standout at most sports, especially in basketball and football, Dad was quite a catch. After graduation, he secured a position as an Art director at KYW, an NBC affiliate in Philly but Dad's family believed it was the oldest son's duty to carry on the family business.

So, even though he was a gifted artist and had studied at the University with great success, there was no question about his career; he had to comply and join his family business. Family and traditions are the bedrock of Chinese life. Being a filial son, he worked in the laundry and restaurant family business when he graduated and Dad played his role well without complaint. Whether Dad was disappointed or not I never knew, but once he started working for Grandpop, he never painted again. My mom believed his disappointment was deep, but what I did know was, he was a hard worker and seemed indefatigable. His three younger brothers except his eldest sister who was my cousin, Sieu Fong's mother, and one younger sister were all born in America making them a family of six. All except my dad's eldest sister went on to college, the younger siblings becoming, a doctor, a dentist, a teacher, and a nurse. Though Dad became a businessman, far from his first love of art, his college years would yield him a great benefit—meeting my mother at a Halloween Party at the University of Pennsylvania's International Club.

As children, we spent time with our paternal grandparents during the holidays, and Sieu's mom would babysit us sometimes. My grandparents held tight to their old-school traditions, mostly with my dad and Sieu's mom. Where my mom's ideals influenced and changed my dad, Sieu's mom kept with the old Chinese traditions and even tried to make Sieu enter into an arranged marriage. Sieu would not have any part in this idea and married the love of her life against her parent's wishes.

My mother, Anna Liu, was born to a privileged family on the opposite side of China in the northern capital city of Shanghai. With a more cosmopolitan family upbringing, Mom and Dad's family had little in common. Mom's father, Matthew T. H. Liu whom we called YeYe, was definitely upper-crust Chinese and he vehemently objected to their marriage. YeYe came to the USA to attend Holy Cross University and then went on to Columbia University to do his Masters. After Columbia, he was summoned back to China by his parents. When he arrived in China, he was told his parents had made a proxy marriage for him and he was thus married to someone he never met.

After his years in the U.S., YeYe, being very Western refused to adhere to the proxy marriage so he left his family and went to Beijing. My grandmother, Betty J. Liu, whom we called, PoPo, happened to be at Dongbei in Mandarin (translated Northeastern University), studying literature at a time when it was uncommon for women to attend college. Because her feet had been bound, for a short period before the custom changed, to improve her marriage prospects, suggests she too was from a notable family and as it turned out, she was YeYe's dad's distant cousin. They dated and then married and went on to have four children, my mother, and her brothers. They lived in Shanghai where my Grandfather (YeYe) worked as a reporter. During WWII he was transferred to work in the State Department.

After the war, YeYe was sent to Japan to represent China at the War Tribunal. The family stayed in Shanghai. When my mom was in the third grade the family moved to join YeYe in Kobe, Japan where he'd been promoted as the first Council General of Nationalist China. The family then moved to Tokyo when YeYe was made the Charge d'affaires as there wasn't an embassy yet. My mom attended the Convent of Sacred Heart (a British school) in Kobe, Japan then the Taipei American School in Taiwan for High School. YeYe had become the head of Foreign Affairs for the European Department in Taiwan. In her sophomore year, YeYe was again transferred to El Salvador where he became Ambassador of Nationalist China, then he moved on to the Dominican Republic, and finally to Cyprus as the Ambassador of Nationalist China.

At the age of eighteen, Mom came to the United States for college and attended the all-girls Beaver College where she studied music. That was not her first love; she wanted to study international affairs and join her father in diplomatic circles. Unfortunately, not only was it

1957, when women were rare in the diplomatic circles, but her father discouraged her. Not knowing what she wanted to do, she tried her hand at business but that still left her unfulfilled. She was a good enough pianist so her professor suggested she majored in music. In her sophomore year, YeYe and the rest of the family moved to Cyprus.

The big house with endless parties, chauffeurs, maids, and a nanny for each child was the life my mother lived. A bit rebellious in her cloistered life, when she met my father, apart from him being attractive, he represented the opposite of the life she knew. The more her father objected to the relationship, the more she gravitated to him over her other choice, a Taiwanese student headed to do his Ph.D. in Aeronautics. She would find Dad more exciting because they were so different. She and my father would eventually marry but as her father had suggested their differing social class was a challenge to surmount.

Assuming her role as wife, she became pregnant about every year for three years, had a five-year reprieve then had another two children in less than two years, and she and their five children wanted for nothing, my Dad being a great provider. Mom went about raising us the way she was raised—open-minded. We took piano lessons and ballet, and Mom who was carefree and tolerant allowed us space to grow. Maybe sometimes too much space. Mom being privy to an international community and used to enjoying the privileges of a diplomat's daughter was quite open-minded and social. Tradition-wise she did not adhere to Chinese customs, so much so that we weren't even allowed to go to Chinatown in Philadelphia, where Dad's sister also had a restaurant. The dynamics of their social class played out in their marriage over time in myriad ways and was especially noticeable in my mother's conflict with my father's parents.

With a mindset of traditional villager beliefs, Dad's parents disapproved of what they thought was Mom's control over Dad. Strictly patriarchal, grandpop was head of his household. Mom tells the story of when she was pregnant my dad's mom forbade her to eat bananas, which she loved. Mom's way of handling the disagreement was to take her mother-in-law to the obstetrician and have him tell her bananas were great in pregnancies. Regardless, Mom would have preferred for Dad to stand up to his parents, but she never showed anything but respect for my father in the home. Their pain and hurt would show up in different ways.

My father worked hard for his family and his parents business. Located in the Germantown neighborhood of Northwest Philly, the businesses were around-the-clock establishments that kept him away from home a lot. Gone before we rose in the mornings and returning after bedtime, we mostly saw him on Mondays, the only time the restaurant was closed. I always looked forward to Mondays as our bonding day. Though Dad had to do all the shopping for the restaurant on that day, he'd also take me to the doctor for my treatments. Later Dad moved our family from Germantown to Wyndmoor, which did not please my grandfather in the slightest. However, when Dad opened another branch of the restaurant in Chestnut Hill which did exceedingly well, he garnered approval.

Wyndmoor was an upper-middle-class, substantially Jewish suburb of Philly and Mom was much happier there. One would have imagined after all his years of service his parents would have turned the business over to him but that was not their way. After some years, Dad was able to purchase the business from his father. One brother-in-law continued to run the restaurant in Germantown and his other brother-in-law took over the laundry. The family had done well for themselves financially, but the conflict would again arise from Dad's side as they thought my mother's influence over my father was greater than theirs. After all, they would argue, why waste money on sending girls to school, which to my mother, whose mantra was education, education, education, was a huge sticking point between the families.

I am unilingual as I didn't grow up with the Chinese language because my mother spoke Mandarin and my father spoke Cantonese. Since they had completely different dialects, we grew up speaking English at home. But I was very much raised with Chinese traditions, culture, and sensibilities on my father's side, and with a cosmopolitan worldview on my mother's. Regardless, being Chinese, my root is deeply entrenched in the family which according to a Chinese proverb, is the first essential base of human society; in other words, family is the pinnacle of Chinese life, and there are few things more important than family. That's how it was in my family. Unlike the Western world Taoism, Confucianism, and Buddhism, all based on the collective had early seeded my dad's values and hence my own. Additionally, my dad was very superstitious; although I think many traditional Chinese are superstitious and that's a trait I picked up from him. Habits like wearing red on holidays and "If you don't eat all the rice on your plate, you will have an ugly spouse." My grandma was the same." One never wears black on a holiday." I mostly adhered to them. Still, I wouldn't necessarily say I'm superstitious—not compared to my dad. Yet I often wonder, when one lives in harmony with universal truths for over three millennia, if these beliefs are ethereal mumbo jumbo, or if they are sage knowledge honed from intuition and years of keen observations.

When my parents were expecting me, they were certain I'd be a boy, since there were already two girls. I suppose intuition is not probability and they only had a boy's name ready—Alan. So, when I showed up they were stunned. "Oh my gosh, another girl." I was nameless for three days. I was finally named Christina after my mother's childhood friend, who became my godmother. Names in my family all begin with A's and B's, and I'm the only C name. All the A's are gregarious, the B's reclusive, and I in the middle, the perfect blend of both. Maybe this should have been the first sign my path would be different from my siblings.

I have two older sisters; Anita, who is two years older, and Betty, who is thirteen months older. They are diametric opposites. After me are my two brothers, Alan, (finally) and Brian, who are five and six years younger than me, respectively. So, it's three girls in a row and then two boys in a row making us a family of seven. If one believes in numerology seven represents a full and complete world. The number seven also represents insightfulness, intuitiveness, truthfulness, and being introspective, intellectual, and wise. It truly represents my beautiful family in many ways. I, on the other hand, had a position in the family of third. This obviously makes me the middle child, but to this day, my mom claims my sister Betty is the typical middle child because she was the middle child first, meaning for the five years before my brothers were born, Betty was the middle child. I find her rationale very amusing and to this day respectfully disagree with her summation. How could that be? I am exactly in the middle of two brothers and two sisters.

Prevailing literature associates the number three as a divine number. One connected to the universal energies, spiritual realm, and spiritual forces, all creeds of one who believes. My life would affirm that I am true to the number three but not as a middle child. Being extremely close to my mother I did not exhibit middle child syndrome which might be the reason my mom sticks to her belief my sister Betty is the true middle child. I love my family, and I love having a big family. It has always been a defining part of who I am. Being surrounded by family and children brings the most joy in my life.

All of my siblings have different personalities, and that made life fun, exciting, interesting, and definitely memorable. My mother, not a hands-on, helicopter, or hovering parent, and certainly not a tiger mom with an open-door policy, allowed us to experience the breadth and depth of our individual personalities. This would cause a skirmish within the family. Mom was driven by her heart and so would I be. Yet sometimes the heart needs to be reined in and my sister Betty would hold this in her craw against mom.

Anita, artistic, creative, independent, free-thinking, and explosive was considered the wild child, a lit cannon, Anita's boundaries were far and wide, and at a young age, she lived a totally experiential life walking on tight ropes, detonating things in her way, and balancing on adrenaline. With no rule book to follow, which she could have used, and my mother's more relaxed *laissez-faire*, anything-goes style of raising us, she had our parents doing hoops, cartwheels, and summersaults to keep up with her. This angered my sister, Betty, to no end. Good thing we lived by the police station as sometimes Mom would get a call to inform her Anita was climbing out the window!

Betty was a by-the-rule-book kind of child, and I think she was that way because mom had no rule book so she developed one of her own. Measured and completely centered, I rarely remember Betty getting into trouble. Alan was pretty laid back and Brian was a bit spicy. To this day we are like a pot of gumbo but we are all and will probably forever be in the same pot.

As my mom tells the story, when I was almost two I was sickly but at almost three years old, I got very sick. I had suddenly gone from being a precocious three-year-old to one who couldn't breathe and was lethargic to the point of not being able to stand up or do anything. Because I was having trouble breathing, my mom finally took me to the emergency room of a hospital in Philadelphia. They gave me epinephrine—unfortunately too much, which put me into a coma. At that time, they didn't know as much about asthma. This was in 1967.

Going into the third day of my coma, my mom decided she just couldn't sit there and watch me like that anymore. She followed her instincts, tussled with the doctor, and against the doctor's wishes signed me out of the hospital and took me to a different hospital. Within a day of checking into the other hospital, over an hour away, I came out of the coma. I celebrated my third birthday in an oxygen tent in the hospital. This would be the beginning of my Tina years. Tiny and all. I don't think my nickname, Tina was because I was tiny, though I was, but a shortening of Christina.

Because my father worked a lot, this left my mother alone with me and half-crazed with worry when he hadn't made it to the hospital during my time in both hospitals. The new hospital was over an hour away and it would take Dad away from the business for quite a stretch. When I asked my mother why she'd moved me, she said, "Sometimes you don't know why you do the things you do, but you have to trust yourself, your instincts, your gut—whatever you want to call it—and hope for the best. I believe things work out for the best, and things work out for a reason."

This turned out to be a statement by which I would live my life. I learned this from my mother who repeatedly trusted her heart and instincts, and it has served me well and primed me for the moments, when I too, had to trust my gut above everything else. I also got my heart from my mother and that has sometimes led me astray.

Severe asthma plagued me throughout my entire childhood. I spent much of elementary school in the hospital. I would spend long durations of time there. Every holiday and birthday I can remember in my youth was spent there. It's no wonder why "hospital" was one of the first words I learned to spell. In the Pediatric ward, I would be kept enclosed in an oxygen tent to help me breathe. My family would call me "the little girl in the bubble" but my dad used to say I was a little China doll, "so fragile." I would wonder in my future if I were a true China Doll.

Nowadays, with asthma one wears a mask or does a breathing treatment, but that wasn't the way in the 1960s. Because of my health, I grew up very sheltered and spent a lot of time with my mom. My asthma was so bad that I wasn't allowed to cry, and my siblings were warned not to make me cry because if I did, it would trigger an attack. I wasn't allowed to run or participate in gym class. My elementary school rooms would have to have special equipment installed to create dust-free environments. Even though I was sick a lot, when not in the hospital there were always friends around. There were days when everyone in the neighborhood would meet up at our house which was the community gathering place as there were five of us and all our friends would come over. I was puny but managed to have a playful childhood. Because I was five and six years older than Alan and Brian I would get to boss them around when we played school as I was always the teacher. I look back now and think it was a most wonderful childhood despite the health issues I faced.

With my dad working constantly at the family restaurant, I was my mom's constant companion. We went everywhere and did everything together. It's uncanny how my adult life mirrors my mother's in so many ways. By the time I was eleven or so, I would spend more time with my father as my sisters and I would work at the restaurant when I could. Anita and Betty worked a lot more than I did until Dad told Betty not to come back as she was scaring his customers away. I liked working at the restaurant because Dad would pay us. I loved even more saving my money and became a good money manager of my growing stash. I did have a vice, clothes, and that's where my money went. As each of us girls had different tastes in clothing, we rarely shared clothes and I loved buying clothes. I even got caught once by my mom when I skipped school to go to a warehouse sale to buy clothes; Mom was in the same line!

Only we girls worked at the restaurant as my brothers were given choices, work at the restaurant or play sports. They chose sports and were always at some sports practice or game. One thing Dad always did was attend my brothers' sports games. Dad would get quite worked up about the games as my brother Brian was always being fouled. I remember once when Brian, who truly was a superb athlete was playing a soccer match. He was dominating the field and someone from the stands shouted, "Get the ball from the chink."

I would attend the games with my mom as well and that was the first time I had seen or heard a racial epithet thrown at my family. My father was incensed but not quite as much as Brian. When Brian teed up the ball, he did so in a manner that when he kicked it, it landed right into the hecklers. Naturally, he was suspended but it was a moment of authority I appreciated. I had not faced racial discrimination and if I had, even in micro-aggressive form, I had not encoded it that way, so to me, my family was as American as apple pie. Racial prejudice had never defined my life but maybe because Chinese were considered the model minority, or because living in a predominantly Jewish neighborhood, people who themselves faced the sharpness of world prejudice, cultural, religious, and racial discrimination, prejudice was not at the top of their list. Jewish people carried the trauma of discrimination in their DNA and they vowed never to forget. It certainly was not anywhere on my mind as my 'type" was blond, blue-eyed, fit guys.

Though Anita was the hurricane that blew off roofs and increased our parents' tensions, there was always an undercurrent that was constant between my mother and my dad that had nothing to do with us, children. Forever my mother's sidekick, I would be the one to hear her frustrations and if I had any qualms with my dad's family it was because of that. I would visit with her friends, go on errands with her, and was always by her side. Mom made sure she provided me with lots of love and activities so I never felt left out of the fun going on around me. From her, I learned how to be a fixer. This bonded me to her in a special way. The funny thing is, I was also by far, the beneficiary of my father's love in the best way he could show it, so I always felt protected by my parents' love. Something about me made my family look to me as a problem-solving helper.

Possibly because I was so grateful to them for caring for me as an ailing child, and always wanting to give back in any way I could I'd be the first to volunteer for just about anything. My hand would shoot up when it was time to get things done and I earned the right to be the family go-to person, gofer in a good way. Nurturing and extreme gratitude became a part of my psyche and over-giving and over-understanding would show up in unexpected ways.

In the summers, Dad would take a week or so off from work so we could visit one of my mom's siblings. She has three brothers, all seriously accomplished. Uncle Jimmy, a polyglot international banker, lives in Singapore. Uncle Matthew was a Math professor in Wisconsin, and Uncle Tommy was in Textiles in South Carolina. We would always drive our Gran Torino station wagon to visit the Liu side of the family. Uncle Tommy lived on this wonder lake in South Carolina and we'd always go waterskiing and boating. I loved my mom's family and always looked forward to our yearly summer visits.

Back in those days passengers didn't have to wear seat belts, so my mom would make a big bed in the back of the car with blankets. It was always the boys and I in the back, because I was categorized as one of the little ones. Anita and Betty would be in the middle and my parents in front. Because we were in what was essentially the trunk, the luggage would be tied onto the rooftop of the car. Once when I was around ten years old, we were driving to Wisconsin. We were on the Ohio Turnpike and it was raining. It was about seven in the evening and the boys and I were lying on our backs, looking up and out the window so we could see everything speed by. As we were driving along, we watched in horror as a suitcase bounced onto the road.

"Dad, Mom's suitcase just flew off the car!" We shouted.

Dad slowed down and pulled off to the shoulder of the highway.

"Okay, someone, go get the suitcase," he said. It was probably less than half a mile back, but it was raining, not to mention the simple fact, it was the turnpike. My sisters glanced back at me before barking orders. "Tina, go get the suitcase." Neither of them budged. My brothers were too young so, yup, that left me.

What! How did they choose me? I was the sickly one and I was all the way in the back. Of course, always ready to help Tina, I did as I was told, jumped over the back seat, and there I was bounding down the side of the highway to grab my mom's suitcase. A driver saw me and slowed, his exhaust-spewing truck coming to a halt. He picked me up in his eighteen-wheeler, I got the suitcase and then he drove me back to my family's car. I thanked him, put the suitcase back on top of the car, and he drove away as did we, and that was that.

"Mom, how could you?" I said as it dawned on me how lucky I was to be back in our Grand Torino. If the truck driver hadn't been a good person, he could have just driven off and kidnapped me! "Am I the dispensable one? Is it because I'm always sick, it'd be easier to be done with me?"

"You know," my dad teased. "If it wasn't for you and your medical expenses, I'd be driving a fleet of Mercedes."

We laughed about it. But was it funny to me? It seemed so but I wonder. Did I somehow feel guilty about my family sacrificing for me? Was that why I was always so eager to help? I don't know what compartmentalization I was doing, though I am sure there were subconscious impacts. But with my family I was safe, I didn't feel burdened or impaled in any way, but that story stands out always as an example of our family dynamics. If someone needed to step up and do something, it was usually me. A problem solver, maybe I was really perceived as the "firstborn son" and that it was my duty to take care of the family. But I believe too, that my prickling mind and musings knew how grateful I was for their sacrifice. When I had means I was able to help pay for my brothers' college and gladly whatever they needed while there. I may have been the odd one out with two older girls and two younger boys, but I'm not complaining because I loved my position and role in my family. It prepared me well for the next chapters of my life.

By the time I was a teenager, I was getting nearly thirty-five shots weekly for all my allergies. There was nothing to make it tolerable except I was spending time with my dad who'd take me to get my treatments on Mondays. Since they could only inject six or eight shots per arm, I'd have to wait an hour before they could give me the rest. It would take all day to get all of my shots. Today they'll mix all those different allergens, but when I was a child, they injected each one separately! It's safe to say that I'm not scared of needles.

Despite the shots and medications, the first rule in our house was to avoid allergens as much as possible. I had a strict diet. My father, who used to roll tobacco and smoke it at age nine back in China had to give up smoking cigarettes. He moved to cigars and then a pipe which he could only smoke outside so he eventually gave up smoking altogether. We couldn't have curtains, rugs, or stuffed animals in the house because of the dust. Worst of all, we couldn't have pets. My siblings couldn't have animals and all their stuffed animals had to be kept in our garage/playroom, but that was just part of "life with Tina."

When I was about fourteen, my mom had had enough. "It's crazy that you're getting so many shots," she'd say. Whenever we went to the doctor, she'd asked when I would be done with everything. "Can't you wean her off of these shots?" she'd inquire. "Look how tiny she is! The shots are holding her maturity back."

So, slowly I was taken off the shots, medications, and steroids. It took a couple of years, but I finally started growing and developing when I was sixteen years old—when the steroids were out of my system. In ninth grade I was 4'11" and maybe seventy-nine pounds. I did a lot of growing in college and eventually got to 5'5" and 105 pounds. My mom's instincts and tenacity taught me to be an advocate when it comes to health issues.

My father, who never once complained about his life, was one of the hardest working people I knew and his success gave us, his children, the freedom to be footloose and carefree. I never thought about what it meant to him to give up on his God-given talent for the life he had to live. Were he in China, his succession rite of passage would be just that, but in a country where exploring the psychology of human behavior is a norm, I now can't help but wonder what my father had wished for his life. Did he wish he'd stood up to his parents and fulfilled his life dreams? It seems to me, that the pleasure he derived from his addiction to gambling, which would cost us our family fortune, was his outlet for frustration. Then again gambling is pretty much a Chinese thing, and maybe in Canton, a boat ride away from Macau, it was just part of the culture. I wish I had been able to ask him. His angst with my mother would be around his family who were also all gamblers. Loaded up to Atlantic City he would squander away all our financial security to the point of losing our restaurant. When my father died at age seventy, I understood why the tension between Mom and Dad could have been pent-up frustrations on both their parts.

Story Two

BEFRIENDING A SERIAL KILLER

There was a naïveté about me when I got to high school, some of which remained for a long time, even when I thought I'd come into my own. I was shy, reticent, self-conscious, and never really spoke up in class. Neither did I do anything to draw attention to myself. I think my self-perception was a little jolted from all the years I spent ailing. My childhood sickness, deep inside my consciousness, probably affected me more than I was aware of because I forgave too much, spoke too little, was too much of an empath, and avoided confrontation at all costs. And my self-confidence too, was not the highest.

Because I had been confined to the house a lot, I grew up very close to my younger brothers, Alan and Brian, and though I didn't have what I would consider a boyfriend until I was in college, I somewhat understood guys. As I got older, I became just as close with my sisters, Anita and Betty, which made me "good friend" material when I got to college. To top it off, I was a daddy's girl. Of all the kids, I was probably the closest to my dad. Maybe he felt more protective of me because I was sickly, but whatever the case, I was the light of his eyes until the day he died. And when a girl is the light of her father's eyes, she somehow feels special.

After high school, I ended up going to a private women's college, Hood in Frederick, Maryland. It became my only option as I had not applied to many schools and when they found out my grandfather was an Ambassador, well that sealed the deal. I expected to go there for a year and then transfer, to where I had no clue. The day I was leaving for college, my dad, as usual, was working so mom drove by the restaurant for me to say goodbye. Dad's eyes filled with emotions as he pleaded with me not to go. "Why don't you stay home?" he asked. "Please don't go to Maryland. You don't have to go to college. I will get you everything you need."

That was my dad's love language. "Get you anything you need." I remember when my sister Anita was fifteen, she went with Dad to look at cars and ended up sitting in a red MGB with white stripes. She loved the car so much she would not get out so Dad bought it for her. Of course, Anita couldn't legally drive it yet and I wondered if Dad had thought it through as Anita and a car spelled more summersaults. But that was his way of telling her he loved her, with hopes, I am sure, that she would return to a straighter and narrower path. Dad, a stereotypical Chinese man, was uncomfortable expressing his affections outwardly so buying things was how he expressed his love. My siblings and I knew how much he loved us, but I don't recall him ever saying, "I love you" to any of us.

Saddened but excited Mom and I were on our way to Hood College. Hood, named after its endower Margaret Scholl Hood, was on the sprawling twenty-eight-acre grounds and was beyond my expectations. A gorgeous campus, it exceeded my wish in every way. Chartered as a college to promote the advancement of women it lived up to its vision and became my new safe haven. Going to a women's college was the best thing that could have happened for me. At first, I was always quiet in classes, which probably stemmed from my low self-confidence. Following after my wild sister, Anita, and then my popular sister, Betty, and all else had stifled my identity as the last "Hom girl." I was a blend of the two and didn't quite know who I was then.

When I arrived at my dorm room, my assigned "Big Sis" had gifts she'd made for me with my name embroidered as Chris. I imagined that Christina was too long and she didn't know my family nickname, Tina. So, from that moment on at college, I became known as Chris. Hood was great. It allowed me to be on my own, which helped build my self-confidence, gain my unique identity, and become stronger and more determined to claim my life than I had ever before. In college, I was coming into my own, began appreciating my power, and having a wonderful time. Not having guys in classes led to a non-competitive female environment which was about learning. It was a relief not to have to doll up for anyone or to worry about what a guy thought of me or what I looked like. Success was on my own terms and that really helped me see what was important in life, not to mention it was the first time I had gone above and beyond in my studies, graduating an honor student.

Women develop a different kind of relationship than men do. We formed special bonds which helped me to become confident and independent. School was a canopy just like home, warm and protective. I had lots of friends, some of whom I have to this day, and we did not shy away from partying. I was one of perhaps a handful of Asian students at Hood. Because I was Asian, I was considered exotic and it was truly banal. So banal, one girl actually asked me if my vagina was slanted sideways. Looking back, maybe this was meant to be a racial slur, but I thought it was just stupidity. Being the "exotic" one in my group, my friends often dared me to pick up a guy, so attracting them became a game for me not to talk about boosting my ego. I was great at enticing boys but not fully seeded in my confidence, I had a non-committal attitude.

Annapolis was our unofficial brother school. We had a lot of eye candy and fit men to ogle. After my freshman year, I met who I consider my first boyfriend, Will. Will was a prepper, all the right private schools, and colleges, and a stint at Harvard. His family had money and his choice of career, as a documentary filmmaker, was privileged.

I had a type: fit, blond, and somewhat ambitious. Because most of the guys I dated fit this preppy profile my sister's boyfriend called me a gold-digger. This hurt me to the core and I was annoyed by that simple statement that stuck in my mind and jarred something in my psyche. I would later wonder why that statement had annoyed me so.

Will and I spent the summer of my sophomore year together and unfortunately for me, but good for him, he left for Paris to further his studies at the Sorbonne as he'd already graduated college. It turned out not to be that unfortunate for me either as I had the opportunity to visit him in Paris. But my naiveté was more than well demonstrated during that visit. Because my mom had traveled so much as a diplomat's daughter and knew first-hand the benefits of being a global citizen, she encouraged us to travel. My sister, Betty was in her junior year and doing a semester abroad program, studying in London. For Christmas, mom paid for Anita and me to visit her. Anita's boyfriend came along and we all decided to meet up with Betty and then go to France to meet up with Will.

This was my first trip to Europe and it was one of the most memorable of my young life. All five of us were packed in our rented Renault and not only did we *do* Paris, we went to The Loire Valley and other outskirt regions. Our shoestring budget had us all bunking in a single room as we traveled. The rooms always had double beds, so we would push them together and camp down. To this day my sister Betty, who did not have a boyfriend with her, jokes about the sleeping arrangement. She was always in the middle where the two beds joined. As she said, "she was in the crack," something we still laugh about.

After a week, everyone went back to London while I stayed in Paris with Will. When I was scheduled to go home, I had to fly back through London to catch my flight to the U.S. On the flight from Paris to London, I sat next to a clean-cut guy with a warm smile.

"You're so beautiful," he said. "Do you model?"

His earnest face struck me as nice, so I wasn't unsettled. "No, I don't. But thank you," I answered.

From there it was easy to strike up a conversation. He was a nice-looking guy in crisp slacks and an ironed button-down shirt and he was exceptionally well-spoken. I always go with my instincts, and my gut said there was nothing about him that made me feel funny, nor was I uncomfortable. He truly seemed like a good guy. When I arrived at London's Heathrow Airport, I found that my aircraft had left early, which left me stranded in London. I was booked on a Charter Airline, which was a lot cheaper than British Airways, but they followed their own rules. For example, if they filled up, they would just leave, even if it is not the scheduled departure time yet.

My sisters had already caught their flight back, my boyfriend was in Paris, and I was stuck sitting in the London airport alone, not knowing what to do. As always, my mother came to my rescue calling the American Embassy, who got me booked on another flight the next day. This meant I had to stay overnight. When I hung up the pay phone after speaking with my mother, I saw the man from my previous flight, walking toward me in his classy and appropriate Sherlock Holmes trench coat. He found out I had missed my flight.

"Chris, I'll give you money for a hotel, and when you get home to the United States, you can reimburse me. We'll exchange addresses," he said. "I want to make sure you get home safely."

His kind face only reflected concern, and I fell for it like a bear for honey. We exchanged details and I was grateful for his help.

The memories of that trip were priceless but when I returned home, I met someone else. Things with Will fizzled and I was no longer in a relationship. To my surprise, I didn't spend months behind closed doors crying at my loss.

Life just moved on. Anita and her boyfriend also went their separate ways but remained friends. I started dating again. In fact. I had a few admirers I juggled, including one at Annapolis and one at West Point.

When I returned to school, I sent my Paris-to-London travel companion the money he'd loaned me and thought that would be it. Then I started getting letters from him. I mean real letters as there was no email in those days. At first, they were just short notes telling me about his travels or just to say "hi," but then he started asking me to travel with him. After recalling our conversation on the plane, where he told me I was beautiful, I tried to tell myself I should've known. Apparently, my "China Doll" had struck again, but I never got the feeling that he was trying to pick me up and that he was just paying me harmless compliments. I was on to a new boyfriend by the time he started pursuing me and it was semiserious.

"Thanks, but I'm not interested, I have a serious boyfriend," I said and left it at that.

Then he started writing me letters asking me to forget about my boyfriend and go motorbiking with him in Australia, saying he wanted to take me to Seattle. He would tell me about his adventures insisting that I should be there. One time, he sent me spark plugs, with a silly note that said, "You sent sparks through me." For me this was another Ohio Turnpike moment, the innocence of the naïve. The idea that I could have been in real danger was never at the forefront of my mind.

"Something just doesn't seem right," one of my friends finally said, flipping through the stack of correspondence he consistently sent. "These letters are really weird. Creepy even."

Had I been watching some of the documentaries on duplicitous people I might have sensed this guy's shtick but I was too naïve for all that. All the men in those documentaries relentlessly pursue their victims and seem to have charmed lives of carefree abandon. Then one day up popped a story on the news about a serial killer who was murdering girls. The news mentioned his different whereabouts, which were some of the same places the guy wrote about in his letters. I began to pay more attention though I was not scared.

My friends, however, were jumping up and gasping. "Chris, this is the guy who is writing to you!"

Though I had stiffened, I said, "No." I thought, *No way.*

"Do not write to him, do not answer any more of his letters, just cut it off. You shouldn't be communicating with him anymore.

Don't do it. You listen to me, okay?" My mom undeniably agreed with my friends.

I just shrugged.

Honestly, I didn't know if someone alerted the school or if one of my friends had just blabbed, but the FBI showed up at my school to question me about the guy. They wanted to know what had happened and asked for his letters. They showed me a picture of the guy and it could have been the same guy but I was not about to accuse anyone without certainty. Acting for my best safety, the school removed me from all of their records so no one could trace that I attended the institution. Unfortunately, the man not only had the dorm hall phone number but the address of my school, though not my dorm. I was instructed not to answer the phone, and if the guy called, everyone was instructed to tell him that I had withdrawn from school and was no longer there.

A little time went by and nothing happened, so I started to think all the precautions were silly and people were overreacting. I had to be accompanied by someone wherever I went and I thought it was just unfounded paranoia. Then one day the hall phone rang, and it was the guy again.

He said, "Hey, I'm looking for Chris."

Whoever answered the phone gave him the approved line. "Oh, she withdrew from school."

"What are you talking about?" he asked. "I'm actually in Baltimore"—my school was in Maryland—"and I was coming to visit Chris."

Everyone was in a flurry. "Oh my god, he's coming to kill Chris!" I heard someone say outside in the hall. Somehow during that whole time, I wasn't afraid. I just didn't believe it, even though everyone else was terrified. Perhaps it was too surreal, but I just couldn't believe anything like this could happen to me. Later that day on the news, it was broadcast that the serial killer was spotted in Baltimore. Of course, we were glued to the television to learn every detail. Finally, it came out that he was spotted in New Hampshire attempting to cross the border into Canada, and when the police approached him, he committed suicide. I admit, it's never been confirmed that the serial killer and my admirer were the same person, but everyone else claims it was him. I never heard from him again.

If the guy I met really was the serial killer, I was lucky he didn't follow me to the hotel when he knew I was in London by myself. Was he the killer? Was he in Baltimore? I don't know. I do believe, though, that my guardian angels had surrounded and protected me. So many things could have gone wrong. But I was blessed. Of all the people in the world, why would he have picked me? They say predators have honed instincts to zero in on their victims. What message had he picked up from me if he were indeed the serial killer? That I would never know.

I graduated college much stronger than when I had started from being a sheltered, naïve child to blossoming into my own as a woman. Yet, I had been so protected and school was a safe and trusting environment that despite my coincidence with a presumed serial killer, I didn't grasp there were bad people in the world. Sometimes I question if maybe I chose to see the best in people, and that blinded me to the reality of what really is and the dangers that could lurk within. I would later find out that my trusting nature was both an asset and a liability.

Story Three

OVERCOMING BETRAYAL

The summer between my sophomore and junior year of college, I was dating, but no one too seriously. I had been juggling "friends" when I met Mack. I was four years younger than him and a rising Junior in College. Though he was older and already out of college, he fit my type perfectly with his tennis/surfer body and curly blonde hair. Having an older boyfriend who had graduated college and worked was cool to me.

I'd heard about Mack before I met him. Mack, Anita's boyfriend, who'd traveled with us to London, and his brother, had grown up and summered together in Cape May, NJ. Years later they became roommates. My friend from West Point was also a friend of Anita's boyfriend.

Mack's parents lived about twenty minutes away but his father believed that once you finished college, you were on your own. Our house with its revolving open-door policy was no stranger to transient people, so while he was in between jobs, Mack lived at our house for a while. I was away at college when he'd moved in and when I came home, ever the surfer guy, he was working a temp job as a lifeguard to save money to travel to Hawaii for a stint before getting another permanent job. My home was a perfect place for him to stay and save money and it was perfect as when we began dating I could go home on the weekends to see him.

Anita, being a girl around town and working in Philadelphia, ran in the same circles as Mack so she knew more about his rendezvous than I did. She also knew some of the girls he befriended and would see him out and about town with different girls. The thing is, when she told me these things, I was not hard-pressed to believe them because the day I first heard about Mack he'd been locked in a bathroom with a girl.

Anita didn't understand why Mack was living at our house and thought he was taking advantage of the situation. For some reason, she had a lot of animosity toward him. She said it was because she didn't like the cavalier way he treated me and didn't like the way he acted… completely non-committal. She also thought too, he was a bit of a womanizer.

Mack and I eventually broke up because, I too, now believed he was too much of a womanizer. Looking back, I recognize we were in different stages of our lives and while we were together for a year or more we mostly saw each other during the summertime when we would be together every day. While I was in college we would see each other some weekends, but not every.

Shortly after we broke up, Mack got into a motorcycle accident and was hospitalized. As I am always the empath and nurturer, I helped to take care of him when he was in the hospital. Mack moved back into my parents house and while he was recovering, we rekindled our relationship. When Mack got back on his feet he began working as a sales rep for a Fortune 500 company. We eventually broke up again, because of the same circumstances.

"He's bad news," Anita kept saying. "Forget him."

I didn't have any hatred or ill feelings for Mack after we broke up, which was always the case with my boyfriends. I always felt that if people liked each other enough to be in a relationship, they shouldn't hate one another when the relationship was over.

Instead of devoting my time to dating again, I focused on school. After college, I went back to live at home in Wyndmoor and got a job with General Foods in sales.

The fall after I graduated college, I did have a "secret love" of sorts.

It was a short but passionate, fun, and memorable relationship with a guy I had known since seventh grade. We had always been good friends, but never dated. Then one fall night, I went with friends to a bar we frequented, and my mystery man was working as a bar-back. He was home for a few months before he was scheduled to leave to attend law school. The few months we spent together were some of the best times I had ever had and while I knew that I had fallen hard for him, I was always aware that the clock was ticking on his leaving.

I think because we knew our time was bided, we made the most of it together.

It was easy to be in his company because we'd been friends for so many years, so it was like being with your best friend to the nth degree, with benefits. I used to wonder what would have happened if I had been honest with my feelings of love for him, but we both ended up having wonderful and fulfilling lives. My pride has always allowed me to make decisions that protected me from getting too hurt, so when the time came for him to leave, we embraced and said goodbye, like two old friends. This is how I liked to end things.

After this heartbreaking departure, I turned all my attention to my career. Since we were in the same business, I'd run into Mack a lot. About six months after my hire, I was promoted and transferred to a rural area in the mountains of Pennsylvania called Scranton/Wilkes-Barre, PA. It was my first time living on my own.

I was a sales specialist for one of the area's large food chains. My job was to sell our products to their buyers. The area of Scranton was a good ol' boy type of area, blue-collar and politically red. An industrial city known for its railroads and coal mines, its big sport is hunting and there is little to no diversity, with Asians and African Americans making up one percent of the population while whites made up eighty-four percent, Native Americans usually on reservations, Hispanic and Pacific Islanders made up the rest. Prior to me, General Foods had always had a man in the position and most likely a non-minority. So, the first time I went to see my buyers, they were shocked. First of all, I'm female. Second of all, I'm Asian, so they didn't know what was going on. The buyer said, "Oh no, no, no, we're not dealing with you. We want our old rep back." They called my district manager and said, "Listen, we won't do business if you don't send our old rep back."

Fortunately, my boss defended me and told them that I was the new rep and, "That's that." I appreciated her. She told me to stick around and see what happened. I nodded sternly and tried not to reveal any emotions, but my knuckles gripped tightly around my suitcase and white-knuckled I forged forward. So, I just kept going back day after day, and after about two weeks, the buyer finally decided he'd talk to me. It was difficult in the beginning, but they were intentionally trying to make it tough for me. They wanted to test me, maybe get me to quit. By remaining centered and not responding to the racial and misogynistic overtones inherent in the situation, it ended up being a great relationship and I was very successful.

Initially, I was to be in that position for a year or two, but after six months the district office told me I was promoted to New York City, which was the largest district in the country. *New York City?* I was shocked. I grew up in a suburb of five thousand people—with a sheltered, suburban upbringing at that; I wasn't a city girl at all. Even though New York was just two hours outside of Philadelphia, I never really went into the city. I'd been to the city with my family to see a *Radio City Christmas Show* but I'd never really spent time there. Perhaps I should have been honored because it was a huge promotion, but that wasn't my first reaction at all. When told the news, I started to cry. My boss was sitting across from me at her large desk. She looked at me in horror and pronounced, "Don't you ever cry." She was a very understanding but tough woman. Leaning forward, she started punctuating the desk with her perfectly manicured finger. "I know you might be scared and intimidated, but you can never show weakness." This probably struck a chord with me which I added to the arsenal. I stared at her questioningly. She sighed. "It is a huge honor, and you have to take it or forget your career here." She had a good point. It had only been six months since my last promotion, and I broke the boundary of being the first female in the area. I'd unquestionably proven myself valuable. It was indeed a big deal that they wanted me in New York, and it was going to be a turning point in my career. So, I took the promotion and moved to the Big Apple.

New York was the real kick-start to my independence. Going from this little rural hunting town to New York City was a challenge in itself, but it really was the best thing for me. A corporate transfer, General Foods paid for my relocation and put me up in a hotel until I found an apartment. As my main office was in New Jersey, I moved to Hoboken. At that point, Mack and I hadn't dated for four or so years, but we still had a passable friendship and he was in the same business as me, Corporate Food Sales. Mack's family had a summerhouse on the beach in Cape May, NJ and he invited Anita and me down for the weekend.

I wasn't privy to the fact that Mack and Anita had been dating as it had never come up. Anita had been in London working for a French bank since 1985 but had returned to Philly for eighteen months. Apparently, in the last few months of her stay sparks flew between her and Mack but she was due to go back to London when they realized they liked each other after all these years of being friends.

We had been out at some bars with a bunch of people before going back to the house. I was upstairs getting washed up, and when I headed back downstairs, I found my sister and Mack kissing. I just stood there staring, shocked, and hurt. I felt betrayed, mostly by my sister and to a degree by Mack. I kept wracking my mind as to why he would invite Anita and me. I was still under the impression that Anita didn't like him at all, so it completely blindsided me. Now I was wondering if she didn't like him for me because she liked him for her! Why invite me to his house if this was his plan? Was he trying to figure out which one of us he liked better? These were all questions with no answers as I hadn't been privy to their connection at the time.

"What is going on?" I exclaimed when I recovered my voice. Fury blinded me. I tried to blink it away, but the longer I stood there in that house, completely helpless, the more I threatened to explode. I was so mad that I ran back up the stairs to pack, more than ready to storm out. Anita and Mack came up after me. It turned out that it was not to apologize but to quiet me down as Mack's parents were sleeping in the next room. After a resolute snap of the suitcase, I slipped out of the room. I stormed downstairs and left in the middle of the night. From there I went to Betty's house because I didn't want to have to explain to my parents why I was showing up so late.

Betty and Kevin had recently married and built a house twenty minutes from our family house.

Distraught, I told my sister and brother-in-law the whole story. They consoled me and said while it wasn't a nice thing to do, they made me question what it was that made me so mad. I hadn't been romantically involved with Mack in four years and I didn't have any romantic feelings for him. Betty, my always protector, made me see I was completely in my ego and so she just shook her head and suggested that I get some sleep. In the morning, after I told my mom (of course since I told her everything and we spoke every day at least once a day) I headed back to my place in Hoboken. I needed to think about Betty's question but I was still too mad to care. I thought it was insensitive no matter which way you looked at it…they could at least have told me.

I didn't speak to Anita for about five months, and for me not to be on speaking terms with one of my siblings was a huge deal. It wasn't until Anita got a promotion and was moving back to London that my mother called to help change my mind. "Anita is leaving from a New York airport," she hinted. That was her way of telling me that I should get over the hurt and make amends with my sister before she left the U.S. So, of course, I followed my mom's advice and went to see Anita off to her next new adventure. No apologies were uttered; we just knew what was important and that was our family bond. Mack would join her in London, and they married a few years later.

Anita and Mack have been married for thirty-five years and have two amazing children, who like my other nieces and nephews are very dear to my heart. Mack was not my destiny but Anita's. His circuitous path to her as a friend, then lover was their journey. I happened to be the in-between. We are all very close and have spent many vacations together. I believe that the family is a priority and that love within the family is the most important element. I've always believed that what was meant to be, would be, which is the attitude that helped me heal from what I considered a betrayal which was not a betrayal but my ego. Had I set aside my ego immediately, I would have remembered what is most important…family.

My life would be very different had I stayed where I was comfortable and protected. So that promotion to what I call my "New York Life" would reveal a side of me I had not yet come to know as Christina. With sickly Tina and refusal to commit Chris behind me, New York would bring Christina into full view.

Story Four

LIVING A TRADER'S LIFE

I loved life in New York. I'd made a lot of friends and we would start our weekend partying on Thursday nights. Labor Day weekend 1989, I was out and about with my girlfriend, Cee Cee, a model/actress who worked in marketing for Ralph Lauren. The bouncers of the establishments we frequented loved us so we could get into just about any bar in the city. We were "questing," our silly term for going out on the prowl and it was great as both of us were single at the time. Wanting a new experience from our old haunts, we decided to go to the new happening spot on the Upper East Side, Sam's Café. This was Mariel Hemingway's place, and it was a really, really hot spot frequented by the yuppies. The place was packed to the gills and we were trying to squeeze our way in when we walked into these six or seven banker-looking guys trying to block our way.

"You'll have to hang with us if you want to get in," they said. As we bantered back and forth they were quite funny. Finally, they let us pass. Inside they started talking to us, buying us drinks, and we ended up hanging out with them all night. Being me, I started checking out the men to see who was the cutest. One was cute and came close to being my type. Fit, cute, suave, and maybe a little dangerous.

"Hey," the guy sitting to my left teased his friend, "You're taken, and your ball and chain is at another club?"

He was the loudest, brashest, and liked being the center of attention. Not my type of personality but I found him funny. Encouraged, he told me his name was Travis. He wasn't exactly my physical type either, usually blonde-haired, blue-eyed, and fit. Nor was he as tall as I liked. He had dark hair, a little stocky but honestly, he was not bad-looking...maybe he was even handsome, but his personality was big and he was infectious. Cee Cee was wearing red pumps that night so he called her "Dorothy." Everything he said was in good fun, and he made me laugh. By the end of the night, we are huddled up in the corner of the bar kissing. His huge personality had taken me totally off guard and I'd had a few whoo-whoo shots.

It was time to leave and I was headed to my car...I had a company car. Travis wasn't shy about asking me to drive him home. I ended up giving him a ride to 100 UN Plaza and thought him a jerk for asking me to drive him home. He asked for my number, and I gave it to him, not something I would normally do. Yuup, I could kiss them and leave them without a backward look but with this Travis guy I was doing things I never did. He seemed like a nice enough guy—charming, cute, loud, and the life of the party. He wasn't necessarily my type but he had plenty of personality, unlimited energy, and unending jokes that kept me intrigued.

That weekend I went home to Philadelphia for a bridal shower and returned to find a message on my machine from someone named Jeffrey. *Who the heck is Jeffrey?* I wondered. I called up my friend Cee Cee and asked, "Was one of the guys we met named Jeffrey?" At first, she didn't remember but thought it could be one of the guys we'd met at Sam's Cafe. She remembered one of his friends calling him Jeffrey. On the message, he left me a number and said, "Give me a call." I was curious to see who it was, so I dialed the number.

"How do I know you?" I asked.

"I just met you on Thursday night at Sam's Café, silly," he said and proceeded to explain who he was.

"I thought your name was Travis!"

"No…I just made that up. I thought you'd have guessed that," he said, laughing. That was Jeffrey; he loved pulling practical jokes. After a fun conversation, he ended with, "What do you think about joining me for dinner?" I hesitated because his lie about his name struck a sour chord with me as it was somewhat odd. Still, he was very comfortable to talk to and somehow I felt a connection to him. So, that Wednesday night we met at Lusardi's an Italian restaurant in New York. It was a very romantic restaurant with dark, old wood, red velvet chairs—the whole nine yards. He must have been a regular because the waiters seemed to know him. As soon as I walked in, the maître-d said,

"Oh, let me take you to Mr. Wilson's table."

Jeffrey was young, all of twenty-eight years old. To be called Mr. Wilson meant he was a heavyweight. I would be dishonest if I said I wasn't impressed. As a child, I was enthralled with fairytales. This felt like a fairytale moment. At the table I was shown to, Jeffrey was waiting with a chilled bottle of Dom Perignon champagne. Being a take-charge person, he ordered our meals. I found this quite mature and out of courtesy I ate what was ordered, some kind of creamy fettuccini though I am lactose intolerant. I would pay the price for that as when I took Jeffrey home I started to feel queasy and had to use his bathroom. I was so sick I sprinted to the restroom and as I was upchucking, all the jerk of a guy could say was, "Close the bathroom door will you?" I should have hightailed it back to Hoboken but I was too sick to drive. Despite what I considered insensitivity, we were together from that first date on.

I soon found out that Jeffrey worked on the American Stock Exchange as a trader. He had an exciting life, was doing very well for himself, and lived in one of New York's luxury buildings. But it wasn't always that way. Jeffrey's background was pretty similar to mine: He grew up in middle-class suburbia in Stamford, Connecticut, and went to public schools. When I met him he told me that he'd graduated from Harvard University but years later I found out that was another "Travis" prank or a lie and that he had attended Northeastern University in Boston. After he 'graduated,' he was a credit short but they allowed him to walk, and Lehman Brothers hired him. He quit after only a few months because he hated wearing a suit and tie every day, as to him, that was constricting. Like them, I'm sure, his quick mind had me captivated but his inability to conform should have given me pause.

Jeffrey truly was incredible with numbers, not just with calculations, he could figure out fractions in seconds and could memorize numbers and large chunks of information instantly. This made him the perfect card counter. With a photographic memory and visionary mindset, he was respected on the streets. He even wore a jacket with the words "Mr. Big" printed on the back. In the late eighties and early nineties, people were raking in and shoveling money as it was the birth of technology as we know it and Jeffrey always had the uncanny ability to see what was next. There was no question he was one of the more brilliant people the Street had seen, a genius of sorts who walked the fine line between genius and madness perhaps.

Around that time, New York had a lot of private gambling clubs under the guise of exclusive clubs where people would go play backgammon or bridge and bet fat stacks of cash. Wall Street guys flush with cash would flock to them because trading is a lot like gambling—a love of risk and quick reward. Jeffrey with his strategic mind was a good backgammon player and decided he'd make his living going to these clubs and gambling. Because he was so good with numbers and trusted his ability, he was sure he'd beat the odds. At the time, since he'd left Lehman, he was making ends meet with his gambling. He was living in a walk-up lower west side apartment with several guys, so he didn't have huge living expenses, just food and his portion of the rent so the risk-reward ratio was perfect especially since he always won. When he didn't have enough money for food he'd go to happy hours that had free smorgasbords and make a meal of the offerings.

After a couple of weeks, while playing backgammon, a man approached him.

"Why are you doing this? You should be down in the stock market. You should be trading and making real money," the mystery man said. The guy who may have been a scout for traders with extraordinary talent obviously, could sense Jeffrey had a knack and could strategize and see moves well beyond the next move.

"What would I have to do?" Jeffrey asked.

"Listen, I know this guy down in Florida who funds traders like you. His name is Neil. He backs guys enough to get them started in trading options, and you give him a percentage of what you make until you're even again. Go talk to him, see what happens."

Neil, a Wall Street man himself, and his wife, Joyce would normally be in New York but they wintered in Florida and it was the cold months. Naturally, Jeffrey flew down to Florida to meet with Neil. He even put on a suit! He'd used the last of his funds to buy a ticket and pay for a hotel as he was low on cash back then. Neil, who'd just returned from a trip to Africa, was quite sick as he'd contracted Malaria while traveling.

When Jeffrey called, Neil's wife Joyce answered and said he was unable to see him. Jeffrey called back every day and after three days she agreed to let him come over. Seems Neil liked him enough to help him by giving trading a shot. Jeffrey was hired and left Florida with a hundred thousand dollars account or something like that to start him off. The deal was a sliding scale with a sixty-forty split (Neil/Jeffrey) to an agreed-upon number and then a fifty-fifty split until the principal was paid back. Then the split would go down again (say, sixty-forty for Jeffrey and Neil) until Jeffrey earned a million dollars, then he could trade on his own. Ever the risktaker, Jeffrey never flinched about taking money that was not his and that he could lose and still be on the line for the money…he was undaunted because he had so much confidence in his ability.

Jeffrey went back to New York and under Neil's guidance and training, started making a lot of money. Once Jeffrey felt he understood everything there was to know, he started taking bigger risks. He would do things he probably shouldn't have done and would be cautioned by Neil but he continued making bigger trades than advised because he was a gambler at heart. Jeffrey was options trading, which is the ultimate gambling. In the eighties, trading options were big as technology advancement was skyrocketing. Traders would buy and sell securities on put or call bets that a stock might go up or down. If in your favor you win big…up or down. It was fast in-out, risky, and was just up Jeffrey's alley. But it worked out, and it didn't take long for Jeffrey to make the million dollars and split off from Neil's company. The split was mutually agreed upon and Neil continued to be the voice of reason for Jeffrey. Jeffrey had also taken quite a shine to Neil's wife Joyce, often calling her his mom.

By the time I met Jeffrey in 1989, he had his own company, Rockrimmon Securities, which consisted of a few friends and Jeffrey. They began making a lot of money. More than they'd ever seen. I was working for General Foods at the time, which was owned by Philip Morris, and they were trading Philip Morris, which we thought was a funny coincidence. As an options trader, Jeffrey only traded with his funds, and like Neil, he backed the traders with his money. Buying and selling large amounts of a stock quickly sometimes took just minutes and it was not at all like an investor who buys a hundred shares when a company starts trading and hangs on to them for years to make a million dollars. For Jeffrey, sixty seconds would be a long time to hold on to a stock. But the mindboggling amount of stocks he was trading at a time was enough to make or lose enormous quantities of money in seconds.

Eight days after our dinner, the following Thursday, Jeffrey asked me to pick him up at the AMEX building. My job was pretty cushy and flexible. I just had to make my numbers and it didn't matter how much or little time it took. I was usually able to get everything done in a couple of workdays so I was available to be with Jeffrey on demand, which he loved. Another perk was my company car as Jeffrey didn't have a car in the city I was his designated driver. When I picked Jeffrey up, he said, "I decided to go to my place in Florida for the weekend. Can you drop me off at the airport?"

Place in Florida! I thought, *Really? Can you pick me up? Drive me to the airport? This guy is so damn rude! Who did he think I was? What a Jerk.* Still, I shrugged and said, "Okay, whatever." I was thinking I'd drop him off and break things off for good. I admit I tend to err on the side of bad boys but he was a bit too much. When we arrived at the airport, Jeffrey said, "My flight leaves in two hours, so how about we have lunch inside the airport?"

These were not the days of TSA and security checks so anyone could walk into the airport and sit down for lunch. I nodded my head in agreement wondering where my break it off thought went. I parked the car as he went inside. When I met up with him, he handed me a ticket.

"What's this?" I asked.

"We're going to Florida for lunch," he said. His eyes sparkled mischievously.

My jaw fell to the floor. *This is crazy. I've known this guy for all of a week. There's no way I am going to do this.* "I'm sorry. I really can't. My mom would kill me."

"Come on. It will be fun. Call Cee Cee and see what she says."

Jeffrey knew I was really good friends with Cee Cee and might listen to her. So, I called Cee Cee, who'd been there when we'd met, and I asked her opinion. "Are you kidding?" she shrieked happily. "Go! It'll be a blast!"

I still insisted I would not go.

He interrupted my internal freak-out and asked, "If I can get your mom's permission, will you go?"

I probably should have been thinking of the serial killer from London about now but I wasn't, so out of my mouth comes, "Sure." Smug inside because there was no way Mom would agree, I dialed my mom and handed him the phone.

"I've been dating your daughter for the last week," Jeffrey says. "I have a place in Florida, and I'd like to take her there for the weekend, all expenses paid."

I am waiting for him to hand me back the phone after the flat-out no from Mom but he continues to talk.

"Does she have clothes or a toothbrush?" I heard my mother ask on the other end.

"No, but I promise you as soon as we get there I'll take her shopping for clothes and toiletries. She'll call you every day. Everything is going to be fine, I promise." Jeffrey could talk anyone into doing anything.

I just stood there, baffled at my mother's response.

"It sounds nice," Mom said. "Go and have a good time."

I couldn't believe it! "Give me a moment," I told Jeffrey.

My mom, who'd met every boyfriend and girlfriend of her five children, some even living in our house, must have probably felt she could trust me as I am level-headed. And then I remembered once when Anita had gone off with a bunch of guys as the only girl in the group and the cops, whose station was next to our house called to say Anita was at the station with a bunch of guys. When they asked Mom did you know she was out with a bunch of guys, my mother simply said, "Yes…and I know every one of them and I trust my daughter."

I was still blinking in disbelief at the response Mom gave but could no longer find a valid reason not to go. Since everyone else seemed to have agreed with Jeffrey, I said, more like muttered. "What the heck. I'll go."

He handed me a first-class ticket for the flight, and I think that was when I realized that life with Jeffrey would never be dull. He was everything the eighties represented on Wall Street: young, rich, and excessive. He wasn't the only one as it was the heyday of the technology glut and young guys like Jeffrey were all printing money and living the high life.

Landing in Florida, though his parents lived there, he immediately took me to meet Neil and Joyce, whom he called his mother/best friend. They were a lovely couple but I guess Joyce didn't think too much of me, thinking, of course, I was just the next girl Jeffrey would pop over with. She was with her mother and the first thing her mother asked me was, "So, what department store do you work for?"

"Who me? I don't work for a department store, I'm in corporate sales."

Her tone might have softened a bit but I was curious why she would assume I was a department store worker. I never asked but would later find out that Jeffrey often dated such women because he could use their employee discount to get all his fancy stuff and he would extend that benefit to his friends. It wasn't like he couldn't afford it but it was a win and everything was a game to Jeffrey.

Jeffrey's parents had relocated to Florida from Connecticut to a house in nearby Delray Beach. The next day we went to visit them. I noted that Jeffrey didn't seem as close to his family as he'd seemed with Neil and Joyce, except with his dad. I remember thinking how much Jeffrey was like his father: bold, loud, happy, and a gambler. Jeffrey had some ownership in a trotter, along with his grandmother Florence, which they raced in Harness races. Jeffrey, his parents, and Florence loved the thrill of gambling. This was not strange to me as my father was a gambler and that was another level of comfort Jeffrey depended on. I've always had the capacity to love people with imperfections. We spent a lovely, whirlwind weekend in Florida, and like a tsunami, I was swept away. It was probably more like being swept up in a tornado, but that was Jeffrey: larger than life. His favorite saying was "Livin' large."

By the time we returned, I was ready to give this thing a real try. I was young and the life Jeffrey led was sparkling bright. I liked sparkles. Who wouldn't at twenty-five? From that moment on I entered into the unexpected life I'd come to live.

I spent all my available time with Jeffrey and eventually moved in with him. Being so young, and with an inborn knack for living on the edge, I often wondered if some trauma Jeffrey could have experienced was the catalyst for all he was to become. Or was he truly walking the thin line between genius and madness? Or was he just Jeffrey, period?

Although he was a risk-taker, Jeffrey also had an incredibly disciplined work ethic. No matter how much partying he might have done he was ready for the next day. Like my father, he worked constantly and he'd come home every night and do research to prepare for the next day. He knew exactly what stocks he had, and how much he traded, and he read all the papers. He spent time going over what he called "his sheets" which listed all of his stock trades. His trading skills weren't just luck, he had skills and he'd put in the work. At that time, he was trading about four blue chip stocks: Phillip Morris, the United Airlines, Dell, and XMI (the AMEX Major Market Index).

Jeffrey lavished me with gifts like mink coats, Chanel suits and matching bags, and Gucci shoes because he always wanted me to look my best. He loved having me on his arm as his exotic partner as we painted New York different colors. He was very proud to have me on his arm and I was equally proud to be on his as he proudly presented me as his girlfriend. One Thursday night we went out with some friends and stayed out late. When we got home, Jeffrey was too tired to go over his sheets, deciding he'd get up and take care of his trades early in the morning. But he overslept and he went to work unprepared. That day strangely turned out to be Friday the 13th, the day the Stock Market had a mini crash when the United Airlines leverage buyout failed. Within minutes the market took a nosedive and Jeffrey ended up losing all of his money—not just a little bit. All of it! The market closed, and there was no way to make the money back or correct anything. But there was Jeffrey undaunted as if to say easy come, easy go!

Jeffrey's work was so stressful. I tried to provide him with a wonderful, stress-free environment to come home to every day. In the midst of the whirlwind of our lives, I too found myself giving away way too much of myself and doing way too much to accommodate Jeffrey's desires. At the time I felt it was the right thing to do. It was the heyday of the stock market so when people lost their money and physically had heart attacks on the trading floor, others would just keep trading around them. There was indeed a callousness to the Titans of the street. I felt our home needed to be a sanctuary.

Jeffrey was always in the heart of the trading. Everyone knew him. He was an active trader and his loud, huge personality was hard to ignore. He was one of the big traders on the street and while he would come home and do his research, he never brought the stress of his work home with him. No matter what had happened, his temperament never changed, and I admired that in him. That day, when Jeffrey walked through the door, I already knew he'd lost a ton of money. But he said, "Well, I had a bad day. I need to figure out where I go from here."

Over the weekend, he did a lot of research and talked to a lot of associates, and Neil agreed to loan him some funds so he could have another shot at making the money back. And, sure enough, Jeffrey went back to work on Monday and started to make his money back. Jeffrey's company, Rockrimmon Securities, was made up of friends whom he'd taught how to trade, and they were again doing very well. At the time they were clearing their trades through Spear, Leeds, and Kellogg, owned by Peter Kellogg. The company was again doing very well and then boom, Black Wednesday's ripple effects of the big crash of the UK market in 1992 brought sobering results. Again, Jeffrey and his traders lost everything, as a lot of people did, and this time it was five or ten times more than before. But again, Jeffrey never got too upset at home. He talked to everyone he could, and then he decided to go directly to Peter Kellogg this time. Jeffrey at the time, was their largest clearing customer.

Jeffrey's personality, brash, bold, and self-involved was one that you either loved or hated. Fortunately, Peter Kellogg loved him. Peter said, "Jeffrey, here's the deal. I will loan you ten million dollars. I want you to hire about thirty traders and teach them all how to trade because you *know* how, but the problem is that you take too many risks." Here was Neil's voice echoing in his ears. "Until you pay me back, you're not trading. That, or we're going to limit your trades." Peter told him. "You choose."

Ten million dollars was a vote of confidence and was a testament to Jeffrey's skills as a trader but Peter also understood Jeffreys's edge that leaned into the addiction of chasing the high above his business savvy. It was a huge opportunity and Jeffrey took the money, hired a team, and taught them the ins and outs of trading. As usual, he was successful and the company was making good gobs of money.

Peter then advised Jeffrey. "You need to diversify. I want you in Philadelphia, the New York Stock Exchange, the San Francisco Stock Exchange, and the Chicago Board of Options." More good advice to mitigate risks.

Jeffrey did everything Peter told him to do. Jeffrey was great at speculating stocks, and although he was a risk taker, he started restricting his traders' risks. He taught his traders to study the way he did it. Within a year, he'd made the ten million dollars back to pay off Peter and was able to start trading on his own accord once again. At this point we were young, we were rich, we were in love and Jeffrey was unstoppable. I am not sure life could have gotten any better. My ability to love Jeffrey the way he needed to be loved was maybe not over-giving or acquiescing but the result of two souls who fit each other's needs coming together. I'd come to truly love him.

Jeffrey always said all he wanted to do was make twenty million dollars he could stash it away and we would live the life he wanted to. Again, I'll admit it was seductive to be able to do and have whatever I wanted but money had never really been my driver, and deep down, Jeffrey and I were different, if complementary people. I was his exotic love he had sewn up with the high life but I was also a woman of my time. With more and more money life became flashier, louder, more extravagant and Jeffrey became happier and more invincible. I, on the other hand, had never been beholden to money so I mostly thought of it as Jeffrey's thing. I was happy in my job making fifty thousand dollars a year.

After working for four-and-a-half years, Jeffrey told me, "It's crazy that you're working for fifty thousand dollars a year. I make that in a day." He wanted me to be at home and said that I should be "living the good life." I don't think it was the money I made or the job I had; Jeffrey just wanted me home when he was there. He said he wanted to spoil me and buy me things and wanted me to live a life of leisure. I wasn't so sure about all that.

"That's ridiculous," I'd scoffed.

While I shot down the idea, it got me thinking about at least changing my career. I did eventually end up leaving General Foods and took a marketing position in New York. It was on Park Avenue and that exposed me to a whole other side of New York City. The East Side as opposed to Mid-Town was sedate and had deep, deep pockets. Quiet money. The trust funds set from old, old money were unassuming and secure in their lineage. Midtown, on the other hand, alive and vibrant, matched people who were more edgy like its landmark, Trump Towers. Ostentatious glitz, and more glitz, it fit Jeffrey to a tee. Jeffrey was not as bodacious as the Towers' owner but they exhibited some personality traits in common: sarcasm, the need to be seen, and an overinflated sense of self. As Jeffrey's net worth increased the more his personality tipped into this realm.

I didn't love this new job as I had my previous one, but it was in the city. I was barely at the job for four months and for myriad reasons it just didn't work out. One was because when the stock market closed at four-fifteen p.m., I would still be at work and in meetings until late at night. Jeffrey, who needed me at his beck and call, hated arriving home without me there. He wanted me to be available to go out and eat or meet up with our friends at the drop of a hat, but I was always working. For whatever reason Jeffrey could not be alone—he always needed someone around, preferably me so he had an entourage. One-on-one Jeffrey was the sweetest guy in the world but when he had an audience he would be loud, always needing to be the center of attention. Knowing his desire for me to stay home with Jeffrey's encouragement, I quit that position and started helping him out at the AMEX. He was always excited to have me there, dressed to kill and ogled by drooling traders. It made him proud. It was another way for him to be admired. Back then the mini skirt was in vogue, and mine were really mini. The trading officials would say I was a distraction! By then, Jeffrey had more than forty traders.

One of the things that solidified my deal with Jeffrey was his honest-to-God kindness. He not only gave to his family, he also gave to mine and just about anyone whether they needed his help or not. He was a giver like I had never seen before. My brother Alan had interned for Jeffrey the summer of his senior year of college. After graduating he'd go on to work for him at the exchange for an additional two years before moving on to his first love: professional sports. Alan, a star athlete, was drafted by the Pittsburgh Stingers, and until he got into a bad accident that left him without the use of his legs, he was active in professional soccer leagues. Alan's legs were so badly crushed they said he would never walk again but my indefatigable brother, not only walked, but he would also once again become an active player. After his accident, Jeffrey re-recruited Alan to help him open his Day Trade business in Boca Raton. He taught him everything he knew and Alan was the trader to open the office in Boca. Brian too was one of Jeffrey's summer interns and would later, for a short time, become one of his Day Traders. But Brian, an introvert wanted nothing to do with this world…it was just not for him. He'd go off to live a life he envisioned somewhat apart from the fold.

"Here's the thing to remember, Christina," Jeffrey always told me, staring at me with a passion that dripped from each word. "A workplace should be like a family. Don't settle for less." Jeffrey practiced what he preached: he got involved in the lives of his traders and we were out with them constantly. We even took the entire company and their spouses on trips to the Caribbean Islands. Jeffrey always thought that if he were good to his traders, they'd be good back to him—and more importantly, loyal. Everything for Jeffrey was done on a handshake. Jeffrey lent out millions of dollars without contracts. The traders could've made their money and left, but as he said, they remained loyal. Everyone who worked for or with Jeffrey loved him. But it didn't stop there. He gave to this cause and that cause and to people we hardly knew and it was not about showboating. Deep down, though not actively observant, he was a man of faith and he genuinely, from his heart, loved and wanted to help people. Though he would come off as caustic, everyone who has ever known Jeffrey will tell you that behind his bravado was a heart of gold. I recognized Jeffrey's enormous, generous heart and loved him for it. I would hold on to these memories in the many years to come. Not that he minded the endearment generosity earned him, but his big heart was my true driver.

Jeffrey was not a person anyone, including me, could say they knew through and through. I think mostly because he never knew himself. If I'd ever wondered, which I didn't, if Jeffrey was looking for love in all the wrong places, I never asked, because whatever his reasons for driving so hard, the results were good.

There was no way to be around Jeffrey and not feel indomitable. For me it was contagious. We were living the high life in New York City. Then Jeffrey upped the ante. We moved into an apartment at 721 5th Avenue better known as Trump Tower. Yes, the glitzy gold towers. Our apartment overlooked the South and West sides of Manhattan and we furnished it with leather couches, marble tables, and lacquered furniture. We had Christofle silverware, Baccarat crystal, and Pratesi linens. I was able to shop in what Jeffrey called the "C-stores" for Christina…Chanel and Cartier. He liked that because he always wanted me to be a standout, much like Joyce, Neil's wife, who to him was a tastemaker. Joyce was always coiffed to the nines and was a woman of means. Jeffrey thought I should be too. I was not opposed because nice clothes boosted my self-confidence; Even as a child, my secret pleasure was buying nice clothes.

We were now far from being faceless New Yorkers. We'd always be welcomed in nightclubs and restaurants where everyone knew everyone and we'd gathered quite a long list of friends by the time Jeffrey was cresting thirty-one. When Jeffrey turned thirty-one, I hosted a private surprise party for hundreds of friends and family at Maxim's, the chic restaurant club on Madison Avenue fashioned after its twin, Maxim's Paris. It was a chic and coveted place to get into. It was a night to remember and Jeffrey was in his element.

Money was flowing in like a river overflowing its banks. Jeffrey was the first person in the U.S. to own the new Mercedes S600 convertible, which we kept in New York since I no longer had a company car. After a year, we sent the car to Florida, where it joined his Jaguar XJSC, and soon after, Jeffrey bought his first Ferrari, a bright red spider. We'd arrived at a stage where we could go anywhere and do anything we wanted, and we did. We traveled the world over London, Canada, Amsterdam, Monte Carlo, Singapore, Malaysia, Bali, Thailand, Hawaii, and more…it was exciting. Because Jeffrey worked so hard, our winter vacations were spent in the islands or other warm-weather places. We stayed in luxurious resorts where we could just lay by the beach/pool and go to the spa. For dinner we always had caviar, pate, and champagne…life was good. We were "livin' large," just as Jeffrey wanted it.

Because Jeffrey loved life and loved people he was extremely generous and believed that when you made money, you should give money to those less fortunate. He took the meaning of "tzedakah" (Hebrew meaning charitable giving) to heart. The more he manifested this life of wealth and luxury the more he felt he needed to give to worthy causes, and the more the universe gave us back. I always used to remind him,

"What goes around comes around."

As a sickly child, Tina, I always read Golden Books and loved fairy tales. I loved the stories of knights in shining armor, princes, and other chivalrous men. At twenty-nine my Cinderella story was playing out right before my eyes. If there was anything to worry about, I couldn't ever imagine it. Life as Christina was truly magical and I was so grateful to Jeffrey for sharing his good fortune with me.

Story Five

UNCONVENTIONAL WAYS

After living together for four years, Jeffrey and I started talking about getting married and having children. Jeffrey had always wanted me to settle down, but my instincts told me he wasn't ready. There was still too much risk in him and I needed to feel certain and comfortable we could go the distance. But as I was approaching thirty, I started to think differently. Was I just being insecure about our future or should I consider marriage? Would I be able to go the distance with Jeffrey? The more money he made, the louder and flashier he became. He was like a beacon shining from a distance. The more he shone, the more hangers-on wanted to be in his company and the more he was debauching. Some of this behavior, this was the eighties the golden age of cocaine, was due to his drug use.

The bad thing about Jeffrey was that he had an addictive personality, which I'd accepted about him, but it was teetering. His gambling addiction was fed through his trading in many ways and was harmless, but he was also addicted to sex. His drug use escalated too which probably increased the need for sex so his philandering became obvious. I, being still quite naïve, and now coddled, never once thought of the demons that might have driven Jeffrey. Why was he always chasing a high? Jeffrey thought nothing of getting high on cocaine. I on the other hand refused to do drugs. As enamored and seduced as I might have been by this outer life, inside of me were Tina, Chris, and Christina and one of them had a backbone. I knew I was with a complex and conflicted man and what gave me pause was real, but his kind heart got me every time.

As I understood his insatiable need for sex early on in our relationship, when I knew Jeffrey was stepping out I told him, "Listen, Jeffrey, if you want to have sex with someone, you can, but I don't want to know about it. As long as it's not a relationship and it's safe. No phone numbers, no names. I don't want girls calling nor can you bring me home anything unwanted."

I questioned myself if I was truly willing to tolerate his infidelity, especially during this period when AIDS was a real conversation. When I mentioned it to my closest friends, everyone who knew about our relationship thought I was crazy. But I knew sex to Jeffrey was a stress relief of sorts and fed his ravenous need for adoration and acceptance. There were times I now wanted to know more about what made him tick. Was there a psychological driver he didn't understand himself? Jeffrey was respectful to his mother whom he always called by her first name; but didn't have the same kind of relationship he had with his dad. I might have briefly wished in our moments of true intimacy and vulnerability that he would be moved to share the man behind the mask with me, but that never happened. Life was too fast and furious and Jeffrey would never allow himself to be alone long enough with his mind to think that deeply. That was just life with Jeffrey, surface deep. I think his sanity depended on his keeping moving.

Still, there was no question in my mind that Jeffrey loved me in the only way he knew how. I was his possession and his tight ownership rights were skillfully balanced by his kindness and generosity. So, I accepted it all, right or wrong and turned a blind eye to it. I felt we had an honest relationship, which was most important to me. As long as everything was out in the open as I couldn't abide lying and expected total honesty from those I love, I moved forward in the relationship. I didn't feel the need to reciprocate his cheating—if you could really call it that. Since he wasn't having clandestine relationships, and I had given him permission, I decided to wait him out. If he'd been in a serious relationship, I as the other woman would have been concerned as Jeffrey called me incessantly, day and night, when we weren't together. Jeffrey would call to talk to me because, for some unexplained reason, my voice brought him a certain peace. He probably recognized that few women would tolerate the chaos of insecure success but I, on the other hand, he trusted to be in the foxhole with him no matter what. He could have his cake and eat it too. I might have been naïve but I was not *non corpus mentis*. I had a protective shield over my heart that buffered me from unbearable pain. Because I had a father, who despite his gambling addiction, loved me, I knew love and judgment were different beasts. I was therefore a woman who knew how to love and protect myself and I could love Jeffrey for who he was—if not totally unconditionally, at least with a great deal of understanding. For what is love but the acceptance of all there is? Yes, I loved Jeffrey in his imperfection and his love for me was a trump card I owned.

In that light, when Jeffrey said he wanted to get married and have children I had my doubts he could settle down. I'd grown up with the fairy tale dreams that my Prince would come one day and together we'd live happily ever after, but I'm now well aware that even a Princess's life was not without trials. I didn't believe in divorce and a huge part of me felt I didn't need marriage as Jeffrey was already emotionally committed to me. Maybe I could have hedged my bets and married him, and if it ended in a divorce I could have claimed half of what he owned. But I was not who Betty's boyfriend had called me…a gold digger. I can't say I wasn't charmed by the lifestyle Jeffrey afforded me but if ever there were doubts, I knew then for sure I was not that. I was not with him for his money. I had simply fallen in love with a man who had a lot of money.

Financially I never worried about money with Jeffrey. There was no "yours" or "mine." Jeffrey set up joint banking accounts and we had joint credit cards. I was free to spend as I pleased and he trusted me to handle all our personal finances. He set up companies in my name to make me feel financially secure. We already lived like we were married so I was in no hurry. Jeffrey made me feel completely taken care of and totally provided for me. But Jeffrey kept insisting we marry and I'd wonder late at night: *Is this the one I'm going to be married to for the rest of my life?* I really battled that, especially since Jeffrey had wanted to be married after only six months of us being together. In my upbringing, one does not just marry a person, they marry a family, and though initially our families got along, there was tension as I believe they considered me somewhat of a usurper of their successful son and maybe an outsider. Jeffrey, as I said, was generous to his family. They wanted for nothing. Still, he was conflicted with their sense of entitlement so I was the one to visit when Jeffrey didn't want to. One thing I know for sure is that I had always disliked his family calling me a Shiksa—derogatory Hebrew slang for a gentile woman, and our relationship was fine until it wasn't. Jeffrey's Aunt Fran and Uncle Herb were the exception. Both Jeffrey and I adored them. They've been married forever and had a great relationship. I thought maybe Jeffrey and I would be the same. They were good influences to emulate so there was hope.

Once when they came to Boca, they stayed with us for a few days. Uncle Herb felt they were an imposition so Jeffrey wanted them to feel more comfortable hosting them at Mar-a-Lago. Uncle Herb always tells the story not because of their stay at Mar-a-Lago but because when they were leaving, Jeffery and our son, Sam took them to the airport and Jeffrey was able to go on the plane with them and Sam got to sit in the cockpit.

All our friends were getting married and starting families. I have always loved children. *Why am I waiting? What's the exact reason?* I would mull this over and over in my mind. I wasn't getting any younger and I'd been on birth control forever. My sister Betty had a hard time getting pregnant and had to take hormonal supplements. I figured if she had problems, then I would definitely have issues after having taken all those steroids for asthma when I was young. It could be years until

I gave birth so I went to my high-risk OBGYN for a consultation. I shared my concerns and he suggested I go off the pill and give my body a rest. After telling Jeffrey the doctor's advice, we decided that I should go off the pill. I figured, if it is meant to be, it will be.

It'd been Jeffrey's dream to get married in Israel. Jewish, though not particularly religious, he was a man of faith. He occasionally went to Temple on the High Holy Days and celebrated Hanukkah and Passover. It was more of a loyalty to his heritage or a feeling of belonging than anything else. Jeffrey was very dedicated when it came to supporting Jewish organizations. He was donating a lot of money to the Jewish Federation, which supports Jewish organizations worldwide. Around that time, the Federation was hosting a mission to Israel, so Jeffrey signed us up to attend with the notion that we could get married. Since it was only October and we were scheduled to leave in April, I had time to think about getting married. Maybe my days as noncommitment Chris were truly behind me.

Right before Christmas, I went to the doctor because I wasn't menstruating. I figured the changes from stopping the pill were affecting my cycle. Instead, I found out that my holiday gift was that I was pregnant. I could hardly believe the news. "Are you kidding me?" I asked my doctor, who just smiled.

"It's great news! Just be careful. Don't go on to the mission. I'm not confident about the medical care you'd receive in Russia," which is where the trip would commence.

I was elated. I loved kids and I knew I would be a good mother. Jeffrey was home when I got in. I sidled up and said, "I have good news and bad news. Which do you want first?" I knew he would say the bad news, as that was always his way. So, I said, "Bad news is that I can't go on the mission in April," to which Jeffrey gave me a worried look since we went everywhere together. Jeffrey had access to me 24/7 if he wanted and he was none too pleased as he wanted to get married in Israel. Quickly, I added, "The good news is, I am pregnant." It took a second for my statement to register. Jeffrey stared at me blankly. In that seemingly endless space of time, my palms started sweating. Then he shot up.

"Yes!" He started jumping up and down and cheering in excitement. He was literally jumping for joy. After Jeffrey's celebration, I broke the last bit of news. "There is just one more thing. There is no way we are getting married now. I will not have anyone think that I trapped you into marriage."

I'm headstrong and made the decision that we weren't getting married, but we were definitely having a child. I did not believe we needed to be married to be committed any more than we already were. I am not someone who feels the need to conform to what is viewed as the norm. I don't care what other people say or do; I do what I feel is right for me. With my beliefs and superstitious nature, I took my getting pregnant and not being permitted to go to Israel as a sign I wasn't supposed to get married at this time. Since I am always tuned into the universe I pay attention to signs and for me, this was a big one. Jeffrey didn't agree but obliged my conviction and most of all, he wanted me to be happy. He went on the trip to Israel and I stayed home. It never crossed my mind that what goes up can also come down and often does, because our balloon just kept rising and rising.

The mission was a couple of weeks long, so for the first time, I had some freedom and independence. When Jeffrey returned, he was excited about the friends he'd made, one being the popular NY Pediatrician, Dr. Barry Stein, and coincidently another guy, Jimmy, whose wife was also pregnant and not able to make the trip. Of course, Barry became both couple's doctor, and Jimmy's wife, Bridgette, became my dear friend.

Jeffrey loved Israel and we agreed that one day we would return as a family.

We didn't get married and we welcomed our first child, Samuel, on September 3, 1994.

Everything happens for a reason.

Story Six

LESSONS FROM AN ANGEL ON EARTH

When I stopped working for corporate America, I wanted my free time to be well spent. It was wonderful to have no set schedule but there is just so much idling about one can do. I enjoyed lunches with friends and shopping and I loved clothes but there is only so much meaninglessness one can engage in and I needed more in my life. With Jeffrey, I knew I was fortunate to live the way we did, and I needed to give back. My heart was and is always for children. While Jeffrey was at work I started getting involved in different charitable organizations.

I was introduced to someone working for the American Cancer Society at a time when New York had just started a group called Young Friends for the American Cancer Society. It was made up of young philanthropic-minded corporate people who planned events to raise funds for the ACS. The group had a "Buddy" program that paired a child with a volunteer. It was the perfect opportunity for me. They matched me with a little boy named Willis, who was in remission from stomach cancer. He was nine years old and his family, from the

Dominican Republic, didn't have a lot of money so they'd turned to ACS for the support they needed.

My role was so rewarding. I got to spend time with Willis, taking him to sporting events, going bowling, or taking him to events at the ACS. It was just my responsibility to have fun with him and it was the furthest thing from "work."

When I first met Willis, he was healthy but still being monitored for cancer. He was still bald from the chemo and bloated from the medications but had the most beautiful, heart-stopping smile and flawless brown skin. We were buddies for a few years, and I loved every day I was with him. Right before I got pregnant, Willis's cancer came back.

I had never been around someone who was terminally ill. I felt helpless. To think this was just a boy! He was only twelve. Here was this young child, with stomach cancer who had the most positive outlook on life.

Every time we got together he was so appreciative of our time. "Thank you for spending time with me," he'd say, his eyes twinkling after I'd hugged him goodbye. He was just the happiest, most positive, most gracious child. The ACS told me that Willis had to have a bone marrow transplant. He was going through different procedures, so I would visit and bring him gifts in the hospital.

When Jeffrey was away in April, Willis started getting very sick. I realize one should never argue with God's plan as I had all the time in the world to spend with Willis when Jeffrey was gone. He was at Columbia Hospital so I'd take a taxi up there and spend time with him and his family. The reality was sobering. We all knew he wasn't going to last very long, so one day I asked Willis, "If there were three things you could have in your life, what would you want?"

He scrunched his face up and thought for a moment. Then quietly said, "A game console."

"Okay. What else?" I urged.

"I want my favorite DJ to call out my name on the radio so everyone can hear!"

The third was that he wanted to meet John Starks, his favorite player from the New York Knicks.

The first one was easy, so I got Willis a Nintendo right away. This provided immediate entertainment and he had a lot of fun with his games which made the days in the hospital a little better. I called the American Cancer Society and asked if they could help me with the DJ and, on a long shot, also asked if anyone there knew John Starks.

The DJ was more than happy to mention Willis on the air, and he even made him a music CD. Willis's face lit up when he received it. It at once warmed and broke my heart, but I only gave him smiles. John Starks, on the other hand, was a problem. The Knicks were in the playoffs, so of course, they were busy. But we left a message and told them that there was a little boy named Willis up at Columbia Hospital and his dream was to meet John Starks. We left it at that and didn't figure anything would come of it.

Days later Willis called me ecstatically. "Oh my God, Christina, you won't believe it!"

Against all logic I was thinking, *He's cured!* But I asked, "What happened?"

"John Starks was here! You did it, you got him to visit me."

"What do you mean John Starks was there?" I asked. It was too good to believe!

"He was here, and he spent the morning with me. We took pictures and he brought me all this stuff."

I said, "Willis, the team just left for Dallas. How was John Starks there?"

"You gotta come up and see all this stuff!" Willis was just completely overjoyed.

When I arrived at the hospital, the nurse told me that John Starks walked onto the ward in a hooded sweatshirt and asked her, "What room is Willis in?" The nurse was in disbelief as she instantly recognized the superstar NY Knick.

John brought Willis a duffle bag full of his jerseys, t-shirts, and photos. Then he spent time talking with Willis, autographed the items, and took photos with him. After a while, he told Willis, "I've got to meet the team. Wish us luck." Then he added,

"Cheer for me!"

I was humbled. The goodness in people, which I always looked for, was strengthened and I was never more grateful. There was never a word about the visit in the press—John Starks didn't want publicity or credit at all. That's not why he had done it. Willis was the happiest that anyone had ever seen him. I believe his life had been fulfilled. The next afternoon, Willis called me and he sounded really weak. I said,

"Willis, what's going on?"

"Christina, I'm just calling you to say goodbye," he whispered.

"Willis, what are you talking about?" I started to feel nauseous, nervous, and sad.

"You know I'm really sick. I'm not going to make it, but I want to thank you for everything you did for me. I know you're going to be the best mommy ever because you have been so good to me."

"Willis, what are you saying?" I couldn't believe that a kid his age was saying something so sweet and kind and filled with acceptance. Despite my desire to remain strong, tears coursed down my face and I choked back sobs.

"Don't be sad, Christina. I'm going to be okay. I just want you to be so happy and be a good mommy."

Within the hour, his parents called me and said that Willis died shortly after I spoke to him. I was absolutely devastated. I got into bed and sobbed while I thought about Willis's brief but impactful life. He always saw the positive side of everything. He would never let things get him down. He taught me that whatever you are given, you have to accept and try to be your best—that it's your outlook in life that's really important. Willis never felt sorry for himself, and he always tried to help the others around him feel good and happy. I had to believe.

It was the first death I'd dealt with from someone so close to me, and I felt so helpless. Willis taught me so much about life in the few years I spent with him. I know he was brought into my life for a reason: to teach me. He taught me to always be humble, to see the love and beauty in people, to give my heart openly, to live life with strength and faith, and to always smile, no matter how bad things are in my life. Indeed, Willis came into my life to prepare me for the life ahead. The life of humility and understanding I'd embrace.

I made a mental pact to be the best mommy ever in honor of Willis. I have always felt sorry that I didn't give him as much as he gave me. I am comforted knowing that he is happy, healthy, and pain-free in heaven looking down on me with his beautiful smile and I thank him for including me on his short journey around the sun.

Story Seven

SOME AMAZING AND HORRIBLE FIRSTS

Jeffrey and I spent the summer of 1994, between New York and Connecticut since I was due to deliver on September 13th. A childhood friend of Jeffrey's wanted to go into the nightclub business in Stamford, where Jeffrey grew up. I didn't object because Jeffrey always wanted to own a nightclub but I still felt cautious about the nightclub scene and Jeffrey's high-risk addiction and behaviors. They got together on the project, and the club was set to open Labor Day weekend. I wasn't planning on going to the opening with my due date approaching so soon. I told Jeffrey to go without me but make sure he didn't stay overnight so he left with some of his friends and I stayed back in New York. I still had some things to order to prepare for the baby and welcomed some time alone. According to Jewish customs, you do not have anything for a baby in your house before the baby is born, so I only had things on order all over New York.

Jeffrey went up to Connecticut. I tried to get some sleep—or as much as I could, considering how uncomfortable lying down was in my condition. I was in bed watching *Against All Odds* and just as the movie was about to end, I heard the front door open. I glanced at the white numbers glowing on the digital clock and saw it was almost 3:00 a.m.. Jeffrey came into the bedroom smelling like cigar smoke and was stinking drunk. I told him to shower, then, when he jumped into bed, I happened to shift my position when I suddenly felt and heard something like a rubber band snap.

Immediately, I felt a warm wetness on my thigh, so I moved to get out of bed. When I stood up, water came gushing out. *You've got to be kidding me.* It was the least convenient time for my water to break, but that's always the way these things work. Jeffrey was in absolutely no condition to go to the hospital, so I thought I'd try to hold things off for a little while. I went into the bathroom and called my mother. Labor usually doesn't happen immediately anyway for first-time mothers, so I let Jeffrey sleep until about 6:00 a.m. When my contractions were about five minutes apart, I woke Jeffrey and said, "We've got to go to the hospital now."

Jeffrey quickly threw on his standard choice of clothes: a swimsuit, a button-down island shirt, and topsiders. At that point, I was beyond objecting so we could get out the door. He was still a bit drunk when we got to the hospital and started entertaining everyone there. Here I was about to have our child and he was walking around the maternity ward, in a doctor's coat wearing a stethoscope—I don't know where he got it—entering people's rooms and pretending to be a doctor. Who does that? I realized then that everything was about Jeffrey, I was his appendage but I was in too much pain to care. By this time in our lives, red flags were flying everywhere.

My labor only took about four hours. At 10:40 a.m. our son Samuel arrived. I would have delivered him earlier, but his head got stuck for a while and the doctor had to use forceps to help him out. He was absolutely beautiful and perfect. He had a headful of dark hair and big dark eyes. When the nurse placed him on my chest for the first time, I knew there was no one I could love more in the world.

Because I had been up all night and the little complication with the forceps, I was exhausted and was told to stay in bed by the nurse. "Try to get some sleep because it's going to be busy from here on out."

The nurse left and Jeffrey came in. There was a hospital bed for me, then a reclining chair for him. "Hey, Christina, I'm really tired. Can we switch? I really need to get a nap," he said.

Never would I have believed it! Of course, he was tired. He'd only had three hours of sleep and was still suffering from his previous evening's celebrations. But why should I give up my bed? I'd only just given birth to our child! It was so typical of Jeffrey and typical of me too because I said, "Okay" and traded places with him. I was in denial I'm sure, my ostrich head buried deep into the sand. I should have been asking myself if Jeffrey's unreasonable sense of self-importance; his need for admiration; his lack of empathy at the moment; and his need to seek attention in any way possible were signs of illness. But no. I gave up my bed! I also remembered the first night with him when I was throwing up in the bathroom! So, Jeffrey.

A few hours later the nurse came back and saw me sleeping in the chair and Jeffrey asleep in the bed with Sam asleep on his chest. She was irate. She lifted Sam off Jeffrey's chest, put him in his bassinet, and then shook Jeffrey to wake him up. "Don't you realize that Christina just delivered an eight-pound baby and you are sleeping in her bed? This is a first and I cannot believe it. Get yourself up and out, and let Christina get some rest now!" the nurse said, shaking her head and giving me a sad look of disgust. I heard her huff "men" as she walked out of the room.

At the beginning of our relationship, Jeffrey was the one who wanted a baby and was so excited from the moment we found out I was pregnant. But I don't think he'd ever considered the responsibilities in a day-to-day sense. He'd been spoiled during our first five years together as he had my undivided attention, and that's the way he liked it. My devotion and being at his beck and call satiated his need to feel special and I showed off his privilege as his exotic, compliant companion. I was his perfect mate.

Jeffrey never did anything at half-measure, not even in 'love.' He had an obsessive personality, and I was part of that obsession. His possessiveness and jealousy didn't feel entirely like a bad thing as I wanted to feel loved and needed. Plus, he absolutely treated me like a queen. I'd never given him reason to be jealous, even with his carrying-on and I'd given him as much liberty and freedom as he wanted. I was loyal, had given all of me away to Jeffrey, and as long as I continued to do so I would be his everything. I was so sure when Sam was born his arrival would settle Jeffrey down a bit. Now we had a newborn and Sam was taking up the majority of my attention and efforts, especially since I was breast-feeding. A new Jeffrey showed up.

He became extremely jealous of Sam taking my attention away from him. I don't think he meant to be, not consciously, and if ever I should have realized his instability it was then because it made things difficult for me. He would come home from work and want to go out to dinner then would get angry when I said I couldn't. He wanted to go to his club and spend time there, but I didn't want to disrupt my routine and be away from home. He was not used to my pushback and expected me to do whatever he said without questioning him and agreeing to whatever he desired. Well, I might have been long-suffering but when pushed against the wall, Christina, the woman who was her own person, came out to face off with the new Jeffrey.

Obviously, I couldn't and didn't give Jeffrey the kind of undivided attention I had given him for the past five years. Things were changing, but change is necessary once people have children. We needed to progress through different stages of life and relationships. Stagnation wasn't healthy, and I don't think it's something Jeffrey, with his spontaneous, unbridled, and unstable personality, would have enjoyed. With every no, he was losing patience or should I say control, but I was losing patience. Even when my mom was there to help us take care of the baby, Jeffrey was straining at the limitations I put on our relationship. I was surprised at his anger.

"Why don't you come with me to the nightclub?" he pleaded, resting his face on my shoulder, and breathing in my hair. I felt his need to be needed but I turned and looked at him with a quizzical brow. "I'm nursing a baby. I can't just up and leave for Connecticut."

Jeffrey's world changed overnight. So did mine. I was doing everything for Sam twenty-four hours a day, and I loved it. It was all I had ever really wanted. My joy with the job of motherhood was inexpressible. When I realized the depth and connection of the act of nursing—that a child was taking sustenance from my own body—sure, it took time, but it was special. Knowing I was the only one in the world who could do for my child all he needed to become in the world, I was undaunted by Jeffrey's demands. I never considered that because for years I resisted marrying him and now didn't have much time to galivant, that this might have plucked at Jeffrey's self-esteem.

As a result, Jeffrey started spending more time at the nightclub in Connecticut. I soon came to realize that he didn't just have a problem with drinking; he was also doing a lot of cocaine, which I wasn't comfortable with at all. Jeffrey's temperament had always been so calm and collected, but he was becoming visibly unstable. One minute he'd be calm and nice, and the next he was a monster. It was like living with Jekyll and Hyde. A couple of times, I tried to talk to him about his spiraling. "Jeffrey, I don't think you should be taking drugs. It's not good for you, and it's changing you."

Of course, that didn't go over well. It started a fight, and I, for the sake of peace, just backed down. I naturally tend to shy away from conflict and it takes a lot to make me mad, but once I am, you can forget it. People have told me that I keep things bottled up until I hit my breaking point and then I flip out. I know my fuse is difficult to light but turns to a roaring flame when lit.

For the first few months, we had Sam, things were very rough between Jeffrey and me. We fought constantly. He'd go to work during the week and then go to Connecticut on the weekends. And the fighting kept getting worse. I was immovable. My thirty-first birthday was coming up in July, and Jeffrey asked if I'd bring Sam to Connecticut for my birthday weekend. Sam was nine months old at the time, and I agreed. Jeffrey had recently opened a deli called, "Sam and Kyle's." (Kyle was Jeffrey's partner's first son's name.)

The morning of my birthday, I awoke in the hotel with Sam to my right and Jeffrey to my left. I tapped Jeffrey and asked, "Are you going to wake up and celebrate my birthday with me and Sam?"

Something set him off when I said that. Jeffrey twisted around in the bed, raging mad. "I'm so tired of all of this. I can't take it!" He lunged on top of me and tried to strangle me. I was in shock. Our child was lying next to me in bed. "Sam!" I choked out, panicking for Sam's safety. I tried to push Jeffrey off of me. Sam started to cry. The sound of Sam crying yanked Jeffrey out of his rage. I didn't know what to do—terrified that anything I did could enrage him further. The best thing to do, as I read the situation, was to stay calm, not bring up my birthday anymore, and not inflate anything at all. And just like that, Jeffrey went back to sleep. So, I simply took Sam downstairs for breakfast. I was shaking. This was not okay and I was not okay. When we returned to the room, it was like nothing had ever happened. Jeffrey greeted us with a smile. "Happy birthday, Christina! I have something for you back in New York."

I decided to let the whole incident go and not mention it again nor did I mention it to anyone but bottled it up inside. I didn't bring it up when we returned home, either. This was not a side of Jeffrey I'd seen before and I had to think.

Our apartment at Trump Tower was a compact one-bedroom. The day after we returned home the concierge called me, a little confused. "Christina, what's going on? You have ten dozen red roses down here."

I thought I'd misheard them. "What? Are you sure that's for me?"

"They're definitely for you."

The roses filled our tiny apartment, all from Jeffrey. The note said, "I love you," but he never said he was sorry. So, he was aware of his behavior and I knew he was feeling guilty about what had happened.

Then, the doorman returned with a familiar red bag, inside a small, wrapped package. *Cartier, what else?* Inside was a diamond and gold Panther ring. *He was feeling guilty.* Although Jeffrey claimed he'd ordered it when I gave birth to Sam, I felt it was a gift of remorse. I am not thinking and am not even privy to this as a sign of remorse from batterers. But this was the first time something like this had happened and being a person always looking for the good in others, I accepted the gifts with gratitude toward Jeffrey for trying to apologize and forgave him.

The experience shook me and I didn't want to tell anyone. When it dawned on me that I didn't want to tell my parents, especially my mother who I've told everything since a child, I knew I was about to become a woman who kept secrets. I rationalized that because I was very close with my mom, hearing about the incident would hurt her, especially since she adored Jeffrey. He thought of her as a second mom. The secret stayed buried within my heart. Over the next few days, I started examining my behavior. I had a new child, so I couldn't just spend less time with Sam. On some level, I was neglecting Jeffrey, but wasn't that the nature of parenting? Each had to give some of their time to the new person in their lives! On the other hand, I wasn't the one who didn't want to adjust to reality, or the one running off to Connecticut, doing drugs, and behaving badly all the time. I wasn't entirely to blame for the situation and it was time Jeffrey stepped up.

For a while life was peaceful and Jeffrey was truly remorseful. I was hopeful we'd arrived at a new normal. It was then that Jeffrey decided we should move out of the city. We'd been looking for houses in Connecticut, but we just hadn't found anything we wanted. Jeffrey suggested that we should fly down to Florida. He thought maybe in Florida he'd be home more, (certainly for his shorts and floral shirt) life would be relaxed, and everything would improve.

We flew down and found a house in Boca Raton. It was a beautiful one-point-two-million-dollar mansion. We were both optimistic about the move. It was going to be like a fresh start. We spent Sam's first birthday on September 3rd, in Connecticut and then moved to Boca Raton the following week. How could things be anything but great in sunny Florida? We were the youngest owners in our exclusive gated golf community and I thought it was perfect to be amongst older, successful, and mature people. It would be good for Jeffrey. Things went pretty well and we relaxed into a new routine. Jeffrey was getting used to Sam and he loved his little man. He was expressing the kind of parental love for which I had hoped. As spontaneous as Jeffrey was, I began to understand that he needed his home life to be stable and predictable as that was what grounded him. Once he'd adjusted to Sam their lovefest began and he was a great dad.

Just as we were developing our little family life and routine, I realized I was pregnant again and this time I was worried. Sam's birth had thrown Jeffrey into a tailspin and an unstable period for us but he had tried and he was coming into his own as a father. I had weaned Sam from breastfeeding when he turned one and thought I couldn't get pregnant while nursing. When my pregnancy was confirmed I wondered how I would be able to love another child as much as I loved Sam. I also wondered how Jeffrey would handle the news since he saw it as dividing my love. Now I would have to divide my love into four when he was barely adjusting and things were just starting to fall in line. To my utter surprise, once again, Jeffrey was elated over the news. I had to believe more than ever, we'd be okay. Valleys are a part of any life's journey and though they had been frustrating, we had survived them.

Story Eight

I'M OUT

Things remained stable and our little family was growing. I committed to trusting Jeffrey and the current shift the new baby would bring. At the beginning of the third trimester of my second pregnancy, we decided to take a last trip before welcoming another baby. Jeffrey loved cruises. He always won a lot of money gambling in the cruise casinos because the blackjack rules were different, more relaxed and the fact that he could count cards was in his favor. The cruise casinos used fewer decks of cards, which made it easier to count, than the six to eight decks in the U.S. casinos.

Having won big once again, we arrived home with a duffle bag full of cash, three hundred thousand dollars which Jeffrey left on the kitchen counter before he headed down to South Beach, which was becoming his new hangout. South Beach to me was bad news. The level of depravity and decadence going on there was not in our best interest, and certainly not the right environment for one with addictions and hubristic tendencies. The next morning, I was cleaning the kitchen and moving the duffle bag out of my way, when Jeffrey walked in from his all-nighter. He was in a horrible mood, hungover, and had a scowl on his face.

"What are you doing? Trying to steal my money?" He barked.

"You are insane. Your lousy three hundred thousand dollars means nothing to me. Anyway, what's yours is mine, and what's mine is mine," I said sarcastically. I set the bag down and started to walk off, but he suddenly grabbed my shoulder from behind and threw me to the ground. Here I was visibly pregnant and all I could think was here we go again. I was once again surprised about Jeffrey's split personality and at the same time worried about the baby. While my tush took most of the fall, I was so big and pregnant that it was scary. I guess the sight of me and my protruding belly sprawling on the floor scared Jeffrey too as he took the bag, put it on the counter close to me, and said to me, "Here, this is for you." Another batterer's remorseful behavior. I was doubtful I could go through what we'd been through with Sam's birth but I didn't say anything. I got up and went into our room and called my OB/GYN. I was worried about the baby inside me. I took Sam, brushed past Jeffrey, and went to have a checkup. I told my doctor I had fallen. Now I was making up typical excuses for battered wives. After checking the baby, I was cautiously instructed to take it easy for the rest of my pregnancy. While I was relieved that the baby was okay, I was filled with worry and rage. *I could have lost the baby. What if I am not so lucky next time?*

One of my voices, Tina, or Chris, said, *"Christina, you can still turn things around. You can make the difficult decision."* I gulped. My bettering the situation could only result in one thing: leaving Jeffrey. He was going to be out all day, so I called my mom and asked her to meet me in Orlando. I was no longer willing to keep secrets. I must have sounded distraught.

"What's going on?" Mom asked. "Are you okay?"

"Yes, but I have some difficult decisions to make...." I couldn't say the truth aloud, so I quickly added, "I'll tell you later."

After I packed our bags, Sam and I got in my Mercedes Station Wagon, my Thanksgiving present from Jeffrey, and drove the three-hour road trip to Orlando. I didn't leave a note. Nothing. I was done. It was over. We were gone. I had reached my breaking point.

One of the reasons I adored my mom was because of her understanding and her ability to be non-judgmental. I did tell Mom what happened but not once did she bring it up and never once did she bad-mouthed Jeffrey. I imagined because of her own experiences with Dad, she thought it best to handle it the way she had handled her ups and downs with him. To her great credit, she offered no opinion and wholeheartedly supported me. She was there as my mother and she gave me the breadth I needed to internalize what had happened without running commentary. When I hadn't answered Jeffrey's thousands of calls, he knew me well enough to figure if anyone knew where I was it would be my mom. And indeed, Mom's phone was blowing up with phone calls. All from Jeffrey.

"I'm just going to answer it," Mom said, throwing her arms in the air. They'd always been so close and I was worried it would complicate things for her.

I held my breath as Mom answered.

"Hello?" she began.

I analyzed her facial expressions as they spoke. "Yes, Sam and Christina are okay. No, Jeffrey. She isn't coming home." Mom paused for a second before saying, "I'm sorry, but this is your doing." She hung up.

After about a week, Jeffrey went to an attorney to have me ordered back home.

I didn't bother to check if he could do that since we were not legally married but threats were being bantered about jeopardizing my position as a mom as I'd removed our child from home without his father's knowledge. I didn't want to get into any trouble with the law and I surely didn't want to do or risk anything as far as my children were concerned. Although my mom had been communicating with Jeffrey to let him know we were okay, she refused to reveal our location. When Jeffrey and his attorney called my mom with orders for me to come home, we were surprised.

Jeffrey, in his right mind, was a kind, generous and loving person. He'd go to the end of the earth for Sam and me. But when Jeffrey's conflicted subconscious roused, altered by all the drinking and substances he was doing, I was convinced more than ever that it wasn't just the wild eighties and nineties. But rather that Jeffrey had issues behind the mask he wore that concealed his feelings of inadequacy. I had to act rationally for both of us until he could get help by setting clear boundaries. I loved Jeffrey and I wanted the best for him and us but something had to give. I had no intention of being an abused partner, and I truly was getting tired of walking on a tightrope when Jeffrey was in an altered state.

"I'll come home under one condition," I began firmly, with the phone clutched against my ear. "You must go to therapy with me. That is non-negotiable."

"Therapy? Sure, that's fine. Anything you want." I could tell it rolled right off of Jeffrey's back. "I just want to be with you and Sammy again. You are my family. Remember, I chose you to be my family."

It was a pompous way of saying it, but he meant it and my heart softened. All everyone else saw was the outer shell of Jeffrey. I was the only one to get even a glimpse into Jeffrey's complex and complicated personality. I had been speaking to an attorney a friend had recommended and she said she'd coordinate everything. Jeffrey needed a reality check. An appointment was set with a marriage counselor. I was worried because Jeffrey had very little respect for most people he considered beneath him. His contemptuous behavior was not only to strangers as he had such relationships with a few family members.

We were reunited at the therapist's office for the first time in weeks. I never doubted Jeffrey's love for me or Sam, but love cannot be about control or jealousy. My love for Jeffrey was unconditional but it was starting to become a concern even for me. Maybe Jeffrey loved me the best he was capable but I was not his toy. I was the mother of his soon-to-be two children. Being the mother of his children was always how I'd rationalized his bad behavior and the reason I'd forgiven him for his fragilities, but this time my eyes were wide open. Integrated as Christina, I was no longer willing to excuse his abhorrent behavior.

Story Nine

WELCOME BABY #2

Jeffrey didn't exactly love therapy but he honored his word and showed up.

It showed me that deep down he cared about and was committed to our family. Of course, being Jeffrey, he could manipulate a situation to get what he wanted but sometimes he was genuine. He once told the therapist how much he loved me and how much smarter than him I was and he respected that. Many times, the therapist tried to push through Jeffrey's defenses trying to get him to open up about things other than our relationship but Jeffrey never revealed a single thing about the demons that plagued him. They were probably buried so deep, that he consciously could not access them, yet like autonomic responses he obeyed them.

Once the therapist asked him if there was anyone in the world he respected besides me. To my surprise, his answer was my sister Anita and his best friend in New York, who was a fellow trader but who had never worked for Jeffrey. I would never have guessed that and I wondered what else could I not be privy to deep in his mind...the demons orchestrating play.

In my thirty-eighth week of pregnancy, I went to the doctor for my routine appointment. To my surprise, I was told that I was three centimeters dilated and needed to immediately go to the hospital. Luckily for this appointment, Jeffrey had decided to accompany me. As we got in the car, I told Jeffrey to take me home. I said that I needed to have some time with Sam, as this would be the last time it would only be him. I was having big doubts about being able to love another child as I couldn't imagine my heart feeling more love than it had already. Reluctantly, Jeffrey went along with my wishes and took me home. I prepared Sam for his new sibling's arrival and after about an hour or so later, we knew we had to go to the hospital.

On May 20, 1996, we welcomed our second son, Jacob, into our family. This time Jeffrey was sober and he bought everyone in the delivery ward sushi while I was in labor. This was a step up from last time. Jacob was born without any complications and only took three pushes to arrive. He was two weeks early and small compared to Sam. He actually was considered a preemie, since he dropped down to 5 lbs. 7 oz. before we left the hospital. Unlike Sam, Jacob was fair-skinned and virtually bald with beautiful slate-blue eyes. Had I not known, I never would have thought he was mine. This time Jeffrey didn't ask to switch places. Like me, Jacob would be called Jakie then Jay, what he goes by now.

Two months after Jay was born, we were still going to therapy regularly. The valley was not so deep this time. The therapy helped a lot. Jeffrey loved having the two boys and would spend a lot of time with them, especially with Sam, since he was walking and talking now. Sam became Jeffrey's little buddy and his shadow. He took him to Miami Heat games and Florida Marlins games all the time since we were season ticket holders with seats on the field and in the third row of the arena. He even started going to a "mommy and me" class with Sam, which Jeffrey called "daddy and me." I was proud of Jeffrey's effort and appreciated his earnestness. He was in love with his children and a good father. I thanked the heavens for our good fortune of surviving the hard times and settling into the family I had always wished for. Jeffrey was still philandering about but by now I thought of these women as casualties of his internal war. I was holding the coveted seat and Jeffrey now knew I was not a woman in a gilded cage.

One day in therapy, Jeffrey said he wanted to get married. He told the therapist that if I would go to Israel with him by myself, in two days, and got married, he would give me eight million dollars. I couldn't believe my ears. It was the ultimate manipulation to test my commitment to him! I had his two children, how much more committed could I be? The therapist was shocked by Jeffrey's offer.

"I would take it," he said with bug eyes.

I was more than a bit annoyed by his response, I was flat-out furious and it set me off.

"I don't need to be paid to get married," I promptly replied. "We already have two children and we are a family. If we want to get married, we can plan to do so in the future but coercion will *not* work. I am not leaving our children and running off to Israel for a week."

"Are you serious?" Jeffrey asked. He seemed genuinely taken aback.

Both he and the therapist thought I was crazy, but the therapist and Jeffrey didn't understand I had never been with Jeffrey for his money. While having a lot of money made life convenient and afforded me a dream life of having no financial stresses, all I ever wanted was a healthy loving environment for me and my family. I knew Jeffrey's true heart and soul. For better or worse, I was committed to being with him for the long haul if we maintained a civil union. Without a doubt, I was secure in his love for me, as Jeffrey loved me more than anything in his life, even more than he loved himself. Truly, I was fine with our little unconventional family. What I didn't understand then, was that one can never love another until they love themselves and that Jeffrey was a far way off from loving himself unconditionally. So was I.

Story Ten

AND FINALLY, MARRIAGE

We'd survived the worst. There were times in our crazy spell when I couldn't relax but deep down I wasn't overly concerned when Jeffrey's outbursts happened. My ability to de-escalate Jeffrey's demons over the years had served to calm his restless spirit and together we had endured what I thought were the worst times in our relationship. Life was once more on cruise control and I hoped I'd seen the last of that kind of behavior.

In November 1998, Jeffrey arranged for our family to go on another mission to Israel. We were going with a large group which included his family and we were touring Masada. While there, the rabbi was scheduled to perform Bar and Bat Mitzvahs for the thirteen-year-olds on the trip. Masada, the famed fortress noted from Israel's battle against Rome, overlooks the Dead Sea. Even at the time of the year, it was over 100 degrees. I told Jeffrey that I was going to take my mom and the boys down the mountain to get ice cream. Jeffrey kept insisting that we had to stay back for the ceremonies, as he had a part in it. But when the ceremonies were about to begin and Jeffrey was up front with the rabbi, I decided to do as I had planned. A few hours later, Jeffrey and the group descended and we got back in our tour buses. Jeffrey was very solemn, and quiet, and only said, "You missed out" to me. He seemed to be sulking as we drove off so I asked, "What's the matter with you? Are you upset that we didn't stay for the ceremonies?" He looked at me with tears in his eyes and said, "We were supposed to get married up there."

Oh, here we go again. *Is he delirious from the heat or just plain crazy?* Then I thought, how typical. *Who else would plan a surprise wedding?* I looked Jeffrey in his eyes which were moist from disappointment, and my heart reached out to him. I said, "Maybe you should have asked me to marry you first?"

He proceeded to tell me his dream was to marry at Masada, high above Israel, and the world. Another of his grandiosity but I could tell he was really sad and meant every word he said.

"Why don't you ask me now, we're driving past it at least," I said.

So, as only Jeffrey would do, he knelt on the floor of the moving bus and said, "Will you marry me?"

This was just too good. Jeffrey on his knees, being vulnerable was a rarity. He was willing to show the entire bus how much he wanted me as his wife and there was nothing I could do but say, "Okay."

Everyone cheered and Jeffrey was happy.

Our next stop on the tour was lunch before going to the Wailing Wall in Jerusalem. My mom and the boys were tired, so she took them back to the King David Hotel for naps. At lunch, the rabbi, who was a good friend of mine, came over and asked me what happened and why I had left without getting married. I told him that I didn't know about Jeffrey's plans for our marriage and he laughed. He said it was just as well as Masada was a place where wars took place and he suggested that we get married at the Wall, the most sacred place in the world to the Jews. There was some gravity to this as the Wailing Wall has great significance in Judaism, Christianity, and Islam as part of the three faith's intertwined history.

As if my own beliefs were not to be left out, coincidently, although I don't believe in coincidences as everything happens for a reason, I was wearing a red suit jacket. This was perfect with my Chinese superstition. Red is the color of the life force itself, and wearing red for good luck on holidays and special occasions is a Chinese tradition. I did have on a black skirt too, but I didn't think too much about that. With my father's mother, this would have been taboo as black represents disaster, sadness, cruelty, and suffering and should never be worn in wedding ceremonies. The other color of clothing with meaning in Chinese superstition is white, symbolizing a mother's milk. It is considered the balance between red and black. I was not wearing anything white, but I surely had my mother's milk.

At the wall, men and women were separated and directed to different sides of the wall to pray. Before we entered the rabbi had us stand near the entrance where we could all be together for the ceremony. Our friends, Chris and Daniel Golden were our witnesses and other friends from our mission were in attendance. I had told Jeffrey that I didn't want to disrupt our children's nap schedule, so we didn't call the hotel to inform my mom. And so, we were married at the entrance of the Wailing Wall. It was a short ceremony and we then parted ways to our respective ends of the wall where the men prayed on one side, and me, and the other women on the other side of the Wall. I would later convert to the Jewish faith as I wanted the boys to be raised in their father's religion.

When we returned to the hotel, Jeffrey was so ecstatic to tell my mom and the boys, even though I don't think they understood at two and four years old what marriage meant. That evening, the rabbi honored us at the mission's dinner event and announced to the whole group that he had married us. We had a toast and Jeffrey was as proud as a peacock. His dream had come true. We might not have been high above the world looking down but we had married in Israel as he had always dreamed. It made me happy to see Jeffrey so elated. He was always the one doing things for everyone else without ever asking for anything in return. To him, this was the greatest thing someone could have done for him and I felt honored to be able to give him this sense of happiness. For me, nothing changed. I always felt we were one together and we already had the perfect family.

Being married was just a formality, although now I, Christina not Chris, was officially in it for the long haul as I didn't ever want to be divorced, especially with two children.

Back in the U.S., to make our marriage legal, we had to go to the Justice of the Peace to get a marriage certificate. It was December 31, 1998, and the laws for instant marriages were going to change after the new year. The new law stated that couples would have to attend three marriage counseling sessions before they could marry. Jeffrey categorically did not want to go to counseling again, so he insisted we had to get married that day.

It was three p.m. and the County Court House was closing early at four-thirty p.m. for the new year. Jeffrey called and said to me, "I have huge positions on and I need to get out of them before the market closes. Take the boys to the courthouse and I will meet you there." That only left fifteen minutes for him to get to the courthouse and that was just about how long it took to get there, but I followed his instructions.

The boys and I were the only people left in the County Clerk's office at four-twenty p.m., other than the employees. Luckily, the clerk helping us loved the boys and was very nice. I told her about our surprise "wedding" in Israel and she thought it hysterical. It was four-twenty-eight p.m., and the employees were getting anxious to leave. I called Jeffrey and he said he was close. I told the clerk, Katie, that he was on his way. Katie was having fun with the boys, so she said she would wait. Finally, at 4:40 p.m., Jeffrey came barreling through the door. His hair was a mess and he was still in his standard attire, his bathing suit and island shirt. Katie looked up at Jeffrey, who was laughing as he ran over, kissed the boys, tussled their hair, and said, "This is him?" I could tell she was laughing on the inside too. Who gets married in bathing trunks and an island shirt? Well, Jeffrey.

The forms were filled out and ready to go, so we just had to sign and we said the boys were our witnesses. A few minutes later, not only were we officially married, but we were the last couple to get married under the old law. After nine years with Jeffrey, I could truly say, for better or for worse, there was never a dull moment. We headed home as Christina and Jeffrey Wilson and our little family, in Jeffrey's eyes, was now complete. I wondered if he now felt he possessed me completely and if things would change again. Jeffrey had adjusted to family life even if the road had been rocky. He adored his children, but even that was not enough to slow down the unrestrained life he lived. He was always gone so for the boys, nothing changed.

Story Eleven

I WANNA BE RICH

When Jeffrey had started trading, the stock exchange was just as depicted in the movies—traders/market-makers crowding on the floor, shouting at each other, and waving their arms in the air. If you were considered "someone," and if people liked you, sometimes you did better as the floor monitors, or Specialists would preferentially take your trade. In that regard, it wasn't science, it was who knew whom, who had the most stock, and who could catch the most attention. Who could get in and out of the stock best could win big.

For years, Jeffrey would wake up and blast the song, "I Wanna Be Rich," by Calloway, on the stereo and he would dance to the deep, hypnotic, drumbeat singing, "I want money, lots and lots of money, I want the pie in the sky…." It truly was an anthem of his life.

I used to laugh and tell him, "That's one way of putting it out there in the universe!"

I am a believer in universal laws, superstitions, and have an appreciation for psychics, though Jeffrey made fun of my beliefs. In my opinion, in life, you reap what you sow. I prayed we were sowing the right seeds. One day a young man visited Jeffrey claiming he had a computer program that could trade stocks faster than a trader on the floor. In trading, executing one second faster is a big deal. Huge companies were spending millions to lay cables underwater just to eke out seconds for faster trade. Here was this guy, another Jeff who said he had the program that could do this, but he needed funding for it to fully realize its potential. No surprise there. People were always coming to Jeffrey for money to start up their companies. He had funded our driver's friend to start a ticket brokerage business and gave a waiter at a restaurant we frequented ten thousand dollars to start his business, so Jeffrey and this other Jeff went into business together. They perfected the software and then loaded computers with the program, hired some young guys just out of college and taught them how to trade. Now that they had the capability of trading at lightning speed over computers, the advantage was obvious: one could buy and sell whatever they wanted at the click of the keyboard button. It was a revolution in the stock market industry…day trading was born.

In the early 2000, day trading hit the world like a storm. Grandmothers were behind their computers trading and a lot of people won big and lost big. As with anything that had probability upsides, people's greed came into play. To be a great day trader meant one had to be disciplined beyond belief and be able to resist the minute-to-minute ticker that is seductive. Setting goals was important. Goals meant selling if the stock goes up three to five percent even if you think it could go higher.

The day traders were making serious amounts of money. One hundred thousand dollars in a day was common, although they could lose the same too, but net-net they were printing money.

"This thing is big," Jeffrey wondered aloud one day. "I have a piece of the company, but why not my own?"

I said nothing because whenever Jeffrey had an idea, he'd instantly act if he wanted. I didn't voice my opinion as I believed Jeffrey's responsibility was his work and mine was our family. He'd been doing great so far so why comment? Jeffrey proceeded to set up his own company, Broadway Trading, and then he became a freight train—simply unstoppable. He rented office spaces in the cities where he had traders and made some of his best floor traders/market-makers managers. Erik and Andy were two of the founding partners in Broadway Trading. Both had worked with Jeffrey at the exchange. Andy was Jeffrey's assistant and was barely twenty-four years old. He taught them and had them teach the newly hired people how to trade. In no time, the business was booming like nothing we'd ever experienced.

Jeffrey was accustomed to making millions of dollars a year, but this was insane. There were days when the company made millions of dollars in one day. Do the math. And this was just a sub-business to all Jeffrey had going on all around the U.S. Jeffrey expanded rapidly setting up offices in Miami, Boca Raton, Atlanta, Long Island, and Philadelphia. The company got so big he no longer knew who was trading for him anymore. There were hundreds of traders and eventually his managers were setting up classes to teach individuals with their own money how to day trade for a fee.

The more money Jeffrey made, the more he spent, and the more his life was spinning out of control. I feared the wheels would just fly off. The high was too high and things started to escalate again. He was gambling, not just on the trading floor but at the casinos. Jeffrey had a million-dollar line of credit at casinos all over Las Vegas, Atlantic City, and The Bahamas. We were living in so much excess, it was ridiculous. To commemorate our marriage, he bought me an 8+ carat, internally flawless, fancy, yellow diamond ring. We had a twelve-person custom stretch limo and a full-time driver. He bought Ferraris, Porsches, Mercedes Benz, Range Rovers, and a custom-made Bentley for over four hundred thousand dollars and, added to all that, our Learjet and helicopter. I could barely fathom a car could cost that much money. "Are you sure we need this?" I asked.

"Who cares if we *need* it—we can have it! It's a Mulliner, number three of four in the world." He boasted.

The song lyrics had come to pass. He was rich, rich with an uppercase R.

Our son Jay loved jet planes, so as a treat, I'd buy him some two-dollar Matchbox jets and his favorite videos of Jay Jay the Jet Plane. We'd go to the airport to watch planes take off while we ate lunch. In 1999, for Jay's third birthday, Jeffrey came home and said, "Jay, I got you a fighter jet for your birthday."

I was expecting a model or toy of some sort, but Jeffrey had a mischievous gleam in his eye. "We named it Jay-Jay. Do you want to see it?" he asked.

We went outside and Jeffrey had the limo waiting. "What are you talking about, Jeffrey? Where is the plane?"

"In the hangar."

There is a private airport in Boca Raton where we kept our Learjet and helicopter. Jeffrey took us to the airport and presented Jay with a Russian MiG. A *real* Russian MiG. Jay looked at the jet and went back to playing with his toy jet. He didn't grasp the concept, understandably. *What the heck would a three-year-old do with a real fighter jet?* I thought incredulously. *This is stupid.*

"I'm training for my pilot's license," Jeffrey said, tousling Jay's hair. "I'll be able to fly this thing in no time."

"Whatever," I sputtered. I was speechless. It was just way over the top, but that's the way Jeffrey was. He was untouchable, spiraling out of control, and the Lord of the World attitude was bordering on hubris. Now in my superstitious world or whatever you might want to call it, hubris is an offense to God. I began to worry. He'd gotten everything he'd wanted, marriage, a family, money. What else would satiate his insatiable ego and desires? More money, more toys? More drugs, more women? No, the high was unattainable and this led to Jeffrey's drug use escalating and his grip on reality deteriorating.

Don't get me wrong, I had really nice clothes, hundreds of pairs of designer shoes, and lots of jewelry. But by now I clearly understood why money could be the root of all evil. I just prayed it did not destroy us. None of this "livin' large" meant anything. I didn't care a bit about the money, the jet, or the cars. All I ever wanted was to be loved and for the boys to be healthy, grounded, and get a good education. I didn't want to fly all over the world and live the *lifestyles of the Rich and Famous* that Jeffrey loved. But none of this was about us.

It was about Jeffrey.

Marriage didn't change things much. The more money Jeffrey made, the more absent he was from our home. The boys and I had a daily routine that didn't include Jeffrey. We led our own robust life filled with activities, their friends, and their interests. Sam took after my family and was an avid baseball player and loved just about any sport. We'd later visit almost every major baseball stadium around the country. I always thought he would become a sportsman and encouraged his playing. Both of our children were in private school and both had a knack for numbers, which they may have inherited from their father. Our lives were full and flourishing. When Jeffrey was home he was like a playmate for the boys, playing in the pool or in one of our kid's playrooms. He did love his sons but I was feeling more and more distant from him, knowing he was out in South Beach with strippers, and I wanted no part of that side of Jeffrey. In some respects, I was relieved that I didn't have to fulfill his insatiable sex drive. I had long graduated from all the partying and fast life and was content living my life as a mommy.

Even after getting married, Jeffrey didn't agree that time together with the family counted as our time together as a couple. He wanted his "exotic girl" as he called me in his arms and he wanted some semblance of our old life back. We could afford to hire round-the-clock nannies, but that was not my idea of family and I could never bring myself to entrust the care of my children to anyone other than my mom and maybe our housekeeper, Amy. I felt we'd already had our time together as a couple, running around, partying, and staying out all night. This was now the stage where you grow up and work on your family. He didn't understand that at all, no matter how many times I explained it. My Peter Pan man had no intention of growing up! I was firm in my decisions and I believe my refusal to play his game anymore was a blow to Jeffrey.

It wasn't that Jeffrey was all parties, girls, and the wildlife, though that was a big part of his life. He worked relentlessly, was involved with a lot of charities, and loved being part of the philanthropic community. He'd fit in well there, but that party side of him just nagged at him, tempting him beyond his control. He was not just going to South Beach anymore; he was getting overly intrigued with it and becoming a part of its anything-goes decadent culture. If New York was good, Jeffrey thought South Beach was even better. In New York people partied, but they still maintained their jobs and normal lives. But South Beach was just degenerate. People were superficial; they felt others' value came from the amount of money they had. It was all sleek sports cars, drunken pool parties, VIP lounges with private tables, strip clubs, and excessive drugs. I knew immediately that no good would come of it when it seemed Jeffrey was practically living there. His entourage grew and so did the women who thought they possessed him.

When I would give my opinion of the whole scene, Jeffrey would say, "Well, I look pretty damn good standing on top of my wallet."

That was it in a nutshell. *So shallow and pathetic.* I would tell him that all the "FOJs," "Friends of Jeffrey," as my girlfriend Tracy dubbed his entourage, were nothing but hangers-on, groupies. Most of them were just along for the ride and the generosity he provided them. They didn't love him. They loved his money. Jeffrey paid for everything: the elaborate dinners at exclusive restaurants, the VIP champagne tables at the hottest clubs, the drinks, the drugs, the strippers, whatever anyone in his entourage wanted. I once told him about an Oprah Winfrey quote that says, "Lots of people want to ride with you in the limo, but what you want is someone who will take the bus with you when the limo breaks down."

He didn't get it, or if he did he didn't care. Had my accepting his behavior all these years been detrimental? Did I enable him to sink further into the abysmal life he was living? In my heart, I always felt Jeffrey's old and trusted friend Adam, who he would stay with in Miami, was an enabler of Jeffrey's destructive behavior. Was Jeffrey's need to be worshipped by anyone so great that he would squander his life in the shallowness in which he existed?

In the words of Johnny Lee, Jeffrey was "Lookin' for love in all the wrong places."

Story Twelve

LIFE WITH A WHALE

Before we had children, but especially after we moved to Florida, Jeffrey liked to go to casinos or on cruises. It was a game to him. The nice thing about Jeffrey when he gambled, was that to concentrate on his playing, he needed a clear head, so he never did drugs like he would when he went to South Beach. He would have a drink or two, mostly for show, as he was constantly being watched by the pit bosses and by the overhead cameras. To look like the average gambler, he would accept a free cocktail every so often. So, when we did casino and cruise trips, he was not high on drugs, which meant we got the fun-loving and calm Jeffrey.

The day trading companies were just "printing money left and right." The thrill and excitement were gone and Jeffrey got a little bored with trading. Always chasing that next "high" and seeking out every ounce of excitement in life, Jeffrey turned his focus to casino gambling. Blackjack, the game that started it all was his go-to game, but he would play roulette, baccarat, and poker for fun. The casinos refer to high rollers as whales, and Jeffrey was one of the big whales. With his million-dollar lines of credit at each of their casinos, the casinos in Vegas, Atlantic City, and the Atlantis resort in The Bahamas would all compete, upping the ante on "special comps" to get Jeffrey to go to their casino.

They would send private Gulfstream Jets to transport him and his entourage and sometimes our family, and they would give him additional lines of credit to play with (sometimes another million dollars), and their largest suites for free. Everything during the stay would be "on the house," including ringside seats to all the big Mike Tyson fights. Basically, anything he wanted he would get.

We were in Vegas one Valentine's Day weekend and were invited to a private concert with Elton John at the MGM Grand. There were maybe ten couples, all high rollers, at the party. We were staying at MGM's exclusive villas, The Mansions, reserved for high rollers only. While Jeffrey and I went to see Elton John, my mom and Sam, who'd accompanied us on the trip, were treated to the best seats in the house to see David Cassidy. Jay was too young so he was at the Villa with our housekeeper, Amy. For my Valentine's gift, in addition to the trip, Jeffrey took me to Gucci at the Forum Shops at Caesar's Palace where I could "buy whatever you want. It's on the house." Needless to say, while I did buy some beautiful things, Jeffrey went to town! It was like one of those game shows where someone has ten minutes to fill a shopping cart with anything in the store; except we were in Gucci Boutique and had endless amounts of time and spending ability compliments of MGM.

Another eventful casino trip was to the opening of the Atlantis in The Bahamas.

The opening was a star-studded event with A-list celebrities and performances by Michael Jackson, Grace Jones, and more. While we were usually given the Tower Suite (the suite that goes across the two towers), we were told that it was part of the negotiations with Michael Jackson that he stay in that suite so we were given an enormous three-bedroom suite.

One morning at breakfast, Jeffrey's casino rep told him that the owner of the Atlantis Paradise Island, Sol Kerzner, wanted to invite us to join him on his private yacht for lunch. It turned out to be a star-studded event. We met people like Marlee Matlin, Star Jones, Richard Grieco, and several other celebrities. It was a small group of people and the boys were the only kids there and they became the centers of attention. There were buffets of lobster, caviar, and other decadent delights, along with champagne or whatever anyone wanted. We went out for a short trip on the Atlantic. Everyone was dressed casually as we were out in the hot sun. Nobody got out of hand, as it was a select group of classy individuals.

That evening, we went to a private party in one of the restaurants in the hotel where waitresses handed out Cuban cigars on silver trays. I was standing at the bar when a young kid came up to me and asked me where everyone was getting the cigars. I told him to look for the women with the silver trays and he said thank you and walked away. When Jeffrey traveled to casinos there was an entourage of trader friends whom he had taught how to count cards as well as other folks who traveled with him. It was his little side hustle job and he would front cash to the traders and they would bet, splitting the winnings with Jeffrey. Of course, not everyone won all the time, but they definitely did well overall. They were not big betters like Jeffrey, so they never drew too much attention from a pit boss. Some of these were the friends who'd accompanied us to the party and I was standing together. A squeal left the group, "Oh my God! Do you know who that is?"

I hadn't a clue. Not one to be star-struck, and quite honestly having two babies, one right after the other, in 1997 as it was then, movie stars were not at the top of my list nor did I have time to go to the movies or watch television, other than Barney. So, I replied, "Who, that boy?"

The women looked at me like I was an alien. "That's Leo… Leonardo DiCaprio!"

He just starred in the movie, *Titanic!* Of course, I didn't know who Leonardo DiCaprio was and did not see *Titanic* until years later. I wasn't living under a rock but, to be fair to my ignorance, he was only twenty-three years old at the time and truly a baby face. He'd starred in a few movies before but *Titanic* was the movie that made him a household name. I mean we were in 1997, the year the movie came out...I gave myself a pass.

We had been to other casino openings before, like the Bellagio's, but the Atlantis opening was one for the ages. Indeed, all these trips came with an understanding that Jeffrey would be gambling a lot. Not only did Jeffrey gamble, but he always brought his group of friends with him. My brother Alan traveled with Jeffrey to many of these events but Jeffrey would always put him up elsewhere just so he wouldn't be privy to the debauchery taking place. While there he'd usually meet up with other "whales" like Roger King, of King World Productions, or Dan Borislow, Magic Jack founder, and they'd be given a private table in the VIP gaming section. The exorbitant amounts of money on the Blackjack table were mind-bending. Jeffrey himself would play three or so hands starting at ten thousand a hand most of the time but it was not unusual to see several hundreds of thousands of dollars on those tables. Like any gambler, Jeffrey always claimed he was ahead of the game, in terms of winning money, but there were many times I could see him lose hundreds of thousands of dollars and not blink an eye. I would be sick to my stomach.

I was never one who enjoyed gambling and thought it a complete waste of money, but I felt that it was Jeffrey's money so he could do with it as he pleased.

Story Thirteen

THE HIGHS AND LOWS

To appease Jeffrey, and to keep up pretenses we decided to have an anniversary party in September of 1999. It would mark our first year of marriage and ten years together. We hired Barton G. to plan this anniversary party, which was going to be a party like no other. It was such a farce as Jeffrey and I weren't getting along again. I had started wondering if we'd even make it through to the anniversary. Jeffrey was doing all kinds of drugs—ecstasy, GHB, and things of which I hadn't even heard. He was chasing the better high; the bigger high. Money, girls, and gambling weren't enough anymore. Numbing out altogether allowed him to keep rolling along.

But we did made it to the party. We were expecting a few hundred people from around the country. Friends and family from all stages of our lives. The night, completely over the top, was a night to remember for all the wrong reasons. It was loud, ostentatious, kitsch, and downright ridiculous. We rented out the Palm Beach Polo Field and built a facility that had three great rooms. The first was for cocktails and was a Florida scene, complete with live flamingos and animals. The next room was the dining area, which had three stages that had entertainment going on each stage. We flew in some Las Vegas Cirque du Solei performers, had drag artists dressed as famous actresses and a Michael Jackson impersonator who sang and danced. We had caviar and *pate* flown in from Europe. Bottles of Cristal Rose Champagne and Chateau Petrus wine were everywhere. Waiters were walking around with silver trays stacked with Cuban cigars. The last room was a Miami Beach Nightclub scene. We had naked women and men in cages dancing, a trapeze, and dancers on a high platform. South Beach's hottest DJ spun the music until six a.m. To say that it was "over the top" is an understatement. Ostentatious and to me excessive, the party cost well over one million dollars. It probably was, and still remains, one of the most talked-about parties in the area and it was, without a doubt the most flamboyant. That night as Jeffrey stood tall on his wallet and donned his crown, though I didn't realize it then, I believe he'd slipped completely out of reality.

After the party in September Jeffrey's partying whirled completely and dangerously out of control. He was spiraling and like a corkscrew, he was going down. What is there to strive for when in your mid-thirties you are a "Master of the Universe?"

The excess and his addictive personality were combustible and had finally caught up with him. Fearing the worst, in a ditch effort to save our family and probably his life and grasping that I hadn't put my foot down hard enough throughout the years, I tried to cajole Jeffrey to go to drug rehab. I even attempted an intervention.

Joyce, our dear friend who adored Jeffrey as he adored her, was heartbroken. She would say she was expecting a call someday that Jeffrey had destroyed himself. Neil, who had started Jeffrey in trading, and often his voice of reason, was unable to get through to Jeffrey. Because of my SOS call, Joyce came over to try to help me convince Jeffrey to get help. He so loved and respected Joyce I was hoping against hope her voice of concern would reach him deep in his psyche, and added to mine, he might be able to hear our plea to help him.

"Rehab!" He'd boomed. "Have you gone loco lady?" he callously scoffed at Joyce. "I don't need any rehab and don't have a drug problem.

You and your friend, Christina here, are insane and stupid. Don't bother me with your nonsense." He'd pushed aside the covers, as he'd been napping. "Leave me alone," he snapped before walking out of the room.

I shrugged my shoulders as I looked at Joyce, who was shaking her head but looked sad. I was at wit's end. My brows were now furrowed constantly. I started questioning everything. This could not be my Prince Charming, the man I was going to be with forever hoping… we'd settle down and have a quiet and secure family life. My happily ever after? I didn't envision drugs, fast cars, fast women, and heavy gambling as a part of that dream. That wasn't me at all, and that's not what I wanted for the kids. I wanted them to be grounded. Anyone who knows me will tell you above all, my kids are my priority. If there was going to be a reason for me to walk out on Jeffrey it would be to protect my children. The kids didn't need to think about money, excess, and the material things that flooded our lives. I didn't want them to think that a fighter jet for their birthday was normal. I didn't want this life for them. And I didn't want them to see their dad this way. Thank goodness they were young.

In hindsight, I wondered what might have happened had I recognized Jeffrey's personality disorder as one stemming from unconscious trauma buried under years and years of denial? His lofty goals; his need for validation; need to control; to be loved; to possess; for insatiable sex; to have his consolatory "exotic" me, by his side, who perfectly fits his personality; the roller coaster life; the barrage of women calling; were all signs indicative of mental trauma that I had missed. Was I living with a narcissist? Our life sure fit the profile, a life of spectacular, almost perfect breathtaking existence followed, by emotional aggression and abuse, but Jeffrey's heart, despite all the bravado, said something else. Was the next step, imminent, the predicted precipitous fall after a meteoric rise? I wouldn't know because I had not asked myself any of these questions.

Jeffrey was spending all his time in Miami, and I knew he was out with girls, gambling, and drugging. In a way, it was good but only because it kept him out of the house in this "undone" state. When he did come home, he'd be coming off the drugs and in a bad mood and we, his family, got the absolute worst of him. Things just kept escalating and the madness was back in full force. Jeffrey was again jealous of the children and my attention to them. That jealousy came out as sarcasm and threats toward me. If I look back honestly, Jeffrey had been verbally abusive for a long time, but I didn't view it that way back then. When he would call me "good for nothing" instead of using my name, I got so used to his labels, that it wouldn't even affect me. Even when OJ Simpson was being tried for the murder of his wife Nicole, Jeffrey would get angry with me and say things like, "Nicole, you better watch it. One day I'm gonna take you out to sea, kill you, and nobody will ever know." But I knew that Jeffrey was a big talker and murder wasn't in his nature. I didn't take him seriously. He was trying to erode my self-esteem and shake my confidence but I had a trump card…I could walk out the door. But all the things Jeffrey had done I had not expected, so God knows what could happen in a drug-induced psychotic state.

I had two things working against me to stand up to Jeffrey as I should have. Being raised in a Chinese home. I wasn't conscious of this, but my parents upheld their cultural norm. In Chinese culture, the wife is the "property" of her husband, and divorce is frowned upon. The second was that I was also unconsciously battling my own self-esteem issues from being so sickly and therefore never truly feeling desirable. These were not conscious behaviors, but deep down I knew they had impeded my decision to walk out the door.

After Jeffrey and I had gone to marriage counseling, I started seeing a therapist on my own. Years of working with Tisha Hallett helped me recognize my self-worth. Initially, I couldn't verbalize that I deserved to be loved and to be happy. After a lot of therapy and deep introspection, I finally knew that not only was I a goodhearted person, I deserved and had every right to be loved, cared for, and respected. The stronger and more independent I became, the more confident I became in my relationship with Jeffrey. I'd known if I held back from making Jeffrey feel loved by me, it would weaken him and give me an upper hand in our relationship. It had been my defense against him but it only drove him to engage in more and more destructive behaviors. I decided to do a reversal.

I never, ever thought Jeffrey would carry out his idle threats. I saw them as empty and ridiculous. The more I didn't react to them, the more frustrated he would get and give up, and the more destructive to himself his behavior became. A shift was occurring in our relationship and I felt stronger than I ever had before. I could have been wrong but I knew how to read Jeffrey well and I would stand by this statement even today.

However, one day after finding drugs on the floor, I was so incensed I told Jeffrey, "If you're going to do drugs, you have to keep them out of the house. You're carelessly dropping pills all over the place. We have kids, and God forbid what happens if the boys eat one by mistake?" I wasn't going to take that risk. I continued. "Here's the deal. If you're doing drugs, don't come home. When you come home, you have to be clean and sober."

"You're crazy," he said (as I predicted). Tight-lipped, he never admitted to any addiction at all. My admonishing did nothing—he still came home with drugs, which I would take and throw down the toilet. Each day the weight on my shoulders to protect our children became heavier, and it was just a matter of time before I cracked but I had to keep up a happy, loving, and playful front for our boys so I became very good at masking my feelings.

Our tension finally came to a head the afternoon before Thanksgiving 1999. I was talking to Joyce on the phone about meeting up with our kids for dinner. When I hung up the phone, I saw Jeffrey swinging through the front door. His eyebrows were knit and his jaw stuck out, making him look Neanderthal. He was completely wasted. If I didn't know it was Jeffrey, I would have thought it was a deranged stranger. He had come undone! Jeffrey could be unreasonable when he was in an altered state so I would manage his undone-ness by staying out of the way.

"Oh look," he said sarcastically. "It's the slut. Don't act like you have no f---ing clue," he followed up.

Initially, I was hesitant to inquire what he meant by these statements; judging by the look in his eyes, I recognized the danger. Unfortunately, I let his disgusting behavior get the best of me and the question ballooned in my chest until it popped out of my mouth. "What's your problem?"

"Your cheating. Your lies." His eyes flashed maliciously and he immediately started cursing at me and rambling about my "affair."

I couldn't believe it. Nothing could be more ludicrous or further from the truth. "I'm taking care of the kids twenty-four seven, three-hundred sixty-five days a year," I said in a deadly tone. "Just because you sleep around with every bimbo in sight, don't put me in your low-life level," I said repulsed and with a disgusted snicker.

"I want to see your phone," he snatched my cell phone away from me and went through all the numbers. "I know you're doing something behind my back," he accused, scrolling through my calls.

"Jeffrey, you're crazy."

Without any evidence to worry about, I just walked away. I got the kids ready for dinner then went into our bedroom. "I'm taking the kids to dinner," I told him, "and I don't want to drive without my phone."

Jeffrey was lying on top of the bed talking on his phone, so I reached out my hand to take my phone back that was lying next to him. Instantly Jeffrey turned on his side and karate kicked me on my left side. I felt a searing pain in my hip. My hands shot to the source of pain; the blow had knocked me sideways onto the floor. Gasping on the floor, one sentence flitted across my mind: *I'm done.*

The verbal abuse was one thing—the threats of murder another and even though that wasn't normal, loving husband behavior, it wasn't like I had felt oppressed. I never felt like a battered wife, yet I was. I was a victim of a deranged man. But that day I realized something: I had made enough excuses for him. In truth, I knew Jeffrey felt I didn't love him and that I only cared about the children. But his hurt feelings were selfish and his jealousy was ludicrous. This attack was absolutely the last straw. I admit Jeffrey loved me more than I loved him at this point and I used this knowledge against him if needed, but I genuinely cared about my husband and was committed to my family. His accusations were paranoia as I had never strayed. I was his wife and would have been till death do us part.

But enough was enough. I had to show Jeffrey that I was not who he thought I was. I was not his plaything…I was his wife and the mother of his children. Cautiously rising to my feet, I ignored the pain and walked out of the room. I went into the garage, as the boys were outside with our neighbors and I called 911. *Maybe the police will come and scare him. It'll force Jeffrey to get the help he needs.* I called Joyce and told her what happened then called my attorney. He must have suspected I'd called the police because before the police arrived, he jumped in his Porsche 911 turbo.

"I don't think that's a good idea, Jeffrey!" I yelled.

He wouldn't listen—he said something under his breath and yelled, "Whatever" mocking the word I habitually said to him. As he was backing out he yelled, "You'll regret this." Then he peeled out of the cul-de-sac, not even caring that there were kids in the area.

My heart pounded. At that point, I'd woken up and I wasn't about to take his threats lightly. When the police arrived, Jeffrey was gone.

"Ma'am, what's his cell number?" one of the officers asked.

Reluctantly I told them and waited to see the aftermath of Jeffrey's actions. They called him on his cell phone, and surprisingly, he picked up.

"You need to come back to the house now. If we have to come after you, things are going to be a lot worse for you."

Jeffrey must've said no and started arguing because the policeman employed the use of more threats. "Look mister, you don't want us to have to dispatch any more police to chase you down and arrest you like a criminal in public, so come back to your house!"

The whole scene was making me sick. I started to feel dizzy and sat down on the stairs. *Just do it, Jeffrey.*

Somehow they finally convinced him to come back.

"Now, when he comes back, I need you to stay upstairs with the kids," the stern-faced officer said. "I don't want them upset or involved."

"No," I swiftly replied, "of course not."

Surprisingly, I didn't hear much when Jeffrey returned—just his muffled voice downstairs. They arrested him, handcuffed him, and hauled him out to the squad car. It wasn't until a female officer came in and photographed my hip, which had already developed a deep, nasty-looking bruise, that I realized what was going on. "You might want to get in touch with your attorney," she advised, "and," she passed on the number for AVDA: Aid for Victims of Domestic Abuse."

I didn't dare imagine the scene of his arrest. Our neighbors must have been onlookers to the horrible scene and surprised by it. I don't think they had ever imagined what went on behind our closed doors. I hadn't wished for Jeffrey to be arrested. That was not my intent. I simply wanted the police to scare him. Only now, I realize that Jeffrey didn't scare easily. I called my attorney again when the police left. She said the police really should have asked what I wanted them to do—if he needed jail or help. But they just arrested Jeffrey and took him to the station. After spending the night in the Palm Beach County Jail, Jeffrey was released on bail on Thanksgiving Day. I had no idea which one of his friends paid the bail but the judge was determined to make an example of Jeffrey.

Six months prior, Jeffrey had been named one of the Top 50 Jewish Community Builders of South Palm Beach County. We did a lot for the community and had gotten a lot of recognition for his charity work. But the judge was tired of people like Jeffrey taking advantage of their economic status and thinking they were above the law.

"But I don't want to press charges," I'd protested.

The judge now had the photos of my injury and the State was pressing charges. There was nothing I could do. I thought Jeffrey was going to kill me for this.

I was issued a restraining order against Jeffrey because of the violence and the drugs. Overnight our entire world changed. He wasn't allowed in the house, wasn't allowed to talk to me, and wasn't allowed near the kids. We could only communicate through our attorneys. I was sick with worry about what our future was going to entail. If Jeffrey were convicted of a crime, he would lose his trading license and we would have to move out of our community because they didn't allow felons to reside there. If Jeffrey couldn't trade, what would become of his companies? Are the kids going to be the products of a nasty divorce? Jeffrey is going to hate me.

While matters were being considered, Jeffrey rented a house in Miami and sent an employee over to get some of his clothes. It was like a forced separation. I'd always tried to tell him time and time again that, "there are always consequences to one's actions. What goes around comes around." Since the moment we'd met, Jeffrey called me all the time. Sometimes he'd call every half hour just to see what I was doing. In the uncharacteristic silence of my home, when both kids were asleep, I finally stopped denying that Jeffrey had a control issue—and had had them for ten years. For some reason, whenever he heard my voice, it reassured him that I was still with him, on his side and loving him. Constant contact and reassurance also helped Jeffrey justify his actions. Now that we were forced not to contact each other, it was the first time in ten years that he couldn't talk to me every moment, and it was undoubtedly driving him crazy. But it was also the first time that I had any freedom from his control. Once I tasted it, I realized how nice a peaceful home could be.

I crept into Sam's room and looked at his little chest rising and falling with his sleep's slow breathing. He looked peaceful—so peaceful. Fortunately, neither of the boys was affected by or witnessed any fighting. We managed to contain ourselves around the boys for the most part. When Jeffrey was with the kids, he was more of a buddy to them, not a parent. They were never negatively influenced by his actions or behavior. Since Jeffrey was always away before, his presence was not missed or seen as unusual by the boys. They were happy loving children without a care in the world. As I had promised Willis, I would do whatever it took to be a good mom.

How did my life with Jeffrey get so messed up? I would lay awake wondering, hoping that everything would be okay. If I knew nothing else, I knew I had to stand up to Jeffrey's terrible behavior and controlling ways. It was time for me to get a backbone and have some dignity. After a few years of therapy, I was finally enabled to say, I don't deserve this. Being able to say this provided me with the strength to understand that I could be okay on my own with my boys. This was the beginning of a new me and that it was okay not to be okay was fine with me. No more pretending. No more.

Story Fourteen

WITH A LITTE HELP, CHANGES CAN HAPPEN

Jeffrey was put under a restraining order for his domestic violence, so I felt safe to be in our home with the kids. Since we lived in a gated community with armed guards, and the guardhouse knew not to let Jeffrey into the community, I didn't worry at all. Additionally, Jeffrey knew he was in a lot of trouble and didn't want to mess with the law which was tantamount to messing with his livelihood. Though I was furious, I kept worrying about how Jeffrey would cope without being able to talk with me every minute and not being able to see his kids.

Two months into our separation, in preparation for trial, I was scheduled for a deposition. Jeffrey's attorneys had to get my side of the story. That they represented Jeffrey and needed to "get their client free from the charges of abuse," my attorney warned, meant they would not be nice. It was a big deal as criminal charges against Jeffrey would change his life forever.

There were two attorneys in the room. Jeffrey's civil attorney and a criminal attorney. True to my lawyer's warning, Jeffrey's criminal attorney was a tough, intimidating, and no-nonsense man. Apart from being tough, he was condescending and did his best to bully me, which I did not allow. He would ask me unrelated things such as my belief in psychics, making fun of the fact, "So do things levitate and spin around the room?"

I don't know what picture Jeffrey had painted of me, but with my back ramrod straight this guy would get to see the new, unflinching Christina. I didn't cower or take his bait. We started the deposition, and I began telling my story. It was easy to speak as it was the truth. About an hour into it, Jeffrey's criminal attorney interrupted. "Let's just stop here."

I couldn't imagine what was going on.

"This is just crazy," he said. "I've worked on some horrible cases. Crimes where people have been killed out of hate. This case is ridiculous."

What the heck is he talking about? It wasn't his hip that was almost dislocated! I crossed my arms defensively but said nothing, waiting for him to continue.

"Listen, Christina," he said." The bottom line here is, in his own way, Jeffrey is in love with you, and it's obvious to me, that you're in love with him. So why on earth is this relationship like this?"

I was so thankful he understood the situation, becoming more affable toward me as things unfolded. The truth was, Jeffrey did love me. I'd always known that. That love was great when Jeffrey was Jeffrey, but when his demons took over that love became an albatross. It's also true that after the children were born Jeffrey didn't love me the way I had expected as the mother of his children, and that was galling. The threats he was making and his treatment of me were likely induced by his drug use, fears, and paranoia that were deeply embedded in his mind. There was nothing I could do to help Jeffrey, unless he became vulnerable, which not even the therapist could get him to be. Despite it all, he did love me as much as he possibly could. I on the other hand had loved Jeffrey unconditionally—until now. That's why I'd put up with his shenanigans all these years because no one is perfect. I wasn't looking for perfection, I'd rather have love. Because of the way I was raised, and my dad's shortcomings, I understood human frailties. But had I understood the man beneath the mask, or myself better, I would never have willingly enabled or fed into his addictions. I may not have liked many of the things Jeffrey did, but I never stopped loving him because of them. Overshadowing all his weakness was his big, kind, and generous heart, and I had chosen the boy/man who just wanted to be loved and I loved him the best *I* could.

Jeffrey was far from stupid or unaware. He might have been in denial but he knew where his love was to be found and where it was not. His fear of losing my love drove him to distractions and to seek emotional satisfaction elsewhere. When he couldn't find it, I became the enemy and his target. In his eyes, I had gone from being his precious, exotic woman to being "Good for Nothing," the name he'd now given me. Instead of saying Christina can you bring me some water, he'd say, "Good for Nothing, bring me some water." And like water off a duck's back, I'd let it slide. Not because I wasn't annoyed, but I didn't need to feed his anger and he knew his statement was so far from true. When he couldn't get a rise out of me, it frustrated him more. If only he could have learned to share my love with *his* children…and only know how much love the children had to give…which was probably equal to or better than mine. He could have found balance…but he did not. All his mind could believe was, I was rejecting him.

His choices for replacing me were not working. Jeffrey knew that most of the people around didn't love him…they loved his money. That made his need to affirm my love for him greater. But the confluence of our second son's birth, leading to less time for him, and his debauchery in South Beach where he thought he'd found the attention he sought but didn't, finally unraveled him. No more could he hide from the demons with just high-risk activities. Jeffrey was at the point where the demons had to be numbed. As his drug use spiraled, he lost more and more touch with reality. If I could only go back. If I could only….

Jeffrey was aware that his money wasn't important to me. Quite the contrary—he never understood that money made things worse for me. It made his world bigger because it brought so many people into it, and the bigger his world got the more constricting mine became. The money was his, not mine. That world was his, not mine. I wanted no part of it. I'd always been a stabilizing force for Jeffrey, even back in New York when he dabbled in cocaine but I never got involved. He counted on me to be in control even if he was not.

The attorney wanted to send us to counseling and set a deadline for a resolution. If we hadn't worked things out by then, we'd figure out where to go from there. The county was trying to make Jeffrey an example, but that wouldn't just affect him, it would affect both of us, our relationship, our children, and our lives. So, the attorney referred us to a counselor named M. Gary Neuman. Gary usually dealt with children whose parents were going through a divorce, but Jeffrey's attorney felt that he could help us. Gary was a brilliant therapist and also a rabbi, so that resonated with Jeffrey.

Gary was highly respected for his work with children. To boot, he was a recurring guest on *The Oprah Winfrey Show* when the topic was divorce. That sat well with Jeffrey. Jeffrey and I agreed to meet with Gary. Part of the problem I worried about with Jeffrey was he didn't respect most people, but he connected with Gary.

Gary was just a wonderful soul, as I discovered on the first day I met him.

"Hello," he said. His eyes crinkled into a warm smile as he shook my hand heftily. *What a nice-looking man. I can't believe that he is a rabbi.* I was surprised I had noticed.

"Nice to meet you," I said sweetly. Immediately I was soothed by his presence. He never jumped to judgment. He worked with us a few times one-on-one, and then he met with us both once or twice a week. Later he started to meet with the kids.

With a restraining order, Jeffrey could only meet the boys and me in Gary's office, as mandated by the court. Alan was the only one who could escort the kids. Jeffrey's demands to see the children at all hours of the day and night were so out of control that he would eventually drive a wedge between him and Alan. Disgusted by Jeffrey and his transgressions, Alan would end up quitting and moved out of Florida, when Jeffrey threatened him and his family.

Because of that, Gary became a huge, central part of our lives. He helped us realize that we both needed each other. He helped us see that we loved one another. Gary told me that Jeffrey loved me to the best of his ability. That his way of expressing his love was providing for us and putting all his trust in me. He said that most men of his wealth would have had a pre-nuptial agreement, but Jeffrey trusted me with everything. He also told me that I needed to give Jeffrey more attention. That if I did, that would help ease his jealousy of the boys. For attention, Gary suggested that as a couple we should have a weekly date night and then also have a family night so we could re-bond as a family. Gary saliently pointed out that though I was a mother, a job I adored, I was also a wife. I was beginning to see once again that while I was blaming Jeffrey's bad boy behaviors they had escalated because I, too, was withholding. I realized too, that I was compartmentalizing. I hadn't made any correlations about my childhood and my life as Jeffrey's wife but there were many things my childhood had impacted.

First, because I was sickly, I somehow encoded I was not as valuable as my other siblings and that whether I understood it or not my psyche was impacted; when on the road trip to mom's family I'd asked if I was the disposable one. For the same reason I didn't think guys would love me so I'd hedge my bet juggling many boyfriends at a time so when we parted I could just move on because I hadn't invested emotionally in any of them. Friction between my parents was there but we ignored it and so I had learned to ignore Jeffrey rather than try to work with him on a solution to our problems. My father had gambled away the family fortune so I was used to Jeffrey's risk-taking behavior. I never stopped loving my father because of it and I never stopped loving Jeffrey either. Yet in therapy, I wondered if each of us was capable of loving the other when to love someone unconditionally one first had to love oneself. Was I really creating a fairytale life that didn't exist other than in the form of wealth?

To be honest, even if these things flashed across my conscious mind it was not until years later and even in writing this book before I could begin to answer the unanswered questions of my existence.

During the challenging period of our lives, I'd kept the kids sheltered from a lot of goings on in our house and because they were young, they didn't seem aware and were not traumatized. The kids appeared to handle therapy well. They didn't know anything about Jeffrey's drug use or that he'd been abusive. Since they were only six and four, they thought Gary was a friend whom they went to see to play games and talk. Gary was skilled at gaining information without causing the children any anxiety. We never sat in with him when he was with the boys but as far as I could tell they enjoyed being with him. When they would play cards and other games Gary would ask them questions about their day-to-day life and I imagine how they felt about me and Jeffrey. He was also assessing the effect our separation might be having. Because the boys were accustomed to Jeffrey being away all the time, so far it didn't present as an issue. Their normal world consisted of me and our housekeeper, Amy, and usually my mother.

At our sessions, Gary would let each of us speak and express our concerns, complaints, wishes, and feelings. Initially, Jeffrey tried to blame everything on me…that I had ignored him and only made time for the kids; that I didn't like his friends, etc.. Gary, having dealt with families going through divorce all the time, did not fall for all of what Jeffrey was saying. Gary would ask Jeffrey to think again about what he was saying and see if he could phrase it in a nicer way. He would try and get Jeffrey to see that he was hurt, rather than mad, and was skilled at diffusing any anger that threatened to surface.

I would respectfully listen to Jeffrey and vice versa. Sometimes, Gary would interject and present a better way to state something or ask a question to help us get our points across. The first few weeks were just back-and-forth bickering, but after a month, we started to put aside our hurt and anger and were able to listen and hear what Gary would advise. We began having more caring and thoughtful sessions. Several times, as it could get emotionally trying, I left crying. We would have to leave at separate times, I imagine for safety reasons, but each time I was driving home from Miami I would get a call from Jeffrey (he was allowed to call me now) and he would apologize for making me sad. He said he hated seeing me so sad, and I know in his heart he meant that.

When I told Gary about the rude names he would call me, "Nicole" or "Good For Nothing," Gary confronted Jeffrey and asked if this was true. Jeffrey laughed and said that it was all a joke and he didn't mean anything by it. Gary then asked Jeffrey if I had condescending or nasty nicknames for him, to which he replied, "No." Gary then explained to Jeffrey how name-calling is actually emotional and mental abuse and is intentionally used to degrade and put someone down in hopes of diminishing their self-esteem and self-worth. He asked if that was what someone who loves someone does. Jeffrey explained that while he always had nicknames for the people he loved, he called Joyce "old lady" or "dragon lady," he called my mom "old lady," and our good friend Suri, he called "fatso" (she is rail-skinny), he didn't mean to be demeaning towards me and he could see how it could hurt me. From then on, the mean name-calling ended.

Gary also came down pretty hard on Jeffrey about his drug use. He reminded him time and again, that not only were they illegal and deadly to him, but if the boys were to accidentally swallow one of his carelessly dropped pills, it would kill them. "Tell me, Jeffrey, could you live with yourself if something like that happened?"

Jeffrey for the first time seemed to comprehend the danger. When Jeffrey felt threatened or angry, he would sit forward in his seat and stare meanly or he would sit back in his chair and act like he didn't care, in an arrogant manner and usually had a smirk on his face. But he was always respectful towards Gary and never cursed or raised his voice and on this revelation, he was all present.

Gary knew Jeffrey loved the boys with all his heart and by making him see the dire effects a potential accident could cause not only in endangering his children but in his wanting to take drugs again, gave Jeffrey pause. It was funny, but not surprising that Gary would tell Jeffrey exactly what I had been saying for months and get him to comprehend it, but he couldn't hear it from me.

Things progressed well with Gary's help. Jeffrey was engaging with the kids, and it gave me the confidence that he was changing for the better. I could now envision Jeffrey being the loving, attentive, and involved father and husband I always thought he could be. I too began to try harder to be sensitive to Jeffrey's needs.

This particular day when we went to see Gary, he said, "Since today is Jeffrey's birthday," Gary's eyes twinkled, "I recommend he spend some time with the kids."

I nodded agreeingly. I wanted Jeffrey to connect with our children. "Okay, no problem" I agreed.

"And then you both should have a date night." Gary finished.

Even though we were still living apart, Gary said that we needed to start having a relationship again, getting back the feeling of being a couple without children and learning what it is to be a couple with children. Now it was painfully obvious that he hoped these interactions would lead us to where we needed to be. I glanced at Jeffrey; he was difficult to read but didn't appear resistant. My heart swelled with hopeful possibilities for our happy future together. With Gary leading the way, I felt more and more confident about its feasibility.

These sessions put us on equal ground without criticism or judgment. For the first time in our relationship, we were engaging in healthy, honest, and positive communication. I thought, *finally my fairytale is coming to fruition. Life is going to be really good.*

On our first date night out, I remember thinking how much fun it was to get dressed up to go out. I tried to look my best for Jeffrey. Before having children, I was the one who loved going dancing, to clubs and nice restaurants, so it made me feel young again. Also, to see Jeffrey so proud of having me with him was a welcome change.

Like Tina's fairytales, there is always some drama, but there is always a happily ever after. So, 35-year-old Christina hoped.

Story Fifteen
GOLDEN ERA

In May 2000 Sam was finished with pre-kindergarten for the summer. The case against Jeffrey was dropped but he was sporadically being tested for drugs, which he continually passed. Jeffrey wanted to move back home, but I was nervous. He had been pretty mean and vindictive before we split and even though things had improved during our separation, I didn't know what I would get when he moved home. Things were so good the way they were and I was scared that if Jeffrey came back, everything would revert to the way it used to be.

I shared my concern with Gary.

"This is my earnest suggestion," Gary said, leaning back in his chair behind his desk. Jeffrey and I sat across from him in separate armchairs. My hands were clasped in my lap anticipating Gary's sage recommendations. "You need to go on a vacation this summer as a family. Spend some quality time together so that you can reconnect and establish a new family dynamic away from Florida and its baggage. A new environment," he further explained, "would give you a fresh start to re-bond."

I was hopeful and looked over at Jeffrey who seemed excited.

"And at the end of the summer, if everything is still going well, allow Jeffrey to come back home. It would be a natural transition." Gary added.

The boys were at home with either my mom or our housekeeper, Amy. I usually went right home after our sessions as they were mentally exhausting but we stayed back and hashed out our plans in Gary's office.

"Where do you want to go?" Jeffrey asked. He was smiling and was truly excited.

After some discussion, we opted for the coastline in the South of France. Joyce and her children often spent summers in the South of France. This was our first time there. The lifestyle was breezy and casually paced for a bonding family vacation. Joyce decided to come along with her kids for a while and that gave me some comfort as Jeffrey and I hadn't been physically in the same space since the altercation. I was excited and hopeful. Jeffrey had put in the months of therapy, was drug tested weekly, and seemed to be back to the guy I first met and loved. With the therapy, we had both matured and changed somewhat. I understood how my pulling away was to Jeffrey a form of abuse. Brene Brown, in her book, *Atlas of the Heart*, explains how, "Jealousy is when we fear losing a relationship or a valued part of a relationship that we already have." She goes on to explain how research shows that high levels of jealousy, which was Jeffrey to a tee, are directly related to problem drinking and to interpersonal violence when drinking. I imagine taking drugs would trigger even more levels of violence, which happened with Jeffrey and his jealousy of my love for our kids and our kids' love for me. He felt left out and not included, which fed his insecurity and thus jealousy. But now with all the therapy, I understood my part in the relationship meltdown too. It is never just one person to blame in a relationship.

There is nothing *not* to love about Cannes. Just up the coast from Monaco, along Rue des Ramparts, the famed French Riviera town (Cannes International Film Festival) boasts amazing sandy beaches and balmy weather at that time of year. We rented a beautiful corner suite at Le Majestic Barriere in Cannes, where we spent the daytime hours at the beach, then we would take the boys to the little carnival along Boulevard de la Croisette or go shopping in all the wonderful upmarket boutiques dotting the avenue. All the while, Jeffrey stayed with us without causing a stir. I could get used to this—Jeffrey's congenial manner.

Joyce stayed with us for the first several weeks and Jeffrey loved having the two women he loved with him. We hired a babysitter a few times when she left so we could go out and have dinner, just Jeffrey and me, husband and wife. We made friends with a loving French family, whom we referred to as our "French family." We loved the area so much that we decided to look for a villa to buy, though that never materialized. I would have loved it. Jeffrey had stayed on in Cannes to look at properties, but never got to finalize a deal before we had to meet up for our Alaska cruise. We felt this was something we could do later. In all our time together bar none, it was the best time of our relationship. Our golden era. If our life could remain on this stratum, I would have indeed found my Prince Charming.

The boys and I flew back to the U.S., and as like several summers before I rented a summer house for my family and their families. This was our once-a-year time together. Jeffrey and I felt it was best for him not to come as I knew my family was still mad at him for the abuse and separation and I needed to have time with them alone to help them understand that things were better. Plus, our family time at the beach still to this day, is the best memories for my boys and all their cousins. It was a wholesome family time and all about love. We agreed to meet in two weeks in Vancouver to take an Alaskan cruise we'd booked for just the four of us.

Alaska was breathtaking. With over three million lakes, twelve thousand rivers and hundreds of thousands of glaciers, the untamed wilderness boasts some of the best seafood which we gladly scoffed down at dinners. This cruise, too, was one of the best we had done.

We spent non-stop time together as a family playing games, sitting at the pool, eating incredible meals, and just enjoying one another. It wasn't me and the boys, then Jeffrey, it was us as one unit, which filled Jeffrey's heart. He was so happy, probably the happiest I had ever seen him, just like in Cannes. Jeffrey spent the entire cruise with me and the boys. He took us on a helicopter ride to the top of a glacier and over volcanoes. We toured the different city ports such as Juneau and Fairbanks. Not once did Jeffrey go to the ship's casino. The extent of his gambling was playing Super Bingo, where we were elated when our youngest "Jakie" ended up winning the Super Jackpot.

At the end of our Alaskan trip, since we were so close to Whistler, British Columbia, we decided to make a pit stop there as we'd never been and heard it was beautiful. A popular ski resort in the winter, the chalet-style village, compact and fun offered great summer sports. My good friend from my New York days, Linh, had a house there and we decided it would be fun to see her too. When it was time to leave, Jeffrey had a strange request. "Let's stop over in Vegas before heading home," he said in a chipper, carefree tone which worried me. I was apprehensive about the temptation to gamble and I wanted nothing from Jeffrey's old life to kick him back into obsession. Still, I didn't want to reveal any lack of trust in him as Jeffrey and I had worked hard on our push to retreat habits and since we were both really trying I thought perhaps it would be harmless. "Really? Okay, no problem." *Guess it'll be a good test.*

Jeffrey's casino host was excited I was coming out with the boys and he invited Linh along as well, and as usual, sent a Gulfstream Jet to pick us up in Whistler. We were again comped at the MGM Mansion, which was a ten-thousand sq. ft. suite/villa, with an Olympic-sized indoor swimming pool, a theater, and butlers at our call. When the boys walked into their room, the room was filled to the roof with toys from FAO Schwartz. My thought: *man, they must have missed him!* We were given private tours to all the Vegas shows and even got to hold the baby tigers from the Siegfried and Roy show. Jeffrey did gamble a bit, and I went with him each night for a while, which made him very happy. He loved having me by his side when he gambled; he said I brought good luck. Gambling made me uncomfortable with the emormous amounts of money he would gamble. At times, he could have three hundred thousand dollars down on the table for a hand of blackjack. My worries were needless because everything went fine. The summer was a resounding success. We were together as a family. We did everything as a family. We interacted as a family. I couldn't have imagined a better family summer. As Gary had suggested, Jeffrey moved back home when we left Las Vegas.

Everything was looking up and Jeffrey went back to "livin' large," but the drugs were no longer a part of the equation. Before leaving for our trip to France, Jeffrey got an offer from E-Trade to purchase his day trading company. They offered him four hundred million dollars in exchange for the company. While he did have some partners/managers whom he would have to pay, the amount of money he would take in was well beyond the twenty million dollars, the exact amount of money he had once dreamed about making for the carefree and abandoned life he envisioned. Over the years, the business had well exceeded those numbers and when the businesses became too big for one person to oversee Jeffrey had made some of his traders, a partner, or a manager. Damien, who I didn't know well, was a significant partner in business outside of the trading companies.

The E-Trade deal would require Jeffrey to sign a three-year contract and to travel around the country to different offices and teach their people how to trade. This to me seemed like it could be a stabilizing force in Jeffrey's life as he loved trading and teaching others. It would also keep him busy and South Beach and Miami would be in our rearview mirror. But Jeffrey had never really worked for someone else and I wasn't sure if he'd take it. He'd always been his own boss and was nervous about signing a three-year contract to work for someone else. I am thinking if this were a non-compete clause opportunity, where Jeffrey couldn't start another company while doing it, he might not find it palatable. Trading was his first love but he'd been there and done that.

"I just don't know. It's great, and it's a lot of money, but me working for someone?" he'd laughed. "What do you think?"

I looked him in the eyes and voiced my honest opinion, "I think it's a good idea because it would give you some purpose." I had also thought about the office being based in California. I'd always wanted to live in California. Our kids were still young, so it was an opportune time to relocate. When I told Jeffrey this, he looked a little more receptive to the idea. So, he hired an attorney to set the ball in motion. In the back of my mind, I prayed he'd make the decision to sell. It was a serious proceeding as a deal like that required a six-month due diligence process and because the market was tumbling from the dot. com bust, E-Trade reduced the offer to three hundred million dollars. It was still a great offer.

Story Sixteen

MEETING WITH THE PRESIDENT

Before and during our split, Jeffrey had become good friends with our congressman, Robert Wexler. Robert would invite us to various events, and we were invited to a cocktail party in D.C. for Bill Clinton. We took the kids with us so they could see the city. At the cocktail party of maybe thirty people, I was introduced to President Clinton and we ended up speaking one-on-one. President Clinton is all that you read about him. When he spoke to you, it was like you were the only person in the room and he gave you his full attention. Very cordially during our conversation, he said, "Why don't you come by the office tomorrow, and you can tour the White House?"

I didn't think he was serious—he probably said that to everyone, or so I imagined. Later that evening, he made a point of finding me in the crowd and repeating the invitation. "If you have time and want to see the White House, let me know," he said cheerfully, his sparkling greenish-blue eyes crinkling as he smiled.

"Well," I smiled back as I responded, "My two sons are with me in town...I'd actually love for them to see the White House."

"No problem! Bring them by, and I'll have everything set up for you." His bodyguard handed me a card and a number to call. Jeffrey was so excited and impressed that the President personally invited me to the White House.

The next morning, I called the number thinking that he was being nice and probably didn't remember giving the invitation, *There's no way that I'm on the President's radar.*

But the Secret Service was expecting us, so I took the kids and Jeffrey along with me. When we arrived at the White House the security guards at the gate looked up our names and welcomed us. A security detail then accompanied us to the White House through a private entrance.

The President was called into a meeting at the last minute, so he didn't get to meet with us on the tour. Still, it was incredible to be in the White House at the President's invitation. The Secret Service opened up the Oval Office to us, and the kids got to sit at his desk. They even let us take photos in the room. It was an amazing memory for everyone.

The week Jeffrey moved back home, he received a call from Congressman Robert Wexler. "I have a favor to ask of you," he said. "President Clinton is going to do a series of dinners before he leaves office, and he specifically inquired if you and Christina would host one of the dinners for him at your house."

It was the kind of offer you just can't say no to. The dinner was scheduled for that October and the Secret Service flew down to map out our house, our community, and the surrounding area to make security arrangements for the event. I was looking forward to creating a memorable event that would make Jeffrey proud and the President welcome. It was not to pass.

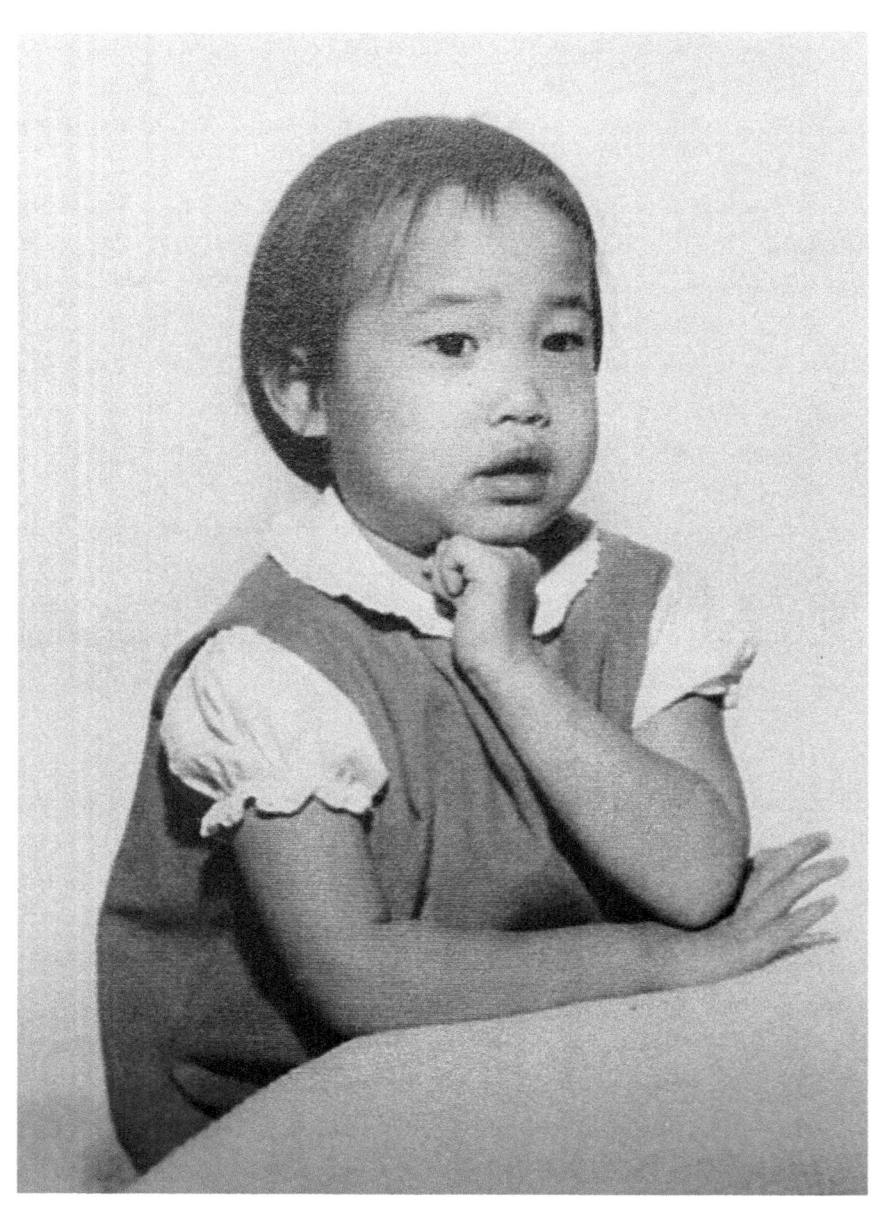

Tina at 3 years old.

Tina at sixteen years old.

(L-R) Tina, Betty, Anita.

(L-R) Betty, Tina, Anita practicing for Miss Bunny's Ballet. I am crying!

(L-R) Tina 7, Betty 8, Brian 1, Anita, 9, Alan, almost 2.

My Kindergarten Class.
Tina, first row on the left.

Daddy's Little Girl.
Tina and Dad, 1971.

Mom and Dad on their wedding day.

My Grandparents (L-R) Matthew T.H. Liu, Betty J. Liu, Sue Fong Hom (in red of course) and Song K. Hom.

My Family: (L-R) Brian, Sieu, Betty, Mom, Me, Anita, and Alan in back.

Me with my Godmother and namesake, Christina Harada.

Me with my Aunt Fran and Uncle Herb Wilson.

The Hood Days
(L-R) Back Row: Jennifer, Stacy, Jane, Me, Christy
Front Row: Betsy, Leslie, Kirsten.

My Boca Besties
Amy Cavayero, Me, and Robin Rubin.

My Boca BFF's
Me, Sheila Fuente, Roxane Lipton, Mara Reuben, and Tisha Hallett.

My Hearts and Hope Group
Me, Ami Reese, Melanie Perkins, Nisa Birnbaum, Brenda Firestone, Lillian Fennell, and Patti Karoussos.

Jeffrey and Me at the infamous 10-year together party.

Jeffrey in San Tropez in July 2000.

Me and Jeffrey as the Simon Weisenthal Centers Honorees.

Our Little Family: Jay on Jeffrey's lap, me holding Sam.

The boys: (L-R) Jay and Sam.

Our family in President Clinton's Oval Office at The White House
Jay in Jeffrey's arms, me and Sam

Sam and Jay with their cousins at the NJ Beach house in 2009.

More Boca Besties
L-R Robyn Chwatt, Me, Johanna DeKama, Brooke Porter,
and Rona Goldberg

(L-R) Joyce Silverman, me, and Neil Silverman.

My 40th birthday party in Beaver Creek.

My 40th birthday in Jamaica.
(L-R) Front Row: Annie Hausmann, me, Marsha Eisenberg
(L-R) Back Row: Eliette Otero-Romano, Gina Ford, Chris Golden, Kim Lindsey, Wendy Zoberman.

My Miami Sisters
(L-R) Me, Gina Ford, Bobbie van der Vlugt, Tracy Mourning.

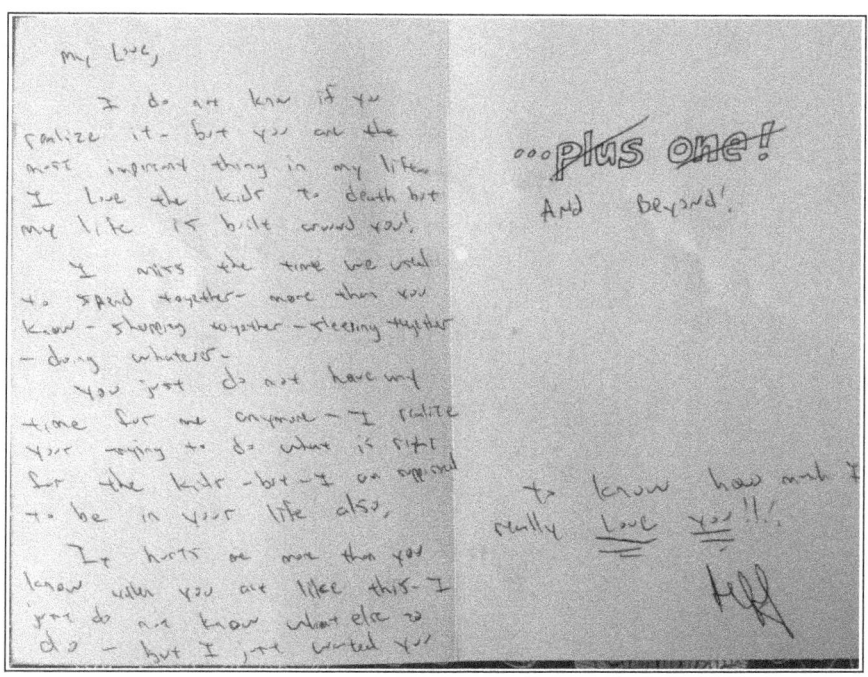

A letter from Jeffrey.

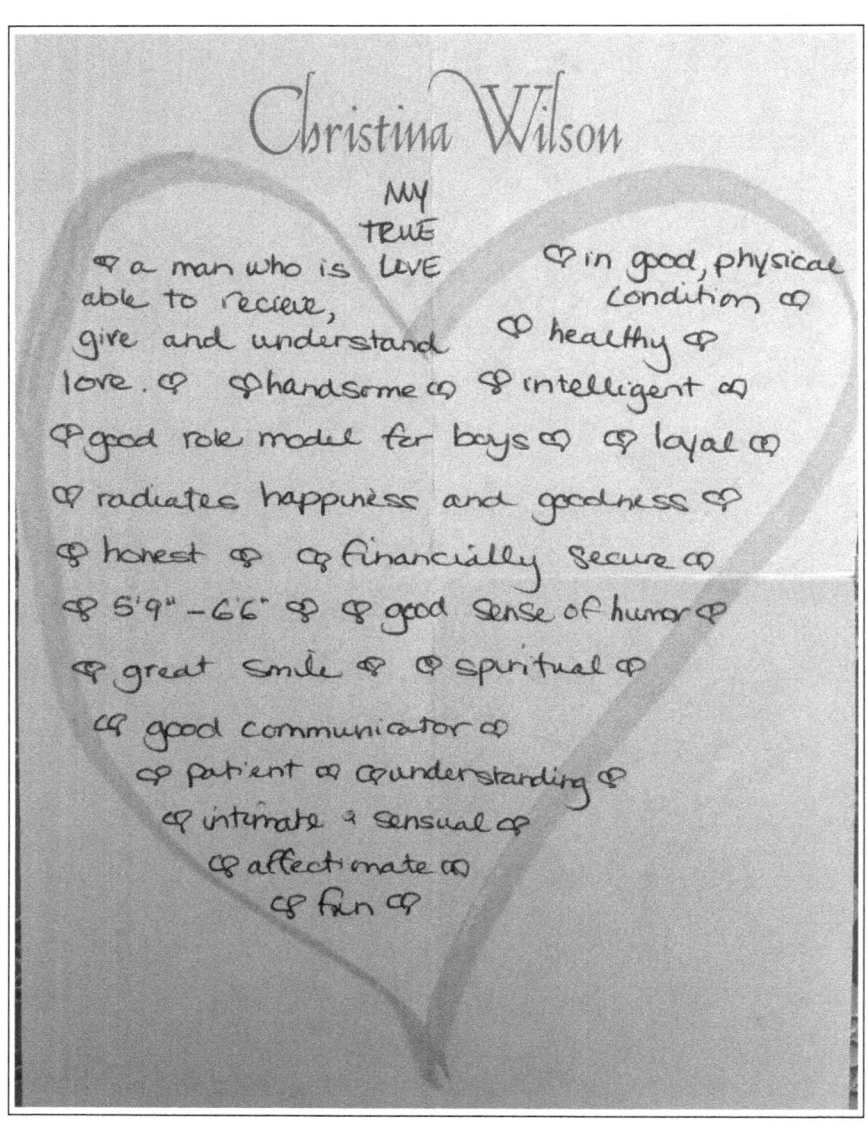

The infamous note with qualities for my ideal partner.

Anthony Liggins, me, and Harold in 2010.

(L-R) Harold Dawson Sr., Rose Dawson, me, and Harold.

Our wedding was officiated by Ambassador Andrew Young.
(L-R) Our daughters Brianna, Katrina, me, Amb. Young, and Harold.

Our Wedding Day (L-R) John Sparrow Cari's Husband,
Cari (my sister-in-law), me and Harold.

Our Wedding Day: Me and Harold.

Sunset in Punta Mita: Me and Harold.

My 59th birthday with the Hom Family.

My Crazy Kids
(L-R): Allen, Brianna, Jay, Katrina, and Sam.

10th Anniversary Surprise Party in Tuscany.
Me and Harold October 2023

Family and Friends at our 10th Anniversary in Tuscany.

My Family in Tuscany
Front row: Me and Harold.
(L-R) Back row: Sam, Allen, Katrina, Jay and Brianna.

Story Seventeen

EERIE FULFILLMENT

Our time away made me more feel confident Jeffrey could be his old affable self, so the next step, as Gary had suggested, was getting back together as a family. After our time in Vegas ended, we flew back to Boca Raton and Jeffrey came home with me and the boys. Jeffrey's first weekend back in our house was in September and we celebrated Sam's sixth birthday on Jeffrey's boat. Our friends and family, including my sister Anita, and her kids visiting from Dubai had a fun-filled day and everyone had a great time.

The night before Sam's first day of kindergarten, I was excited as I got everything ready. I wanted to be the one to take our firstborn, but Jeffrey offered to take Sam to school. Knowing it would be good for both of them, I encouraged him to do so. That meant a lot to both of them because it marked a milestone and for me, it was a blessing to see Jeffrey taking such an interest in family life. Watching my firstborn son head out to his first day of what would be the next twelve years of his life was so heartwarming. Sam was dressed in his light blue polo shirt and khaki shorts uniform and Jeffrey in his standard bathing suit and island shirt. Jeffrey put the top of the Bentley convertible down and had Sam sit in the front passenger side seat. Sam felt special as he knew that he was supposed to sit in the rear passenger seat as a child of six years of age, but fortunately, he was pretty big for his age so it didn't look too suspicious. They both waved happily with big smiles as Jay and I watched them pull out of the driveway. As I watched them drive away, our firstborn and his father, side by side to Sam's first day of kindergarten I felt hopeful. The future looked bright for all of us and my worries started to fade away from unpleasant memories of the past.

In the spring of 1998, I went to my yearly reading with a woman named Iris Saltzman. Iris was well known in the para-psychology space and had even been mentioned in Brian Weiss's blockbuster book *Many Lives, Many Masters*. She was a regular on Sally Jesse Raphael, Larry King, and other shows. She looked like a normal woman except for her unusual bug eyes. I went in with an open mind, knowing only too well some of the traits of "the phonies." Vague generalizations that could apply to anybody and keen observations made then wax convincingly. I was careful not to reveal too much of anything or use my body language to indicate something unspoken but I was floored by this woman's reading. She seemed to be the real deal! She told me things that were so specific I couldn't figure out how she would know them as a complete stranger!

My friend and neighbor, Roxane who had been to Iris before me, told me to be prepared and know my history before I went to see her. So being one to take advice to heart, I made a list of events that happened during my lifetime, so I could be ready for when she brought events up. I sat across the desk from Iris. Her office was dark. Iris introduced herself and said that she was going to go into a trance-like state. I watched as she closed he eyes and breathed deeply. After a minute or two she opened her eyes, which seemed to have become more pronounced and stuck out more. She then began talking. She just rambled on about things and at times I thought she was speaking another language, then she said what happened when you were almost three? Something significant happened. Of course, I understood it to be when I almost died and was in a coma. She then asked about me falling off my bike and bruising my left knee when I was eight or nine, which happened; and I did have a funny scar.

She continued to go on and on about things that didn't make sense, but every so often would ask a question or bring up a name that made sense or was relatable.

"Christina," she finally said, "you need to be very aware of your dreams. Your dreams are always telling you things."

The moment she said it, I thought of that *damn red motorcycle dream*. I told her the dream. With her eyes closed she just blurted out, "It isn't a red motorcycle. It's a red sportscar. But don't worry, he's alone. You should get life insurance on him if you don't have it already."

What the heck? She must be crazy. Psychics aren't supposed to say someone is going to die. This can't be true. I just didn't want to think about it. I wouldn't allow my conscious mind to go there. I continued to listen as Iris talked on and then when she finished and came out of her state, I thanked her and left, my mind feeling burdened.

A new business opportunity had come up and Jeffrey had decided to go check it out. After taking Sam to his first day of kindergarten he and his nightclub partner, Damien, flew to Costa Rica to look into the feasibility of starting this new business: online poker and sports betting. When he got back, he'd planned to meet his attorneys to try to seal the deal with E-Trade. I wasn't too excited about this Costa Rica thing as it would take him away from home but it was far better than South Beach. I was praying he would take the E-Trade deal as it would give him purpose. As usual, Jeffrey was back to calling me many times a day. I'd already spoken to him a few times that day and he was supposed to return that night. On September 10, 2000, at around seven p.m., Jeffrey called me from Costa Rica to tell me he'd decided to stay over to meet with someone the following morning before flying back. I could tell he was a little frustrated with being there. I don't know what had frustrated him but he just wanted to get home. He was already there and it was seven p.m. so I told him another day wasn't a big deal. Why not just stay over and get what he needed to do done?

"All right," I said. "I will see you tomorrow."

Everything between us was so going well, and though it had only been two weeks and my jury was still out on what long term would bring, I was truly hopeful about being back together.

Anita and Mack were living in Dubai at the time so to escape the hot, hot summer months Anita and her two children would come to stay with us or with my parents in Philadelphia. Anita and her kids who were with us, were leaving for Philadelphia the next day. We got the kids to bed and then we settled in for the night. At one-thirty a.m., Jay woke up, scared for some reason, and wanted to sleep in my bed. I pushed back the covers to let him in, holding his body close to me as we slept. The thing about Jay was that he clung to me during the days but at night he always wanted to sleep in his own bed. The situation gave me pause because strangely, it was the first time he'd ever asked to sleep in my bed. He only liked to sleep in his bed with all his "didis," which were originally burping towels that became Jay's comfort blankies. All Jay ever needed to self-soothe was his thumb and didi's. When I could finally shake off my unsettled feeling, I fell back asleep.

I always kept the ringers of the phone off in the bedrooms at night so as not to disturb the children as I never thought of an Emergency call happening. But the phone rang at six a.m. I don't know why the ringer was on, but it was. I jumped up and grabbed it so it wouldn't awaken Jay.

"Hi. Mrs. Wilson please?" the woman asked.

"Speaking," I whispered.

"This is Hollywood Memorial Hospital. We need you to come down. We have your husband here."

My groggy eyes narrowed. "I don't think so. It must be a mistake," I said. "My husband is in Costa Rica." *Stupid wrong number....*

"There was a car accident. We're just going off his license."

I had been to that hospital once—just the week before to take Jay in for an evaluation. Jay was little for his age so the doctors wanted to monitor his development.

"I was there the other day. Did I drop Jeffrey's license there?" I asked.

"No, listen to me. There's been a car accident and you need to come down. This is your husband."

I tried again to explain. "That's not my husband. My husband is in Costa Rica. I just talked to him less than twelve hours ago."

"The only ID we have from the car belongs to your husband. We need you to come down here like now."

"What car is it?" I thought our driver had taken Jeffrey to the airport.

"It's a red Ferrari."

My heart froze. *Did she just say a red Ferrari?* Instantly I thought of the red motorcycle dream and the psychic. I couldn't believe it. *No, this isn't possible*! Jeffrey can be careless, but I was sure, as usual, Jeffrey had Mateo (our driver) take him to the airport. *One of his friends must have borrowed the Ferrari. That was not unusual. To my chagrin, Jeffrey always let his hanger-on friends borrow his cars whenever they wanted. That could be the only explanation.* But my mind constantly flitted back to the dream. Because of that, I headed to the hospital just to be sure. I asked Anita to wake up the kids and get Sam to school.

The weather had been terrible throughout the night, a nor'easter storm had come through, which was somewhat typical as we were in hurricane season. The rains and winds had stopped by the time I woke up. As I rushed to the hospital, I was anxious. I always thought if something bad had happened to someone close to me—to my parents, kids, or Jeffrey—that I would feel it in my gut. I thought I would feel sick to my stomach or uneasy or something, but I didn't feel anything other than anxiousness from the morning call.

On the way to the hospital, I called my mom to let her know what was going on, I called my friends Joyce and Gina, and then I called our driver. I asked Mateo if he was supposed to pick up Jeffrey from the airport sometime today.

"No," he said. "Jeffrey drove the Ferrari to the airport."

My stomach sank. "Do you know if anybody went to the airport with him to borrow his car?"

"I don't know."

My heart sank further. "Can you meet me at the hospital, then?"

"Yes."

Mateo was living in Miami Beach about thirty minutes from the Hospital, so I figured that he would arrive around the same time as me. When I walked into the hospital and inquired about Jeffrey, they told me my husband was in the trauma unit. Taking a deep breath, I walked into this big room which was empty except for one person. Like they said, it was Jeffrey. I was shocked at his physical appearance. I'd expected blood and gore, but Jeffrey looked perfectly fine except he was hooked up to a bunch of machines, and monitor lights were flashing his vitals. He had a couple of cuts and scrapes, but his color was good. Really, he looked perfectly healthy. Like he was taking a nap. I didn't understand what I was seeing. I could only stare at Jeffrey in disbelief. *This is not happening, this cannot be happening. Maybe he is just in shock*, I kept thinking. *He couldn't have been hurt that badly. He looks fine!*

The monitor he was hooked up to was a breathing machine and I noticed this was not as it looked. He was not fine. What I understand now, is that when confronted with sudden experiences, one can go into Fight, Flight, or Freeze mode. I was in Freeze mode as I felt stuck and couldn't move. I am a problem solver, but I was stuck. As I was contemplating what to do next, a trauma surgeon approached me.

"Are you Mrs. Wilson?"

"I am."

"And this is your husband?"

"He is."

"He was in a bad accident. I give him a four percent chance to live."

Just like that? He sounded like he was giving me a weather report. For a minute I said nothing, then I quizzically looked at the man in front of me and spluttered, "Excuse me?"

"He's suffered a severe head trauma, a (TBI) traumatic brain injury, and he probably has only a four percent chance of survival."

That was it. My dander rose like bile. How dare he? How dare he play God! I couldn't believe the arrogance of this man. The nerve of him to walk up to a woman whose husband lay flat on a bed, supposedly dying, and just say something like that as though it was nothing! Where was his bedside manner? Where was his humanity?

Now I'm a tolerant woman. I don't normally fight or do unnecessary drama. These qualities are how I was able to put up with a lot of Jeffrey's attitude through the years. But contrary to what others may think or have thought, I am far from being a pushover, and when I feel backed up against a wall I come out fighting. I could feel my fangs coming out at this ill-mannered guy who was really over the top. My back straightened, my eyes began to squeeze and my heart started beating fast. *This guy is messing with the wrong person.*

"Four percent?" I asked in an acerbic tone. "What kind of a number is that? Tell me, how exactly do you arrive at a number like four percent?" I made sure he knew I intended to be insulting. Being who I am, if the surgeon had been a little more tactful, and had even an ounce of empathy and grace, I might have accepted his professional opinion. "Are you trying to tell me that there isn't a surgery, there aren't any medications, there is absolutely nothing you can do for him? But you can stand there and give me a four percent chance?"

"Look," he said his tone even more deriding, "If I was to cut into your husband's skull, his brain would fly out all over the place, and that would be the end of him."

I was stunned. I was *verklempt!* And I was angry. And I wasn't about to back down on this imbecilic man when it concerned my husband's life. "Thank you for your opinion. I'm going to find someone who can do something." I pushed passed him. So, when faced with this dire situation my brain goes into hyper-solution mode. My problem-solving self was back. Obviously, this doctor couldn't do anything to help, so I was going to find someone who could. I didn't know about the thirty-six-hour rule for traumatic brain injury patients then, but I just felt that time was ticking and I needed to act fast. Because of the doctor's insensitivity I refused to give up. Jeffrey was not going to die that day!

I went straight to a pay phone. I don't know why as my cell was somewhere but I was not in any state of mind to think, and the pay phone was what came to mind. I went into action mode. It was probably seven-thirty a.m. when I started making phone calls. I began calling friends who I knew would help me in my time of need. Joyce, Mateo, Gina, and her husband Tommy Ford, had arrived and I told them about the situation at hand. I called Larry Phillips, heir of Phillips Van Heusen, who thought of Jeffrey like a son and was very connected, and I called Chris Golden, my dearest friend in Boca Raton, who I knew would call everyone we knew, or research who to contact. Chris and her husband, Daniel Golden were neighbors we met when we moved into St. Andrews Country Club and also our witnesses at our Jerusalem wedding. Like Jeffrey, Daniel was a big donor to the Jewish Federation of South Palm Beach County.

The Federation community thought it funny that they both had non-Jewish partners named Christine/Christina. It was pretty easy to guess that we were the "shiksas" at all the Federation events. Chris and I became instant friends as we share an interest in the same thing...psychics and astrologers. I told them, "I don't care what it takes, just get me someone who knows what they're doing."

By ten a.m. I spoke to the nurses and found out more about Jeffrey's condition. Jeffrey was in a coma and his brain was swelling.

His Glasgow Score, a neurological score that indicates the severity of a brain injury and the conscious state of a person, with fifteen being normal and three being the lowest score, was three. This meant he had no response to anything. His ICP or increased intracranial pressure, normal range of seven to fifteen mmHg was in the twenties and going up. How could this be when Jeffrey looked so peaceful…like he was asleep. I had no idea at the time what all of this meant but I knew I had to act even faster.

My calls to friends had set off an avalanche. I had no idea how some people got wind of Jeffrey's situation but by ten-thirty a.m., the hospital was swarming with hundreds of people. My friends, Jeffrey's coworkers, employees, the dreaded South Beach entourage which my girlfriend Tracy had labeled the "FOJ's"—the leeches who went around town saying they were "friends of Jeffrey's" to get into clubs, restaurants, and casinos; and others I'd never even heard of. So many people were there that police officers had to be called in to control the crowd.

I was not happy about the mob of people milling around and I didn't have time to acknowledge them. I couldn't speak to anyone. I kept pacing around the room. I just needed to think and figure this out. Fix this situation. I couldn't be distracted. If I lost focus, I would break down. My focus needed to stay on a solution, for I wasn't going to let Jeffrey die. I knew he wasn't going to die. Not that day. I just had to find him a good doctor. I couldn't believe Jeffrey was just lying there, flat on his back. If I didn't know better I would think it was one of his practical jokes but I did know better because after I had grasped the reality of the situation I realized the tubes coming out of every orifice were the machines keeping him alive.

At around eleven a.m., my friend Chris said, "Christina, we found Jeffrey a doctor. He is one of the world's most renowned neurosurgeons but he's in New York. This will cost a lot of money that has to be paid now. Is that okay?"

I didn't have to think twice. "Get the jet, get the pilot, and go get the doctor. I don't care what it costs." I directed. "We need him down here immediately."

I was relieved and finally hopeful. This was something I could finally do that needed to be done, and it would keep me proactive in helping to save Jeffrey's life. Jeffrey had money, and if there was ever a good reason to use it, this was it.

I immediately called the neurosurgeon, giving my approval for him to come down. Apparently, he was the Chief of Neurosurgery at a New York Trauma Center as well as a clinical professor at Weill Cornell Medical College. But even with his stellar credentials, unfortunately, he wasn't licensed to treat Jeffrey in Florida.

"But listen," he said, "I am going to speak with Hollywood Memorial Hospital and get everything worked out so I can at least come in and evaluate your husband." He asked me to fetch Jeffrey's chart and read him some of the medical information.

I got the chart and read it to him.

He told me not to worry, that he was looking at a twenty-four to thirty-six-hour window to act in this case. "I'll get down there in plenty of time. How do they have Jeffrey set up right now?"

"He's just lying flat in a bed, hooked up to machines."

He told me to have Jeffrey's head up at a forty-five-degree angle to reduce brain swelling. I felt reassured after I hung up the phone. I prayed that everything was going to turn out okay. If this neurosurgeon was as good as they said, I wouldn't go through the whole ordeal alone or in the dark. I hadn't had a moment, and to my surprise, I hadn't cried.

The doctor had, as he'd said, reached out to Hollywood Memorial Hospital. As soon as the hospital realized I'd called in a renowned neurosurgeon from New York to assess Jeffrey's case, his local medical care team came out of the woodwork. Doctors and nurses were rushing in and out of his room, asking me constantly what they could do for me and constantly monitoring Jeffrey at his bedside. Jeffrey was now at a forty-five-degree angle as the New York doctor had suggested and compared to when I first arrived, when he was just lying flat and going to be left to die with his four-percent chance of survival, I felt something good was going to happen.

The chief of neurosurgery of Hollywood Memorial Hospital came into Jeffrey's room shortly after and introduced himself to me. "I can't believe you have this neurosurgeon coming here," he gushed.

"I guess that's what needs to be done for Jeffrey to be treated as he should be treated," I said disdainfully.

"I trained with him in Medical School. He is a genius." The doctor said in awe.

So that's why all the activity. Too bad it had to take all that to get my husband the care he needed.

All morning and afternoon, it seemed like hundreds of people were in and out of the hospital waiting room. I am glad I was too preoccupied but I got the gist of the mayhem. Everyone wanted to claim Jeffrey, best friends, girlfriends, business partners, you name it. I was busy making phone calls and talking to people who mattered amidst the chaos. During the afternoon, a nurse came over and said, rather uncertainly, "Mrs. Wilson, we just got a phone call from the White House, calling to check on the status of your husband and I believe they said the President is thinking of you?"

"Thank you," I said cordially. I had enough to keep me occupied to answer the obvious question lingering in her eyes but in hindsight, I'm sure all the nurses were wondering who the heck my husband was that the White House would be calling. In a month from then, we were to have hosted President Clinton at our home.

It was very gracious of him to call and though I was distracted and focused on Jeffrey's care, I was grateful.

Boca Raton is no stranger to bad weather. I would constantly ask Jeffrey not to tool around in his Ferrari when the weather was bad. We had a fleet of cars to choose from each as ostentatious, and much safer but the extra showy, red Ferrari, represented risk and danger which was right up Jeffrey's alley. The week before the accident, in a similar storm, I had refused to drive with Jeffrey in that Ferrari. Instead, I'd called our driver to come pick us up in our Range Rover, even as Jeffrey insisted the Ferrari was perfectly safe. I believe the accident was his destiny and not mine.

So, here we were in the middle of the bad weather that had caused Jeffrey's accident in the first place and I was desperately trying all I could to save his life. He'd only just come home two weeks before and only last week he'd held his son's hand and taken him to school. Our new beginning was so promising, how could life be so cruel?

Jeffrey it seemed had changed his mind about staying in Costa Rica and taken an earlier flight home. After all the talking I'd done, he'd still gotten into his Ferrari that was parked at the airport—which he shouldn't have done in that kind of weather—instead of calling Mateo to pick him up, especially since he'd flown into Miami Airport over an hour away. The Ferrari, so low to the ground, hydroplaned, spun out and he lost control of it and hit the median. Somehow the door opened and Jeffrey fell out of the moving car and landed on his head in the middle of the Florida Turnpike. That explained why he had no broken bones or other visible cuts and bruises. His head had sustained the brunt of the injury resulting in severe head trauma.

As I heard it, a witness to the accident, headed in the opposite direction stopped his car, jumped the median, and called 911. The Good Samaritan had even held an umbrella over Jeffrey to shelter him from the rain and to make sure passing cars could see them through the bad weather and wouldn't run over Jeffrey. He'd stood with him until the police arrived. When I heard about him, my eyes watered for the first time but I did not give in to the pending tears. Had I broken down, I feared I'd be ineffective and I had to hold it together for Jeffrey. I fleetingly kept thinking I had to find this man. I had to thank this man because he was Jeffrey's *angel here on earth*. Yes, there are angels here on Earth. I know that. I believe that and I am convinced that this man was one of them.

The same storm was delaying the neurosurgeon's take off in New York. I was worried sick. When you've been told you have a twenty-four to thirty-six-hour window to save your husband's life, twelve hours is an eternity to wait for that savior. Finally, I was told the doctors were arriving, so I went to stand outside Jeffrey's room doorway to greet them. As I impatiently looked down the hall, I saw whom I believed to be the neurosurgeon and a younger doctor approaching.

The neurosurgeon walked with an air of confidence that was quite intimidating. His resident also looked confident but had an ease to him that made him more approachable. I introduced myself as they got close to where I was standing.

"I'll talk to you after I see your husband," the neurosurgeon said quickly walking into the room. He had a serious, no-nonsense look on his face and was all business. I understood he was a professional and had to prioritize his patient's needs, but at the moment I couldn't help thinking another demi-god! *Oh great, another asshole doctor.* This time though, I had no verbal reprimand. I was patient. I had to be. He was my only hope.

When he came back into the hallway where I had remained, he finally greeted me.

"Mrs. Wilson, your husband has suffered a serious traumatic brain injury but we can manage him."

"What do you mean manage him?'"

The neurosurgeon explained that they had a lot of experience with cases like Jeffrey.

His tone was softer and more understanding than the other Dr. Demi-God, but I was still shocked at his businesslike matter-of-factness It was great news but *my God, do these guys have no emotion?* I suppose when one sees death every day becoming immune to it is necessary, which of course might be good for them, but terribly insensitive to the families of dying patients. I supposed too, that doctors didn't want to give false hope but there had to be a balance somehow.

He explained that they were going to perform a bedside procedure in which a shunt would be inserted to release the fluids that were building up in Jeffrey's brain. By doing so, this would give his brain more room.

He asked me to sign a consent form permitting him to treat Jeffrey.

The doctors said they could get started on treating Jeffrey right then but would need to get him up to New York for surgery.

My mind went into a tailspin. *Jeffrey is hooked up to machines, he is in a coma, I was told he had a four percent chance to live. Now they want to fly him up to NY. What is going on and what am I to do?*

I felt weakened by that strong dose of reality. Those were the only two options. I surely didn't want Jeffrey to die, so, I agreed to let them treat my husband. What other choice did I have? I just had to hand over the reins and have faith. I truly just had to believe.

"Okay, we'll go to NY," I said softly. With that confirmation and the consent form signed, they went into the room and put a shunt into Jeffrey's skull to relieve the pressure. Within seconds Jeffrey's ICP number dropped. My heart leaped. Seeing this gave me the hope I needed to pick up and go back to where it all started with us...New York City.

I arranged for a med-jet to transport Jeffrey and the doctors to New York. I would follow in our jet. The whole ordeal made me think of my mother's actions when I was in a coma at three years old. She had the faith and the courage to follow her instincts to take me to a different hospital. She took a risk, but she'd saved my life. The similarity of the situation was uncanny. I tried to channel her in those frightful moments. I had the faith to take the risk in the hopes of saving Jeffrey's life.

On the plane, I stared out the window at the formidable gray clouds below. They mirrored the gloominess I felt inside. Joyce, ever the bedrock had flown up with me and planned to stay until we figured out the next steps. I was so thankful to her for leaving her own family to be with me. My mother had now gone down to Florida to be with the kids so I was rest assured they'd have the best care. The boys were accustomed to their Nana being with them and she knew their routine down pat. Anita and her kids stayed for a week with my mom in Florida then they all flew to Philadelphia on that Friday for Sieu Fong's wedding. Sam and Jay were in the wedding.

We arrived at the NY City Hospital in the early hours of Tuesday morning. By eight a.m. hordes of our friends and business associates from New York were crowding the SICU waiting room. I had never seen news travel so fast and so far. It was a testament to the kind of friend Jeffrey was for so many people over his thirty-nine years. Most of them were his friends and many of the people I called friends had also been because of Jeff, including Joyce. The hospital gave us a private waiting room, much appreciated since so many people had shown up to offer support and I couldn't deal with the madness. The trip to New York was now fading into a stressful blur of on-the-spot decisions and emergency surgery.

With a traumatic brain injury (TBI) the first thirty-six hours are critical. If the patient is treated properly within that amount of time, recovery is much more likely. Though Jeffrey's neurological readings were abysmal, luckily we were now in good hands. The first thing they did was a craniotomy, which meant they took out a hand-sized piece of the skull to give his brain room to swell safely without building up pressure inside the skull. *Imagine that, I scoffed thinking about the doctor at Hollywood Memorial, they cut into the skull and his brains didn't come flying out all over!* We were hoping with the pressure released, Jeffrey would begin to recover. Distressingly, they also found that what Jeffrey had suffered was a brain shearing—when the brain shifts in the skull causing tearing of the internal lining, tissues, and blood vessels—and not brain damage as in a puncture to the brain. Jeffrey had one of the worst kinds of brain injury one could have and the prognosis was not good. Often fatal, it at best leaves the victim in a vegetative state. There have been, however, reports of recovery in younger people. Jeffrey was only thirty-nine years old and I prayed age was on his side. After the surgery, he had round-the-clock care and the pressure in his brain was constantly monitored to see his responsiveness to treatment.

The surgery went well but Jeffrey was still in a coma. The first three days were touch and go; it was life-giving over to death from minute to minute. The subsequent surgeries were a blur. At one point the doctors mentioned that it would be so much easier to monitor the oxygen in his skull if they had a certain type of machine. Unfortunately, even at this level-one trauma center, the hospital didn't have one. It didn't seem like a question, in my eyes, so I said, "Let's get one." Whatever we needed to do, we were going to do. If this would make a difference in helping to keep Jeffrey alive and give him a fighting chance for recovery, that's what was going to be done.

"Are you sure?" The doctor asked, baffled.

The hospital immediately went through the process to find the machine. Once it was located and authorized, I paid the few hundred thousand dollars tab—and donated it to the hospital.

I had a lot of pushback from people who didn't think I should be spending Jeffrey's money this way. God knows why I had finally married Jeffrey and this was the reason. As his wife, it was mine and only my decision to decide. I again thanked my angels who had never led my steps astray, not even when things looked dark. I categorically knew there was a reason for everything. I needed to thank M. Gary Neuman for suggesting our vacation away. If the universe was delivering a message, it wanted me to have one of the greatest memories of being with Jeffrey for me and our boys.

The doctors stayed in the SICU room with Jeffrey round the clock, trading off shifts. Joyce and I stayed and slept in the waiting room. We were on day three but I dared not leave as at any minute they might need me to sign consent for more surgery or medication, so I didn't have a reprieve. And a good thing I did because Jeffrey's pressure started going up dangerously. This was absolutely haranguing.

One of the neurosurgeons was European and had performed treatments in Europe that weren't approved by the FDA in the United

States. He mentioned a method he'd used in Europe several times with successful results in improving patient outcomes. But to do a Hypertonic Saline treatment here he'd have to get special permission from the hospital and me. There weren't many other options left to try at this point, and they had to decrease the swelling in Jeffrey's brain somehow. I was perfectly willing to try anything to give Jeffrey a better chance at survival.

When the doctors presented the treatment option to the hospital, it was granted right away. The stipulation was that a doctor had to stay with Jeffrey for the duration of the procedure and then Jeffrey would have to be monitored around the clock. So, the doctors agreed to the bedside sentence. The doctor administered, very slowly, the precise infusion percentage of sodium saline through a central line in Jeffrey's chest. If he'd given too much, too quickly, it could be fatal, so there was a huge risk. Then, it became a wait-and-see.

The treatment seemed like a miracle—Jeffrey's pressure started going down. He went from being on the verge of death to being stable. He was the first person in the United States to have that procedure, which has since been documented in medical journals. I couldn't help but smile as Jeffrey liked firsts. After the fourth day in New York, things were stable. I hadn't left the hospital. I hadn't showered and was in the same clothes since I'd gotten the initial phone call about Jeffrey's accident. Someone, I don't recall who, had booked me a room at a hotel a couple blocks away so I decided to go and take a shower and have a break.

As soon as I arrived at the hotel, the hospital called and said, "You need to come back. They found a clot and your husband needs to go back into surgery." I thought, *My God! What next. I can't even get a shower.*

In addition to worrying about my husband's safety, I missed my kids. Jeffrey was my priority, but I worried about my boys. I knew they were well cared for and that I didn't have to worry, but this was the first time since their birth I had been away from them for any length of time. Confident of the boys' care, I focused solely on Jeffrey.

With all that could be done, it was now all about making it through the hour or the night. I took things moment-to-moment and day-by-day. Thinking too far into the future was unfathomable. I had to stay present. The emotional toll would be too much to endure if I didn't keep to micro steps. But as time passed, about two weeks, the intervals stretched out a little more and then a little more. I breathed a sigh of relief. Knowing we were in this for the long haul, I started to think about finding a home in the city. Thank goodness the throngs of people had abated by now and I could have a more predictable routine. My friend Linh, whom I'd met in the early 1990s at the Peninsula Spa, was my first one hundred percent Asian friend. We always laughed at how she was the first person, outside of family, that I befriended who was like me.

Although Linh was not an ABC like me, she was Vietnamese and born in Vietnam, we were simpatico. She was married to a Japanese man and they lived on the Upper East Side of Manhattan. We'd become fast friends when we were both young women of leisure, without kids, and with unlimited funds. Joyce knew that Linh had just been with me and Jeffrey in Vegas but had returned to her home in Whistler. As Joyce needed to start preparing to go back home to her family, she reached out to Linh and immediately Linh flew to New York. She began to take charge of my life by finding me a place to live and booking rooms for me at the Four Seasons Hotel when the boys and my mom would come up on the weekends. During the weekdays I stayed in a hotel room adjacent to the hospital so I could be more or less on the premises at all times. I had put a stop to any more visits to the hospital by creating a phone line so people could call in to get an update on Jeffrey's progress. Joyce, who'd been with me day and night had gone back home so I had a lot of time to think.

We were going into the third week. Jeffrey had stabilized some and I wanted to see my boys, so Mom would bring them up on weekends on our jet and we'd all stay in a suite in the Four Seasons Hotel. Jeffrey was in a coma for seven weeks and until he was better I waited to take the boys to see him. Eventually, my friend Linh set me up in a furnished apartment and filled the freezer up with her homemade gourmet meals when I realized there wasn't an end in sight. At that point, I needed to come to terms with another phase in my life.

I'd arrive at the hospital at seven a.m. and leave at eleven p.m. I'd just wait, talk to Jeffrey, play music, and talk more, but the doctors were constantly with me. We became very close and would remain so to this day. While at Jeffrey's bedside, I thought about stories of people waking up from their comas. I saw it in movies frequently, and it was always a tidy event: the characters just open their eyes and they're back, talking and answering questions. But it didn't and wouldn't happen that way. It was a slow, long waiting game. I watched over Jeffrey constantly, waiting for a movement or any sign of him waking. Every day I hoped that it would be the day that Jeffrey woke up. Since one thing Jeffrey loved about me was that I was always dressed in skirts and heels, I kept up my appearance just in case he opened his eyes. I didn't even own any jeans or sneakers, so when the nurses would suggest that I wear something comfortable, I laughed and said, "This was how I dress. If Jeffrey opens his eyes and sees me any other way he will close them again," I'd jest.

Every day the doctors would go in and test Jeffrey for reactions to various stimuli, such as pain and light. Finally, Jeffrey opened his eyes. Medically speaking, once the patient opens his or her eyes, that person is considered out of the coma. But Jeffrey couldn't talk, couldn't move, and was still dependent on a breathing machine. His eyes were open but reflected nothingness. Initially, I was full of excitement, but when I saw there was no life behind his open eyes, I went back to hoping and praying to my angels. The funny thing is, I was also mad at Jeffrey. Had he listened to just this one thing I'd asked he would have been alive and spared me and the children the significant life disruptions we were facing.

After two months, Jeffrey was finally moved out of the SICU into a private room. The neurosurgeon told me we needed to do anything we could to get his brain cells to heal. So, I started researching everything I could about brain trauma and rehabilitation. As my concentration in college was research, it is second nature for me to delve in and learn about things. The doctors said stimulating the brain through therapy could help speed up the recovery process. Jeffrey was out of a coma because his eyes were open, but they were so empty. It was like the lights were coming on, but nobody was there yet. Seeing him this way fueled my fire to bring my husband back. I hired round-the-clock private nurses and a companion because I wanted someone to be there with him all the time just in case something adverse happened when I wasn't there. I loved and trusted these doctors and the other staff but they had jobs to do besides sitting at Jeffrey's bedside. It also relieved me to go home once in a while.

Because I thought that it would be good for the kids to have a few weekends at home with their friends, and still get to see me, I headed home. The boys were young, but I believed it best to be honest with them. I didn't want to get their hopes up in case things didn't go well and I am adamant about honesty in general and would never want to give them false hopes. So, when they would ask, "Is Daddy going to get better?" I just said, "I hope so."

I never wanted to promise that he would get better because what if he died? In their grief, they would think I had lied to them and that is what they might remember. I didn't want that for my boys and decided that exposing them to what was happening and being honest would be less traumatic than trying to shelter them from the truth. The thing is children understand so much more than we give them credit for as adults.

After this, the kids took an active role in Jeffrey's recovery. When they came in on the weekends we'd go to the hospital to spend time with Jeffrey in his room. They would hold his hand, engage him with stories and talk to him. Kids take their cues from their parents and because they saw how I spoke to Jeffrey, believing he could hear, they never felt it was unusual to talk to someone who couldn't respond.

At four and six years of age, the boys were incredibly compassionate, caring, and involved. Their kindness to their dad almost brought me to tears. Once again I had to find the courage to be strong for us all.

"Hi, Daddy, it's Sammy," he'd intertwine his tiny fingers with Jeffrey. "This week at school, I got all hundreds on my tests. Miss Silvia is going to institute a new math program for me. She said I need a challenge. The Heat are starting their season soon." And with that Sam was off, telling his stories the way only a young child could. In a bizarre way, it was great for the kids because they were spending more time with their father than ever before and they had his undivided 'attention.'

We began physical and occupational therapy as soon as Jeffrey was out of SICU. We would get him out of bed, upright on a tilt table, and into a wheelchair. Jeffrey would show little signs of improvement, which to me were huge, following us with his eyes, squeezing my hand, and crying. Clinically speaking, Jeffrey was in a minimally conscious state, having moved out of a vegetative state. I knew he could comprehend. I knew he was appreciative though he couldn't express it in words. I only hoped that he finally understood our love for him.

I read about a woman who could use neuro-biofeedback with electrodes, to see if Jeffrey's brain had any activity. So, I flew her up to New York. She and some other doctors, who wanted to see the results, tested Jeffrey's brain. She would ask him questions or say words to see if his brain was active. After the testing, she determined that Jeffrey had activity, but it was still very low. But, she said, "It's promising." That she could record activity, even though he couldn't verbally or physically respond, meant something. We thought in time, with stimulation and healing, brain activity would improve. This gave me more hope and I was determined to get Jeffrey all the therapies and stimulation he needed to get his brain synapses firing like before the accident.

Around Christmas time, going on four months since the accident, Jeffrey was progressing nicely and was relatively healthy. The hospital advised me to move Jeffrey out. With winter illnesses going around, they said there was a good chance of him getting sick from being in the hospital, so we moved across the street to nursing home. We were still close to the hospital and the doctors so I was okay with the move. I arranged to have his therapists come to work with him every day, as well as an acupuncturist and a massage therapist. "I'll get him anything that will help him recover," I said. Now that I wasn't restricted by hospital rules, I could bring in alternative therapists as much as I wanted. I was incredibly open to the possibility of their being efficacious.

When Jeffrey had his accident, the last thing I was thinking about was his businesses. During the first week in NY, Jeffrey's Florida nightclub partner, Damien, had flown up to visit and told me he had a Power of Attorney over Jeffrey's businesses. I was in no frame of mind to get behind the steering wheel of his businesses with all I had on my plate.

"That can happen?" is all I said, perhaps naively. In any case, I was more concerned with keeping Jeffrey alive. In all honesty, I was relieved to know that I didn't have to worry about the business too. I just had no time. The mob scene at the hospital had metered out a bit after a few weeks but they had moved to the phone which, thank goodness, now had a recording of Jeffrey's progress. Everyone was trying to get a hold of me; everyone wanted to know what was going on. I only answered the private line set up for my family and important friends.

"Don't worry about a thing," Damien said soothingly. "I'll take care of the businesses; you just concentrate on Jeffrey. He's like a brother to me, I will handle everything."

I inhaled, then sighed in relief. "That's just fine with me."

From then on Damien would stop in every couple of weeks to give me an update on the business. In October about a month after the accident, I got a call from Damien. There was a problem he needed to discuss with me.

"What's going on?" I asked.

"Apparently in August, Jeffrey's CFO refused to pay the company's medical insurance premium, over a personal issue. The moment he heard of Jeffrey's accident he paid the bills. When the insurance company started getting bills for Jeffrey, they panicked."

I bit my lip. It was probably in the millions of dollars by now—he had major brain surgeries, was on life support for months, had private rooms, the whole works. It was not a cheap accident. I ran my fingers through my hair anxiously.

"And?"

"The insurance company was trying to figure out a loophole so they won't have to pay, and when they found out the premium hadn't been covered for a month, they dropped our coverage," Damien said. We'd had a no-limit insurance policy, so I can wonder why they want out.

"What will you do about it?" I asked.

"Sue them, of course," he said.

"That's well and good, but it isn't going to help our situation," I replied as gently as I could. "We need medical insurance, and we need it right now." If we tried to get a new health insurance policy, it wouldn't be possible because Jeffrey's brain injury would have been considered a pre-existing medical condition. This was not my problem and I was none too pleased. "Figure it out, Damien."

Damien said he'd figure it out and get things taken care of, but I wasn't going to cut back on Jeffrey's care. I told him that if insurance wasn't going to pay, then the companies had more than enough money and they were going to have to pay the bills. Jeffrey had created the businesses and it was his money. I went about what was my business… taking care of Jeffrey.

I'd read about a treatment called Neurodevelopment Therapy (NDT) that had been developed in Scandinavia. It is a holistic interdisciplinary physical therapy program specifically designed for neurodevelopment in people whose brain has been impacted in some way. I contacted the creators of the program and asked if they would come and assess Jeffrey's condition. When they arrived, they said Jeffrey needed to be doing so much more in terms of Neurotherapy. In terms of physical health, we were doing great. Jeffrey didn't have one bed sore, his skin was amazing, and he was gaining weight. He looked great, as if he'd never been hurt, other than the area of his craniotomy, where his hair had now grown back but there was a concaved, soft spot where his skull was missing. Most times we had a helmet on Jeffrey, to protect the area. Eventually, when he was in full recovery the surgeons would replace the missing skull with a plate.

"He needs to be out of bed more," the therapist added. Jeffrey would open his eyes, and I could tell if he was there or not. Even the kids could tell. When he heard the doctor's voice, his eyes opened wider. Again, I was convinced that Jeffrey understood much more than we believed he did, and I think he was hopeful to hear those words. He'd even progress to the point where we could get him to move his head a little bit. These were the little things that indicated to us that his recovery was possible.

We then instituted an NDT program at the nursing home. As the treatment progressed, the neurosurgeon continued to check in on Jeffrey daily and he'd gone from being a hard-nosed buttoned-up doctor into becoming my confidant and closest ally. Many of my single girlfriends had commented on the doctor's good looks and inquired about his eligibility but I had never paid attention. I'd never really noticed before but indeed he was a handsome man. Considered one of New York's most eligible bachelors, I couldn't help but laugh when I discovered that, no wonder my friends were forever prodding me to introduce them. I had been so focused and intent on Jeffrey's condition, that I never really looked at him as anyone other than Jeffrey's doctor and then my close friend.

One day when the doctor came in to test Jeffrey's responses, he frowned. "I don't think Jeffrey likes me," he said.

"What makes you say that?" I asked.

"Each time I come in the room, Jeffrey closes his eyes and ignores me."

I stifled a laugh and decided I'd have to pay attention next time. The nurses would laugh and say, "I think Jeffrey is jealous!" They might have been joking but I was well aware of Jeffrey's mean, jealous streak.

I started watching in earnest and as the doctor had said, I could tell by the change in behavior that Jeffrey was annoyed each time the doctor was in the room. It reaffirmed to me that Jeffrey was indeed in his body.

Jeffrey was making improvements to the point where the doctor thought a rehabilitation center would benefit greatly. There was a well-known place in New Jersey, but when I visited it looked so dark and gloomy I couldn't bring myself to take Jeffrey there. My first thought when I went to visit the rehab was of *One Flew Over the Cuckoo's Nest*, so that would not be an option. *Jeffrey would blast me once he was able to talk if I took him there.*

Another place was TIRR in Houston, TX. So, I traveled to Texas to meet with the renowned Dr. Gerard Francisco. I just had to laugh to myself when I met the doctor because he was another very good-looking man. *Jeffrey was definitely going to be upset having all these handsome male doctors around me.*

Dr. Francisco was incredibly positive and I immediately connected to his outlook and philosophy for care. Rehab should be all about positivity and hope. The facilities at TIRR were so active, optimistic, and bright, that I knew it was *the* place to take Jeffrey.

Story Eighteen
NEXT STOP HOUSTON

A few days after Jeffrey's fortieth birthday, April 27th, we left the nursing home and were off to The Institute of Rehab and Research in Houston, Texas. Life at TIRR was very different from our routine in New York. Immediately we were assigned a team of therapists who would work with Jeffrey. We had a physical therapist, a speech therapist, an occupational therapist, a music therapist, and a coordinator who all worked under the direction and guidance of Dr. Francisco. To keep some consistency in the transition, I had a group of private nurses and our companion, Mary, come out with me from New York. After eight months of solely taking care of Jeffrey, our nurses were overly protective of him and since we had our own self-designed method of care, I felt it was important to have them with us. We had the most capable and skilled group of medical staff working to restore Jeffrey to his normal functioning self. Not surprisingly, this would be the same facility and medical group that would rehabilitate Congresswoman Gabrielle Giffords when she was shot in the head by a zealot in an assassination attempt years later.

From the very start the therapists set up a schedule to have Jeffrey out of bed for the majority of the day. They outfitted him with a wheelchair with support for his head, since he had trouble holding his head upright, and he had a helmet to protect the area in his skull where the craniotomy took place. As I would observe Jeffrey, it never ceased to amaze me how life can change so drastically in a single minute. I was proud of Jeffrey's efforts and drive and I felt as long as we tried he wouldn't give up hope. Jeffrey was a winner, and he knew what had to be done. I think we were both ready to put the accident behind us and move ahead, going as far as we could go.

Dressed in casual clothes every day, instead of pajamas, was another booster. Just seeing him dressed and sitting in a wheelchair seemed like a vast improvement. Every day Jeffrey had a full schedule of therapies, and he would go to the gym where the other patients were and the therapists would work with him. Sometimes they had him sit and work on the side of a table or he would stand in a standing box and track things. Then he would have range of motion exercises and other activities ranging from massages to music therapy and they even had dogs come in as therapy.

Like in New York, I found a townhouse for myself and the boys to reside in when they came, so we would all be together in a home-like setting. The boys would go to therapy sessions and assist in Jeffrey's workouts. Because of the format in which TIRR operates, it allowed for a lot of interaction between the boys and Jeffrey, which was so uplifting and positive for all of us. I continued to stay with Jeffrey from early morning to bedtime during the weekdays and then on the weekend, I tried to balance my time between the boys and Jeffrey.

Once the boys were done school for the summer they came out and lived in Houston full-time with our housekeeper, Amy, and her daughter Lena. When the boys attended Jeffrey's physical therapy sessions their cheering would always get the best performance from Jeffrey. At first, just seeing Jeffrey sitting in a wheelchair was surprising to the boys, but then after a few weeks they would witness Jeffrey take steps with assistance, kick a soccer ball, and he could even arm wrestle with them. Even though Jeffrey was still unable to talk, he did show emotions by smiling and crying. He always smiled when the boys were around and would cry when they left. All these accomplishments, seemingly small, were giant signs of hope for me and the boys. We felt that in time, Jeffrey was going to fully recover. The thought is that there is a thirteen-month window for recovery, so we were right in the midst of the timeframe.

The summer was ending and Jeffrey was still making little improvements. I had a discussion with Dr. Francisco about taking Jeffrey home to Florida. I made plans to have the house renovated to bring Jeffrey home. This meant having ramps installed where there were stairs, the shower had to be widened for the wheelchair to get in and out, the carpeting had to be taken out, and hardwood floors installed and a therapy room had to be created. I had to get a custom van that would be able to transport Jeffrey, hire round-the-clock nurses, find doctors who would be on call, and find a therapist who could continue the therapy. Everything was set in motion and the plan was set to bring Jeffrey home on September 17th. It would be just over one year from the accident. I went to Florida on September 7th to have a party to celebrate Sam's seventh birthday and make sure that everything was going to be ready for Jeffrey's homecoming.

Though it wasn't what I ever envisioned our life would be like, I was ready for the boys, me, and Jeffrey to start a new life.

Story Nineteen

ONE YEAR TO THE DATE

I woke up in the middle of Sam and Jay. Ever since the accident, whenever I was with the boys, we would all sleep together. On September 11, 2001, as I lay silently awake, I thought, *I can't believe that it is already one year ago, almost to the minute, that the dreaded phone call from the hospital woke me.* How much life had changed in the past three hundred and sixty-five days. Jeffrey, who in his own words "lived life large," was incapacitated and completely dependent on others. I, who had been a twenty-four seven hands-on mommy, was now my husband's twenty-four hands-on guardian. The boys thankfully, had my mom who had given up her life to come and care for them, were always aware that their daddy may never be the same. My thought switched, *"I need to stay positive and keep moving forward,"* which is how I'd keep myself strong and happy every day.

Though life would never be the same, in six days Jeffrey would be home and we would start all over again adjusting to a new normal. I had gone deep into the foxhole with him and not for a moment did I regret my decision. I was also able to take out some of my frustration of the past eleven years because I told Jeffrey all that was on my mind through the hours and hours I sat with him for a year. I don't think he could hear me back then, but it did me a world of good.

Most people had gone back to their lives, so after twelve months only our close friends and family had access to us. I didn't have to worry about life in Boca anymore because it would be a while before Jeffrey would be his old self. I hoped too he would come to appreciate that life is promised to no one and would come to respect it in the future.

That morning, I dropped the boys off at school. It was just after 8 a.m.. It'd been so long since I was able to, so I hung around talking to some mothers in the parking lot. They were kind and sympathetic and I was glad to have reconnected with them. We said our goodbyes and I got in my car and headed home. My phone rang. It was my brother, Alan, who was a former trader for Jeffrey.

"Where are you?" he said followed by, "A plane just flew into the World Trade Center." I thought how strange, all the time thinking it was a small private jet or something that mis-navigated.

"Did you hear me? A commercial plane just hit the World Trade Center. The North Tower is on fire."

Immediately I thought of all our traders who worked for Jeffrey at the Stock Exchanges in the area. We even had commodities traders inside the World Trade buildings. My phones started ringing nonstop from traders' wives and friends affected by the tragedy. Still, I couldn't imagine it. I rushed inside, ran past Amy who was cleaning up the morning mess, and turned on CNN. I couldn't believe what I was watching. World Trade Center North Tower was ablaze…huge plumes of fire and smoke billowing from the Tower hit by the hijacked American Airlines passenger Flight 11 at 8:46 a.m. that deliberately flew into it. People were jumping to their deaths, New York was awash in ashes and a second later I watched another plane United Airlines 175 fly into the South Tower. I was frozen in shock, transfixed staring at the television. The towers in no time became infernos, and it took less than an hour for the South Tower to collapse followed twenty-nine minutes later by the North Tower. My phone kept ringing nonstop.

One of the calls was from the boy's school saying it was going into lockdown.

In an instant, I got back in my car and drove over to the school. There was no way that I was going to have the boys locked in at school without me. Not surprisingly, I was not the only parent with that thought. So, I gathered up Sam and Jay and headed back home to safe ground.

The world was aghast as it watched the once-thought-indestructible Towers and other buildings collapse. The morning only got worse as a third plane struck the Pentagon! And a fourth plane went down in rural Pennsylvania! America was under siege in one of the worst terrorist attacks in human history. At the end of it all 3,000 lost their lives and over 25,000 people were injured. The rest of the day was to go from bad to worse and that day is still a blur today. I had been shocked, saddened, worried, and confused by the events of this terrible day so it wasn't until the afternoon when the calls metered out that I thought I had to call Jeffrey. He was safe in Houston, and I was doing all I could to support the distraught spouses and families of our traders.

I called Mary, Jeffrey's companion who had started with us in New York, seven weeks after the accident. "What's going on?"

Mary told me that Jeffrey had been crying all day and she couldn't get him to stop. Mary had finished washing Jeffrey up and gotten him ready for his morning physical therapy at 9 a.m.. Since they were earlier than expected, she positioned Jeffrey in front of his television to watch the *Today Show* until it was time for his therapy. She left the room momentarily to check on something outside and Mary said that was when the news of the attacks came out. Stunned, she was like the other staff members glued to the television. She was a New Yorker. This was her hometown. She was riveted thinking of the level of chaos, and about the many injuries and people who would be rushed into NY Hospitals. Like most Americans unable to comprehend what she was seeing, she did not return to Jeffrey for a while. When she made her way back to Jeffrey's room, she said he was looking at the news coverage and just weeping. She said he wouldn't stop crying. By the time we spoke, he had been crying for hours. If there was a doubt about Jefferey's cognitive ability, it was dispelled at that moment.

What Mary did not understand was that Jeffrey had witnessed, with the rest of the world, the unbelievable tragedy of 9/11. That was his whole world, his livelihood, his love, and he was watching it get decimated and there was nothing he could do or even say. He could not talk or express what he was thinking and feeling, all he could do was cry. I couldn't believe that the one long-weekend, one of only a handful in 365 days I had been absent from Jeffrey's side this would happen.

I tried to console Jeffrey over the phone, telling him that everyone we knew was okay, which was a lie, and that he needed to stay strong and continue his fight to get better. I told him that I would be out to bring him home as soon as planes were permitted to fly as all flights, including private jets, were grounded. I knew without a single doubt that Jeffrey heard and understood me, but the tragedy had hit him in a place way more than he could take. In that moment he had made up his mind what our outcome would be.

The next couple of days were spent trying to maintain a normal, calm home environment for the boys, while inside I was feeling conflicted with emotions of sadness, anger, concern, fear, and anxiety as I imagine most of the world felt too. *How could something of this tragic magnitude happen in the greatest city in the world? What is next? What are we going to do? Who died in the tragedy?* These were all questions that everyone spoke to one another about incessantly. It was the only thing anyone could do to try and make some sense of what happened.

Each morning, afternoon, and evening while grounded I would check in with Mary and speak to Jeffrey, but he just continued to cry. I was told that the medical team had tried the day after the attacks to get back on schedule, but Jeffrey wouldn't cooperate. He just gave up and wouldn't respond to anyone or do anything in therapy.

On Wednesday, our pilot called and said he thought we would get clearance to fly out on Thursday so I called and told Jeffrey that I would be there the next day. I kept trying to reassure him that everything was okay and that I was coming out to get him ready to return home after the weekend. Everything was in order for his homecoming and now all we had to do was get him packed up and ready to travel. I pleaded with him not to give up hope.

On Thursday morning I called Jeffrey's room and nobody answered, so relieved I thanked God they were back in therapy. I was waiting for the pilot to call with our exact clearance time and then we were off to Houston. We got clearance and set out on the two-hours-plus journey to Houston at about three p.m. By the time we arrived, disembarked, and got to TIRR it was evening. Everything on the ward was quiet, understandably so, and everyone was in bed. Everyone was trying to cope with the aftermath of 9/11. I walked to the end of the hall to Jeffrey's room and found it empty. I looked around wondering if I had gone to the wrong room but saw that it was indeed the room except there was no Jeffrey, Mary, or nurse.

After a few minutes of looking for someone to ask what was going on, a nurse on the floor told me that Jeffrey had been rushed to the hospital in the middle of the night and that was all she knew. I immediately called Mary, who explained that Jeffrey had to be resuscitated and was in the ICU at Memorial Hermann Hospital. *No way. No way.*

I rushed over to the hospital and when I found Jeffrey, I was shocked to see him hooked up to all sorts of machines. I couldn't believe it…a week before he was healthy and able to kick a soccer ball in therapy and now here he was again on life support. *What the heck happened? I felt so defeated. Did we start all over again?*

The doctor explained that Jeffrey had contracted an infection, which may have been from replacing his skull plate a few weeks back in preparation for his return home. Also, he had developed pneumonia. He had to be intubated and put on a breathing machine/ventilator due to his respiratory failure. To top all of this off, he was in a coma again. It was all so surreal. In my heart, I knew Jeffrey had given up. The shock to his system had detonated his immune system and here he was once again back at square one. I didn't know if I had it in me to start all over again.

The next few weeks were a blur to me. I continued my routine of going to the hospital every day and sitting by Jeffrey's bedside and talking to him. I was dazed and on autopilot. Because of all the infections that were taking over Jeffrey's body, he was not only in ICU but also in isolation, as he had the highly contagious MRSA, an infection caused by a type of staph bacteria that has become resistant to antibiotics. This meant we had to wear gloves, a mask, protective gowns, and booties to enter the room. Because of all this, I had the kids stay back in Florida. I didn't have a good feeling and I was spent.

I decided I needed to see the kids and headed home for Columbus Day weekend.

For the first time in thirteen months, I was feeling a little defeated. From the moment the doctor told me that Jeffrey had a four percent chance of surviving, I had been in fighting mode. I didn't allow any negative thoughts or opinions around me or the little world I had come to live in. I had been existing on hope and this is what got me through every moment of each day. But, on Saturday, October 6th, I woke up with a bad feeling. I felt off…something wasn't right. I called Joyce and told her that I didn't think that Jeffrey was going to live much longer and said that I couldn't go back to Houston on my own. Of course, Joyce said, "I will go with you." So, on Sunday night we headed back to Houston.

On Monday morning I was told the team of doctors in Houston wanted to have a conference call with me. On the call, the team told me that Jeffrey was at the point where he was being kept alive by the machines. That without the life support, he would not be able to breathe on his own and would die. They said that they had all conversed, consulted on the matter, and knew that I would not be able to make the decision to "pull the cord" so they were making the medical decision to take Jeffrey off the ventilator.

I had done everything possible for Jeffrey. And truly I was spent but I would have kept going. But now even the doctors were ready to give up. The only thing I could say was that I wanted the boys to have the chance to come and say goodbye before they turned off the machines, which they all agreed to. I also said that I wanted all the tubes and machines (not the ventilator) disconnected so the boys would not be frightened. They also agreed. They offered to meet with the boys to explain what was going to happen and tell them that Jeffrey was going to die. I called my mom and told her that she and the boys were going to have to come out the next day. I did tell my mom what was going to happen so she would not be surprised. I made calls to our family and some friends to tell them that Jeffrey was going to be taken off life-support to give them the opportunity to come and say goodbye. Friends and family came in overnight to say their goodbyes to Jeffrey, but it wasn't until I was told that the boys were arriving, that everything all of a sudden slowed down and became real. I prayed for God to *give me the strength to get through this* and headed down the hall to greet the boys and my mom.

The doctors had a private room set up for us to meet and talk to the boys, so I took the boys and we went into the room. I felt like a kid myself and here I was with a five - and seven-year-old getting ready to talk about how their daddy was going to die. With Jay on my lap, his security blanket in one hand and his other thumb in his mouth, and Sam seated on a couch next to me, my free arm holding him close, the doctors came in and said they had some bad news to tell them. They said, "Your daddy has become very sick and can no longer breathe on his own. He has been put on machines to help him breathe and stay alive, but he is not really alive so we are going to take the machines off and unfortunately, this means he is going to die." With the words "going to die," both boys turned to look at me and said, "Daddy is going to die?"

It took every bit of the last ounce of my strength to look at Sam and Jay in their innocent baby faces and nod yes. With that they both started to weep. I have never experienced such great pain as I felt at that moment. There is a saying that "A mother is only as happy as her unhappiest child;" I don't know who said that, but I can attest that it is without a doubt the truth. I not only felt my pain but also the pain of both of my precious babies. All I could tell them was that we were going to be okay, "I promise that we will be okay, I promise."

Sometime later, a nurse came in with crayons and paper and asked if the boys wanted to write their daddy a letter or draw him a picture. So, both boys made pictures that they wanted to give to Jeffrey. Once they finished, Mom and I took them in to see their dad. When we got in the room Sam immediately went to Jeffrey's bedside and told him, "We are going to be okay, don't worry." He then climbed onto a chair to get up onto the bed. He held his picture in front of Jeffrey's closed eyes and told him, "I made you this picture and I love you." Sam leaned down kissed Jeffrey and climbed down.

What was so amazing was Sam's strength, not physical, but rather emotional as he did all this without breaking down and crying. Sam then turned to me and grabbed my hand as if to lead me to bring Jay, whom I was carrying. I leaned over and sat Jay down on top of Jeffrey's chest. Jay looked at Jeffrey and with tears streaming down his face, he leaned over and kissed Jeffrey on his cheek, whimpering, "I love you, Daddy." Then he placed his picture on Jeffrey. I lifted him off and held him close and I let him cry into my shoulder.

I then took Sam's little hand in mine and we stoically walked out of the room. We went into the changing room to take off all the isolation gear and wash up when Jeffrey's good friend Andy came in physically distraught and crying after saying his goodbye. Andy had worked with Jeffrey the entire time since starting out at the age of twenty-four as his gofer on the street. He went on to become a partner in the Day Trading company. Andy was endeared to Jeffrey and was grateful to him for helping when he'd lost a bunch of money he had needed to pay his taxes. Jeffrey hadn't batted an eye, though he gave him a tongue-lashing right before he wired the money to him. Andy was one of the few people Jeffrey trusted and I was glad he was there. Andy was especially distraught because he should have been on the plane with Jeffrey to Costa Rica and would have been in the car coming back to Boca. Destiny had intervened as he couldn't make the trip when Jeffrey had called and said wheels up in two hours. Like the psychic had said Jeffrey would be alone. I gave Andy a sad smile, but Sam walked over patted him on the back, and said, "It's okay Uncle Andy, Daddy will be okay and we will all be okay, too."

Story Twenty

'TIL DEATH DO US PART

Facing Jeffrey's pending death and dealing with all that was going on felt surreal. I could only pray the children were okay. Though they were young these are the kinds of jarring events that if not handled well could affect their lives for a long time. My ever-loving and supportive family and friends were by my side. I couldn't imagine the moment without them by my side. The thought was that my mother and brothers would take the boys to a hotel and wait for me. I was going to stay with Jeffrey until he took his last breath. I had fully expected that once life support was disconnected, Jeffrey would die quickly, so Joyce, who had returned to be with me in those last moments went to the waiting room to give me time alone with Jeffrey. The doctor turned the machine off, took out the breathing tube, cleaned him up a bit and then turned on the morphine IV. I did not want Jeffrey to experience any pain, so the hospital agreed to set us up in a hospice-like setting.

Once all this was done we moved into a private room where we could be alone. Movies and books are so misleading. The first few hours, I sat by Jeffrey's bedside talking to him, reassuring him (and subconsciously myself) that the boys and I were going to be okay and it was okay for him to leave. Jeffrey was afraid of dying. He always said he was destined to die young as his dad and grandfather had, though they were much older than forty. When Jeffrey's father died we were in Bali. His mother had called Joyce who had called us, and partly because of this fear he needed to do everything he could to live "life large" and on the edge. As I sat with Jeffrey I understood that destiny cannot be denied. I might have intervened but destiny had won.

For hours I talked and reminisced about our life together. I told him I forgave him for all the bad things that had transpired between us in our time together and apologized for my part in it too. I thanked him for giving me a good and unexpected life and despite it all, for always providing for our little family. I thanked him for loving me with all the capacity he had available in his anguished life. I wish I had better understood the source of his pain but I know it was his path and mine to discover in each other who we were at our core. It might even have dawned on me that Jeffrey was in my life as a teacher for me to embrace who I truly am at my core. He had shown me my strength, my determination, and my problem-solving skills and taught me how to love someone unconditionally. Even conflicted I loved Jeffrey. I told him not to be afraid and that it was okay to die. To trust his destiny. I tried to assure him that everything would be good in heaven and that he would be whole again. I talked and talked until I had nothing more to say. If somewhere in there he could hear me…all that needed to be said had been said.

The afternoon turned to evening and then the next day. I was so afraid to leave his side, even to go to the bathroom in the room because I thought he would die without me there and I didn't want him to die alone. Friends and family stopped in to say goodbye, but for the most part, everyone let me have time with Jeffrey alone. The hours passed and Jeffrey kept hanging on. The next day came around and I was emotionally and mentally exhausted. Jeffrey's friend, Andy, came in and told me that I had to get some sleep and that he would sit in the room while I slept. I squeezed into the bed with Jeffrey and went to sleep beside him. I woke up a few hours later and Jeffrey's vital signs were still the same.

I couldn't believe that he could hold on for so long. I went back to gently telling him not to be afraid.

After twenty-four hours passed, I started to wonder if perhaps the doctors were wrong and that it wasn't Jeffrey's time yet. It was going on to thirty hours of sitting or lying by his side. I was slowly going out of my mind and started to lose patience. I even got angry thinking this was the last bit of torture Jeffrey was going to put me through testing my commitment and love one last time.

"Jeffrey," I started pleading with him.

"If you are going to die, please do so and stop the torture I'm going through. Truly, I am going crazy and I'm at my wit's end, so if you are going to die just do so already. Enough is enough."

I'd like to believe he heard my pleading and decided to let go shortly after. His body started to show signs of shutting down. I had the doctors increase the morphine because I thought he was in pain, but they claimed that he was not but did as I asked anyway.

His breathing was slowing more and more. I kept telling Jeffrey everything was going to be okay, that he taught me how to be strong and independent and that I would make sure that the boys were always good. I told him not to be afraid and to go to the light. That he would soon be free of the constrictions and pain that he had endured the last thirteen months. I told him that I would always hold him in my heart and thanked him for the life he so generously provided me. I talked until there was nothing left to say once again and waited for him to take his last breath. The time each breath stretched out longer and longer until he took one last gasp of air and stopped breathing. It was all so surreal and peaceful and I wasn't sure that he had really passed until the doctor came in and told me that Jeffrey was dead. It was nine thirty p.m. on October 10, 2001, exactly thirteen months to the day of his accident.

The doctors' pronouncement made it all so real and I think for the first time in the thirteen months of fighting for his life and only thinking optimistically, I realized that this was the end. I touched Jeffrey's cheek kissed him on his forehead and said, "I love you" for the last time. Then every bit of strength I had left came crashing down as I dropped my head on his chest and cried for the first time since this entire ordeal began.

All the tears I had held back for thirteen months flowed like a river.

They were tears of sadness, fear, anxiety, and in some sense relief. As I wept, I felt the thirteen months of keeping myself optimistic and strong, fighting for Jeffrey's life and encouraging him to fight with me, forgiving and apologizing for all that we went through draining out of me. I could finally let go and concede defeat. I didn't realize the depth of my anguish.

"Get a doctor, she needs a shot." I heard a voice yelling. Just as quickly another emotion came over me, *Are you kidding me? I let myself break down for one minute and now they are going to give me a shot like I am crazy or something.*

As a nurse started to approach me, I took a deep breath, gathered up the reserve strength I had left in me, lifted my head off of Jeffrey's chest, wiped my eyes and face with my hands as I stood up straight, tall, and said, "I am fine. I need to go to get my boys now."

I took one last look at Jeffrey's body and walked into the hospital hallway where Joyce was waiting to go with me to the hotel. I didn't say a word and neither did she. We just walked out of the hospital and that was the last time I saw Jeffrey.

I don't know why I couldn't just accept the concerns of the hospital staff?

Why did I have to pretend I was okay? I wasn't okay and I gleaned something in me that needed further examination. It's okay to have emotions. It's okay to break down. It's okay to accept help. What I hadn't realized was that my role as fixer ever since I was a child had also not allowed me to emote. Was that why I could leave boyfriends as though nothing mattered? Was holding back myself a part of what Jeffrey had felt from me. I had no answers but I have learned something about me I never fully understood.

On our way to the hotel, I called my brothers to tell them that Jeffrey had passed. Alan, even estranged from Jeffrey for the past two years, was there to support me and pay his respects to Jeffrey. They had, despite it all had a good run. Alan asked me, "How long ago was that?" When I told him, he said, "That is so strange. Sam and Jay were sleeping and all of a sudden, right about that time Sam sat straight up in bed and said that his daddy came to say goodbye." Then he laid back down and went back to sleep.

The next morning, the pilot called to say the forecast was predicting some bad storms in the area, so we should try to get out ASAP. I told him I needed my morning tea and then I could get everyone together and go to the jet center. By the time we got there the winds and rain had picked up. The pilot said, "As soon as we get clearance, we need to take off," so me, the boys, my mom, Alan, Joyce, and Andy got on the plane to wait for word that we could leave. Brian, always dependable and ready to help had volunteered to load up my Range Rover, pack up the townhouse for me and then drive back to Florida.

The pilot said that three bad thunderstorms were forming a triangle, but there was a small window that would allow us to take off in between the storms and we could get high enough to fly over the storms. He told us to buckle up and that it would be very bumpy for a little bit. There was no easy way with Jeffrey.

We got the clearance and all of a sudden we were taking off straight in the middle of the three storms. It felt as though we were bouncing higher and higher into the air and everyone was frightened. I tried to act like it was nothing so the boys wouldn't be frightened, then Sam yelled, "Daddy, you aren't being funny. Please stop this!" Then, all of a sudden, the bouncing and turbulence stopped and we had a calm flight all the way back to Boca Raton.

Story Twenty-One
A LAST GOODBYE

When Jeffrey's body arrived from Houston to the Boca Raton Funeral Home, the director who happened to be a friend from the boys's school, came by the house to ask for an outfit to lay Jeffrey to rest. The boys and I looked at each other and I asked Sam and Jay what they thought their daddy would like to wear the most for his send-off. Without any hesitation they chose the perfect Jeffrey outfit… his colorful bathing trunks and a "Bye-Bye" island shirt. We knew if given the choice, this is exactly what Jeffrey would have picked out. Because the casket would be closed, only we would know and it was our memory alone how Jeffrey would arrive at his destination.

Sam told us how he imagined his daddy flying around in heaven with his great big wings. I quite imagined the sight of Jeffrey as an angel, with big wings, flying around in his bathing suit, with a big fat cigar in his mouth. The thought relieved the heaviness, if just for a moment.

The funeral was on October 14, 2001, and as one would have imagined, Jeffrey's funeral was no less of an event than anything else he'd orchestrated in his life. To accommodate seven or eight hundred guests that would arrive at the Temple, extra police escorts to manage the traffic would be in place. The service would be held in the main sanctuary to accommodate the amount of attendees. As one might expect, when it came time for me, to manage the arrangements for the funeral, I recognized just how much I was in shock.

Rabbi Singer, who had married us in Israel would preside over the service. He came by the house to offer his condolences to me and the boys and to discuss the services that he would preside over. Fortunately, I had a weekend to prepare for the service and the traditions of a *Shiva* (Jewish mourning ritual) that would commence after the service for five days at my home.

I knew a lot of people would be attending Jeffrey's send-off, even though it was just a month after the tragic 9/11 and many people were still afraid to fly. When he asked about who the speakers would be at the service, Sam immediately told Rabbi Singer that he wanted to speak. Rabbi Singer had smiled in his always gentle way and told Sam that would be wonderful and he was sure his daddy would love that. Along with Sam, we had Jeffrey's best childhood friend, a couple of family members, representatives from some of the Charitable Foundations that Jeffrey donated to, community leaders, friends from NY, and Damien speak. My sister Anita represented my family and my dear friend Gina's husband, Tommy Ford, who would later die also too young, gave the main eulogy. Although I do not like public speaking, I thought after thirteen months of being isolated and unavailable to almost everyone we knew and associated with, that I should speak.

No matter what the circumstances, when you experience the loss of your spouse, the grief is devastating and completely uproots all understandings of normalcy. While most of the day was a blur from the shock I was in, I do have one impactful memory. After the attendees were seated in the sanctuary, it was time for me, the boys, and other family members to take our walk to our seats. I had intentionally arrived late with the boys, so as not to keep them waiting and having their time at the funeral as short as possible. I walked out first, carrying Jay and holding Sam's hand, with Rabbi Singer leading us. The moment I walked into the sanctuary, I looked up and saw our dear friend, Shea.

Shea was one of the first of Jeffrey's friends I'd met and he was one of Jeffrey's dearest friends. Shea had been a trader for Neil when Jeffrey started in the business. I hadn't seen Shea for several years because he was always abroad, living in different countries. Shea loved to travel and to live in different cultures. When I saw Shea's face and the look of sorrow, love, and compassion, it jolted me back out of my stupor and back into reality. All of a sudden I felt sick to my stomach. Shea's presence, totally unexpected meant the world to me. That he made the effort to be there for us was something I will always be thankful for and emotional about. To me, that is love when you just show up in the time of someone's need. I had to gather my emotions and inner strength as I knew that I couldn't break down with eight hundred pairs of eyes watching. So, like the professional, I'd come to be, I put on my stoic mask and proceeded along with the rabbi to our seats.

Everyone who spoke had beautiful, funny, and heartfelt things to say about Jeffrey, all recounting his beautiful heart. Then came the time for me and the boys to go up to speak. Sam dressed in his blue blazer and loafers was the first to speak. At merely seven years of age, he'd written his speech about his daddy and how he was now in a better place. By the time he ended there was not a dry eye in the synagogue.

It took all the strength I had in me to hold myself together. I don't know anyone, let alone an adult or other child, who could have done that, but Sam took on the responsibility himself, which was an incredible feat. Thankfully, Jay, with his "didi" in one hand and I carrying him, leaned into the microphone, and said "I love my family" then turned his head into my shoulder to cry. After consoling him for a few minutes, I gave the final eulogy. I honestly don't know how I got through. I was just on cruise control and doing everything I knew I had to do to survive. With eight hundred pairs of eyes and ears on me, there was no way I was going to show any weakness. Sometimes I wonder if this was a good thing, especially for Sam to witness, as maybe this is how he learned his strength at such a young age.

But that day, regardless of all the FOJs in attendance, many who claimed him their own, I sent my husband off to his resting place. After our speeches, Rabbi Singer closed out the service and we proceeded to the cemetery, where Jeffrey's body and casket were placed into a mausoleum next to his father. For the next five days, we sat Shiva at my house, which is a blessing to the grieving. It is a time of remembrance, but also a celebration of the deceased life. Barton G. catered the first night. I have no idea how many hundreds of people stopped by to pay their respects to me and the boys. This was a time for anyone to come by and show their support, so over the five days, we were constantly surrounded by family and true friends.

This was great for the boys, who had their aunts, uncles, and cousins around like it was summer at the beach house. I will always appreciate the extent to which people were there for me and my boys. My dad, Betty, Kevin, Sieu, and Andrew all drove down from Philadelphia since my dad hated flying; we had friends who took a train down from New Jersey because they too did not want to fly after the 9/11 attacks; Shea came from some foreign country even with all the security hassles one had to go through after 9/11; this to me was a tribute to who the Jeffrey I fell in love with was. It was not about the glitz, glamour, or seedy South Beach decadence. It was for Jeffrey, who'd touched and impacted so many lives in a good way, and I was glad to see that in the end, despite it all, the gratitude and love was there.

Story Twenty-two

HOME

Ever since I was a little girl, my mom would tell me how she was strangely awakened from her sleep the night after my great-grandmother died. When she opened her eyes she saw the ghost of my great-grandmother standing in her bedroom doorway. My mother described her as being at peace and healthy and my mom got a warm feeling of love and understood that she'd come to say goodbye. After a minute or so, the apparition disappeared. All my life, I was afraid that when someone died I would see a ghost. For the first few months after Jeffrey passed, I was a bit afraid of waking up in the middle of the night.

I was busy making sure the boys were okay. Every night after Jeffrey's passing my youngest Jay would cry and cry and cry. Sam, who assumed "man of the house," from what people had unknowingly said, took on the role of being unflappable which I knew was not healthy.

I took to playing a game with the boys to help them process their emotions. We called the game our "Happy Sad game" and each night before bed we would go around and each of us would say something that made us happy that day, then something that made us sad, something that made us thankful, something that made us mad, and then a wildcard which could be any emotion we wanted. Every night for a couple of years, when it came to what he was sad about, Jay would cry and say, "I am sad that my daddy died." Sam and I would then together hug him until he stopped and then continue with our game.

At first, this would break my heart and I would hold back tears, but after a while of this consistent breakdown, Sam and I were ready for it and it was routine.

In February, just out of curiosity I called a medium a friend had told me about who could contact the deceased. Although I did enjoy going to psychics every so often, I had never been to someone who dealt with the dead. After a while listening to the woman tell me things about myself, she asked if there was someone I was trying to reach. When I told her that I was trying to reach my husband, she told me that she couldn't reach him because he hadn't yet crossed over and that maybe he was still here "reviewing his life and learning his lessons." She said I should give it more time and try again in a few more months.

I thought it funny and said, "Well it could take years for him to do that."

Although I didn't see a ghost and the medium couldn't locate Jeffrey for me, I began to notice that Sam was taking on a lot of Jeffrey's idiosyncrasies.

Again, I reflected on how little we know about what children understand. Was this because so many people had told him he was the man of the house? I know they had meant no harm but I was against this kind of thing and felt it would be a great burden on Sam. Sam would walk around stretching out his arms exactly like his father, would lick his lips in the same annoying fashion as Jeffrey did, and was doing other little things that Sam never did before. Sam would also say things like, "Daddy told me the answers today at school."

At first I didn't think very much about any of these things, but after months of watching these new habits, I started to get worried that the next thing I would see was Sam smoking a big cigar! I happened to mention my concerns to my therapist, Tisha, who had been my rock and my savior for many years through my turmoil before Jeffrey's accident. I credit her for the strong, self-appreciating woman I had become.

Anyhow, Tisha seemed concerned about what I was telling her and asked if she could work with Sam. Of course, since I have always had great faith in Tisha, I agreed to have Sam see Tisha with me.

After Tisha spoke with Sam for a while she asked to speak to me alone.

She told me that she thought that Jeffrey's spirit was attached to Sam and that he hadn't "passed over" to the spirit world yet. I didn't think anything strange about what Tisha was telling me as she had never steered me wrong before and I knew how intuitively accurate she had always been with me, so I just accepted her thought and asked what to do. She told me to read a book by Dr. Edith Fiore called, "The Unquiet Dead." which would describe what Tisha explained as Spirit Possession. This means that, sometimes a Spirit doesn't cross over into the spirit world and attaches to a living being. We scheduled a session to perform a dispossession.

When I went to my session with Tisha she asked me to close my eyes and try to visualize Jeffrey. As Tisha is a hypnotist by profession, her soothing voice and guidance got me to a state of mind where I all of a sudden could see Jeffrey. I saw a vision of him floating in darkness and way above him, far away, there was a speck of light. I shared with Tisha what I was seeing and she told me to mentally tell Jeffrey to go to the light. Tisha told me to convince him that it was okay to leave and not be afraid. As I concentrated on saying these things in my mind, I saw Jeffrey floating higher toward the circle of light, which was getting larger. Tisha asked what I saw in the light and I said there was a figure with her hands stretched out towards Jeffrey. Tisha told me to take a closer look to see who it was and I was able to focus in and see that it was Jeffrey's Grandma Florence who had passed a few years before Jeffrey.

Tisha told me to tell Jeffrey to go to Grandma Florence, to grab her hand, and that everything would be okay. I mentally did so and watched as Jeffrey slowly ascended towards his grandmother. I kept encouraging Jeffrey to go and waited for him to go to his grandmother. Just as Jeffrey reached the light and his grandmother and was stretching out his hand, my cell phone rang and woke me out of my hypnotic state.

I was startled for a moment and grabbed my handbag to turn off the phone.

At the time, I had two cell phones because I had one private number that was just for my mom, the family, and Jeffrey's doctors. I grabbed the first phone I touched, but it was the wrong phone. When I found the ringing phone, the ringing stopped. I picked it up to see who called and the phone said "HOME." I thought, who would be calling me from home on this line?

But then I happened to look at the information again and saw the time and date, which read, "10/10/01 and 1:53 p.m."

I looked again at the numbers with disbelief and shock then threw the phone down. Tisha asked what was wrong and I picked up the phone to show her. As clear as day, the phone read "HOME 10/10/01 and 1:53 p.m." and Tisha said, "Why does it say 10/10/01 when it is March?" I looked at her and said, "That is the date that Jeffrey died." I knew then that, just as he always had, Jeffrey had called to tell me that he made it HOME.

I was filled with different emotions: sadness, relief, amazement, and confusion, to name a few. As a person who believed in source, I knew the spirit never dies but simply transforms; yet it was jarring. Everything in me knew it was Jeffrey. I thanked Tisha for her help and left her office, still in a bit of disbelief at what just happened. I got in my car and picked up the phone, which now read the correct time and date, and called Chris Golden, the only other person I knew who would understand and believe what I was about to tell her. I was driving while talking to Chris, when out of nowhere a red Ferrari Maranello, the exact same as Jeffrey's, cut me off then stepped on the brakes for a second as though they wanted me to see it, and then sped off. I had to quickly brake and I noticed that the car did not have a license plate. I told Chris that I would call her back and pulled over to the side of the road. There weren't any other cars around and the car was well out of sight. I took a deep breath then yelled, "Okay Jeffrey, I get it. I see the signs. I know that you are okay. Thank you."

After that day, Sam stopped with the funny "Jeffrey" habits and was back to being his sweet adolescent self.

Story Twenty-three
ALWAYS AROUND

For Sam, Jay, and me, there wasn't one specific date that represented the tragedy of Jeffrey's death. Unfortunately, due to the circumstances of his accident, there are a couple of days that are always a reminder of our reality. September 11, 2000, marked the date of the accident, and October 10, 2001, the date of Jeffrey's passing. Because he died in Houston, Texas, his body had to be flown back home so the funeral wasn't held until October 14th.

The first anniversary of Jeffrey's accident was September 11th, a day all Americans and the world will remember forever. When the next September 11, 2002, was approaching, I decided the boys and I would remain at home and do nothing. I guess I was superstitious about the date and wanted to be safe and do nothing to tempt fate. While we were sad the date represented two years since Jeffrey's accident, we felt a sense of security being together at home and were relieved when the day was over and we made it through without any tragedies.

Then October 10th rolled in and hit us like running into a brick wall. Marking the first anniversary of my husband's death was a horrible experience: the heaviness of the day; the constant playbacks in my mind of memories of Jeffrey, the tears my babies shed over their father's death. For my sweet Jay, these tears would come every night for years.

And for Sam, who needed to be strong, his grief would play out later in life. For me, who'd spent the year of the accident surviving on adrenaline and trying to be brave while fighting to save Jeffrey's life, the year after his death I fought to provide a normal life for the boys. I was still portraying an air of being okay, strong, and all-together for everyone around me and as always it had become a new habit to wake up and put on the mask of happiness and get through the day. The truth was, I was tired of wearing masks in both Jeffrey's life and death. So, just like every other day, I woke up on October 14th, the day we'd buried him, and continued with my life as I knew it.

Since the accident, my boys had been sleeping with me at night. It provided us all a sense of security that others, who hadn't experienced what we had, could not understand. They would concerningly tell me that it wasn't healthy but since my instincts told me that it was what we needed to do, I did not listen to anyone's advice. Around my family, I was the one making all the decisions and that's just the way it would be.

One night, the boys and I were sleeping soundly when suddenly I was jolted from my sleep. I am usually a sound sleeper, so it was unusual that I would wake up in the middle of the night but on this particular night something had caused me to open my eyes. Checking to make sure the boys were okay when my eyes scanned over them to my shock I saw Jeffrey sitting on top of Sam, who was fast asleep to my right. Never before since the year of his death had I ever seen him. As I would recall the story my mother had told me about my great-grandmother which I had received with a bit of fear, I had wanted to see Jeffrey but I was fearful though hopeful about the possibility of seeing his ghost. So, when I saw him sitting right there next to me, I was shaken.

I didn't say anything and didn't move but instead just looked at him staring out over us. He didn't look at me but instead held his gaze out over the three of us. He looked so calm, so at peace, so strong, healthy, and young. He did not say a word. I shut my eyes to make sure that I wasn't dreaming and when I reopened my eyes, he was gone.

After he left, I felt a strong sense of being safe and the heaviness I had been feeling and carrying around seemed to diminish. I went back to sleep feeling more at peace with my life. When I woke up in the morning, I started to wonder why it was that night he decided to come to me. Then, when I looked at the calendar and saw the date, October 15th. We had not made a big deal of the date after all we'd been through so much on the 10th so the 14th, which marked the first anniversary of the day he was laid to rest, sort of came and went without notice. I started to chuckle. Some things never changed. I think Jeffrey's visitation was two-fold. First, Jeffrey was the kind of person who would not want to be forgotten, especially by me; he wanted to let me know I had forgotten the anniversary of his funeral. He'd always made his presence known and loved to be the center of attention in life, so why not in death? For me to not have made a big deal over this 14th date probably bothered him. True or not…it was something Jeffrey would do.

Secondly, I feel the real reason for Jeffrey's return was to tell us that he is okay and he is watching out over us. He wanted to reassure us that he loved me, Sam, and Jay the best he was capable of loving. Even with all the "high" life he partook in, his true heart was always with me and the boys. He came back to let me know that he will always be protecting us.

Jeffrey's visitation provided me with a new sense of security and I gained a sense of peace "knowing" that he is always around. I was also relieved to know he was okay and in a good place. That visit freed me emotionally and I was able to leave behind the deep grief that I had settled in and that I had been secretly living with under my mask. I began to move forward to regain a sense of peace in my life. Rather than thinking of the thirteen months after the accident as a mistake, I perceived it as a blessing. Jeffrey, Sam, Jay, and I were given thirteen months of closure; a time centered on strength, optimism, healing, and growth; of being a family unit and defining what family commitment is; and most of all, true unconditional love. I, without a shred of doubt, know that Jeffrey died knowing how much the boys and I genuinely loved him.

Story Twenty-four

BLUE JAY

A few months after my visit from Jeffrey I got a call from a friend who is also a psychic. Elaine had met Jeffrey on a couple of occasions and Jeffrey liked to tease her about her profession. One time when she called the house and Jeffrey answered and Elaine asked if I was home, he replied, "You're the psychic, you tell me."

Many people may think my belief in a universal source of all things makes me a loony toon. But no matter one's faith, if there is a universal force it means we are all part of it and can tap into it if we have lived our lives in the belief of I AM; I am one with Source and therefore connected to all there is. But this is not some esoteric theory I made up. Quantum physics, as it relates to spirituality, purports the interconnectedness of the entire universe and the theory of entanglement is a real phenomenon.

Anyhow, Elaine called and said that she wanted to see me. When I walked into Elaine's house, the first thing she said to me was "Damien is a bad person. You need to totally keep away from him."

Considering all that Jeffrey had achieved, all we had; there was no Will. I believed that had it not been for Damien, I would have been lost. Immediately, I told her she had to be wrong this time. "Damien is the only person I can trust." I countered, "And since Jeffrey gave him Power of Attorney before his accident, he must have trusted him too. Damien is the one taking care of all our businesses and finances." I said. "Check again Elaine you have to have the wrong name."

Elaine said that was the name that jumped out when she saw me, but maybe she was mistaken. We sat down and Elaine told me that Jeffrey was always coming by and nagging her. She said he would appear at the craziest times, though it didn't surprise her as that would be what she'd expect from him. I thought to myself, Elaine is not a medium so how could she interact with Jeffrey? Elaine went on to tell me things like, "Jeffrey is sorry for the way he treated you at times, but you were the love of his life," "Jeffrey is so proud of the boys and is always watching out over all of you." I may be gullible but as Elaine talked, I was thinking she was just saying things she thought I would want to hear, trying to console me and make me feel better about Jeffrey's death.

We continued to talk and suddenly a Blue Jay appeared on the windowsill of the window between us.

Elaine said, "Oh look, here is Jeffrey now. He comes to you as a Blue Jay all the time," Jeffrey says that he "especially likes to come to you when you are sitting alone drinking your morning tea."

The bird sat there and looked inside the window at me for a minute or two and then flew off. I didn't think anything of it and then Elaine said, "Jeffrey wants me to ask you why you dressed him like that for his funeral?"

When these words came out, my heart stopped and I suspiciously looked at Elaine and asked her what she said.

So, she said again, "Jeffrey wants to know why you had him dressed like that for his funeral?"

Now, nobody but me, the boys, and the funeral director knew how Jeffrey was clothed.

Two days before the funeral, the funeral director asked me to pick out an outfit to put on Jeffrey's body in the casket. The casket was closed and his body was not going to be viewed by anyone. I asked Sam and Jay what they thought their dad would want to wear and we all agreed on the same outfit, which was his favorite button-down beach shirt he wore every day at home and bathing trunks. This was how Jeffrey dressed at home, was most comfortable, and we all agreed would have been what Jeffrey would have chosen himself.

As a matter of fact, because he was always barefoot, I forgot to include shoes with the clothes. The next day the funeral director had to come back for his topsiders. So, when Elaine asked me the question, it took me by shock.

When I didn't answer, Elaine said, "What did you put on him? Was he in his favorite suit? A tux?"

I shook my head no and said, "Jeffrey hated to dress up in a suit and tie. He quit his first job on Wall Street because he couldn't take wearing a suit and tie every day."

Elaine then said, "You didn't put him in a shroud did you?"

I laughed and shook my head no.

Finally, Elaine said, "Christina, Jeffrey says that he asked you this because he knows that you aren't believing that what I am saying is really from him. He wants you to know that he is really here talking to you. He isn't upset and the choice was right, but he knew that by asking this, it would confirm that it is him."

When she said that to me, a well of emotions built up and flowed out in tears.

I couldn't stop myself from crying. It was all so overwhelming. I never expected that I would hear from Jeffrey again but here he was talking to me through Elaine. This is why she called and said she needed to see me. So, Jeffrey could let me know the things he wanted to say all those thirteen months he couldn't talk.

Through Elaine, he told me that he appreciated my giving him all my time and devotion and stayed by his side almost every day after his accident. He said he heard all the things I said to him and enjoyed the music I was playing all the time. He said he loved the visits from the boys and it brought him so much joy when they were with him. He mentioned that he had been afraid to leave Sam after he died, so he stayed with him until I helped him leave. He said that he watches over us every day and how happy he is to see the boys growing up to be such good and loving boys. He said that I was the mother that he always knew I would be and his leaving allowed me to give the boys all the parenting and love they needed. He thanked me for taking care of him and for all the love I gave to him and he told me that he loved me the best he could and I was the love of his life. He said that he would always watch over and protect me and the boys.

After all this, Elaine said to me, "I am exhausted. Jeffrey completely wore me out."

So, I hugged her, thanked her, and then left.

The next morning, I was sitting at my kitchen table drinking my tea and a Blue Jay flew onto the windowsill. I looked at it and said, "Hi Jeffrey."

I once looked up the significance of the Blue Jays. I was not at all surprised to find that in the realm of spiritual meaning a Blue Jay is considered a mystical messenger that signifies guidance, protection, hope, clarity, and change. Blue Jay sightings may be an omen urging one to speak up, be bold, and to have confidence. If ever I doubted, I believe that the pairing of Jeffrey and me was that we were each other's teachers in this life. There is one other thing about Blue Jays, they symbolize trickery.

Story Twenty-five

I'M HERE, BELIEVE IT OR NOT

While my sister Anita and Jeffrey, though they saw each other rarely as she'd been abroad since 1985, bonded over their love for parties, she would push Jeffrey's button, doing just the opposite of what he wanted or expected to get a rise out of him. Betty and Jeffrey on the other hand were opposites and had a love/hate relationship that was more on the dislike side. Betty, a no-nonsense, Type A kind of person, who never did drugs and barely drank alcohol could not abide Jeffrey's, showy, loud, live-wire personality. She would tense up around him and could never relax. She would often say, "I'd never turn my back to Jeffrey." They were oil and water to some extent and Jeffrey loved to annoy Betty who would not hesitate to tell him off. They did tolerate each other, even if distant, as we were family.

Jeffrey always admired and loved the relationship I had with my family and he felt very at home with all of my siblings. His family was not the cozy, emotive type so he appreciated being around us. Every summer, after I had Sam, we would rent a big house on the New Jersey shore and my sisters, their family, my parents, and my brothers would all come up and stay with us. It was our family reunion and get away from the Florida summer heat. Jeffrey would take my dad to Atlantic

City to play Blackjack, their bonding vice, and sometimes we'd go with them to see a show, but for the most part, we just hung out, relaxed, and enjoyed our family time together.

One time Jeffrey was asked to golf with some people at a famous course in the area. As Jeffrey was a terrible golfer and Betty's husband, Kevin, was a great golfer, Jeffrey took Kevin along as his ringer. Jeffrey, always having to bet on something and be the center of attention to make his life more exciting would bet large sums of money on a hole. Always surrounded by his friends, on the last hole of the round, Kevin was looking at a tough putt. Right before the putt, Jeffrey said, "I bet forty thousand dollars that Kevin sinks this putt." A cheer resounded.

Kevin, a non-gambler who believes in saving his money for the future, the ultimate no-risk kind of guy was appalled. He looked at Jeffrey like he was crazy! Kevin was looking at a difficult putt, and to have the added responsibility of all that money riding on him making that putt was to him insane. But, that was Jeffrey! Kevin sunk the putt and Jeffrey won the bet. In return, Jeffrey bought Kevin a golf shirt from the Pro Shop.

After Jeffrey passed, one day Betty got a call from a former work associate. They hadn't spoken in years. Her friend proceeded to tell her about the strangest thing that had happened to her and her sister. They had gone to a medium and in the middle of their reading, the medium said, "Hey, there's a guy named Jeffrey who was in a car accident and is holding the side of his head here. He wants to tell his boys that he loves them." Betty's friend and sister said they'd looked at each other as if neither knew a Jeffrey.

Days later the friend said she suddenly remembered that Betty's brother-in-law had died from a car accident and had two boys, so she'd called. She didn't know if his name was Jeffrey but she felt compelled to call Betty to give her the message. Betty thanked her friend for calling, but being a non-believer wasn't one hundred percent sold on what she had been told. Nevertheless, she called me to tell me what her friend had said. I told her that was strange as I couldn't figure out why

Jeffrey would go to a stranger instead of to Betty directly. I moved on and didn't think much of it after that day.

My sister Betty had always been a non-believer in astrology and psychics. Some time went by. Betty was alone at home making herself lunch. She went to go into her refrigerator and something invisible physically stopped her in her tracks. Probably because of the call she'd received a few months earlier her immediate thought went to Jeffrey. "Jeffrey, knock it off. Get out of my way." One of the things Jeffrey did to get a rise out of Betty when they were together at the beach house, was to jump in front of her. This would annoy Betty to no end and there was no mistaking the message. Betty said the sensation of being held back was gone after she scolded him. Jeffrey had made a believer out of Betty and of course, got the last laugh.

Anita and Jeffrey were two peas in a pod. Both with extreme personalities, another reason I adjusted to Jeffrey's, they inherently understood each other. Both could do anything they wanted if they put their minds to it and they genuinely loved each other. They shared the same love of life and love of partying. Jeffrey was always pulling practical jokes on Anita as she was a good sport about it. One day, Anita was at her home in California; she was getting ready to go out and went to get the keys that she always put on her counter, but they weren't there. Nobody had been in the house since she drove the kids to school and returned home, so she couldn't understand what happened to the keys. Anita searched all over the house and backtracked her steps several times—still no keys. She rechecked the area around the counter. She checked everywhere until she became frustrated from looking. Then the thought of Jeffrey and his practical jokes hit her. "Okay Jeffrey, you're not funny. Give me my keys back." This time when she went back to the counter, her keys were back right where she knew she had left them. In Shirley MacLaine's book, *Out on a Limb,* she described a similar situation, only her poltergeist was named Tom MacPherson!

My mother and Jeffrey shared a special bond. Despite Mom knowing the hardships and issues Jeffrey and I had in our relationship, she had long loved him and she more than anyone understood as she'd had similar experiences with my dad. Often Jeffrey would call Mom to talk and express how he was feeling, something he did with no one else. Even after eleven years together Jeffrey never once confided in me the demons he wrestled with daily. The reasons he could never be alone. The anxiety of never measuring up. The need for adoration. The origin of his addictive personality. Like me, my mom saw Jeffrey's heart beyond the bravado and would forgive him for his shortcomings. Still, being my mother, she couldn't forget about some of the bad things we went through.

Jeffrey always knew how much my mother truly loved him. After our final altercation that led to our separation, and because Jeffrey did not come to our last family gathering, my mom didn't get a chance to see Jeffrey before his accident. One morning in January 2003 my mom called me and she sounded upset. She told me she'd had a vivid dream about Jeffrey. She'd walked into a room and Jeffrey and Joyce were sitting on a bed. When Jeffrey saw my mom, he stood up, walked over to her, and hugged her. Then she woke up in tears. She said it was so real and that she could feel the hug. She said she remembered thinking happily, "he can walk." I told her that I thought that it was a visit from him. She said she thought the same thing. A year later, my mom had another vivid dream and this time she said to Jeffrey, "I forgive you." That was the last time she had a dream about Jeffrey. Mom got to see Jeffrey almost every weekend during the thirteen months of his hospitalization, but since Jeffrey couldn't speak, he never got to apologize for all that had happened in our relationship. He appeared in her dream to tell her how sorry he'd been.

Not surprising to me, I have had a lot of "Jeffrey" encounters. He is such a strong presence. Every time I go to an astrologer, psychic, or medium Jeffrey always makes an appearance. I see the Blue Jay at random times and at all different locations. I always recognize him and say, "Hi, Jeffrey." I talk to him, I yell at him, I blame him when things go wrong, and I ask him for help when I need something.

One night, after the boys went to sleep, I thought I would clean out Jeffrey's bathroom drawers. It had been a couple of years since his death and all Jeffrey's things were still where they had always been. Even though the boys and I had been going to an amazing group therapy called Hearts and Hope for a while and making great progress, I still hadn't cleaned out his things. It was time to start letting go. I figured that since I had some time before bedtime, I would begin cleaning out his things starting with his side of the bathroom.

One of Jeffrey's favorite things to collect were the soaps, lotions, shampoos, and conditioners from the hotel where he would stay. He had an enormous collection from all around the world. He wouldn't ever use them, he just liked collecting them. I had a few lawn trash bags ready to begin and even though I was feeling a little guilty about throwing everything out, I gathered up the thousands of what I called his novelty gadgets and began throwing them in the bag. All of a sudden, this loud banging started. It sounded like somebody was pounding on the ceiling of the bathroom.

The loud noise startled and scared me. I got up and looked around but couldn't see what was causing the noise. Then it occurred to me what I was doing and I shouted out loud, "Jeffrey, this is all a bunch of junk and I am not keeping it anymore. Get over it!"

Then as quickly as it started, the banging just stopped. Once I had everything in the bags and tied up, I looked up and said, "Sorry, Jeffrey. I know you loved collecting all these things."

Another night, after I'd cleaned out his office and made it my office, I was sitting at the desk when the television, which had been dead for several months, started to blast out sound. The television was in a built-in wall unit with cabinet doors to hide it when not in use. The noise startled me and I jumped up, went, and opened the doors and saw that the TV wasn't on, but a noise was coming from it. I unplugged the TV and the noise stopped. A couple of months later when Anita came to visit, her first time back at the house since Jeffrey's funeral, she went to get something from the office. The moment she stepped into the room, the TV started blaring out the noise. Anita jumped at the suddenness of the noise and yelled to me, "Tina, where's this noise coming from? How can I turn it off?"

I went to check out the situation and recognized the sound was the same as the noise that had startled me a few months prior. I knew I had unplugged the unit but thought, *maybe our housekeeper, Amy, had plugged it back in, because how could it be on otherwise?*

I opened the cabinet and the TV was off and unplugged, but the noise was definitely coming from it. I told Anita what happened to me and then she smiled and said, "Okay, Jeffrey, very funny that you scared the shit out of me. I know that you are here."

And then the sound stopped.

Having Jeffrey around real or imagined has helped me in many ways. It gives me comfort knowing that he is not gone, but somewhere else watching over us. It allows me to be at peace with his physical being gone. I speak to him all the time, sometimes I yell at him when I am angry, and sometimes I ask for his help, but I truly believe that he can hear me. I understand his messages and signs and I acknowledge them verbally to him, so he will send more to me. Although he is not here with me in the physical world, I feel strong connections to him and know that he is always with me and the boys. I am probably more receptive to the notion of life after death and signs from loved ones who have passed, having experienced so many messages. I always say, "The more you believe, the more you receive."

Story Twenty-Six

THE WOLF IN SHEEP'S CLOTHING

The love of money can be, as the Bible suggests, the root of all evil. The love of money will show you who you are every time. Greed, excessive and unethical behaviors, can be outcomes when one's love of money trumps their humanity. I grew up with the belief that how much money you have is a very personal matter. I was a "saver" and would hoard the money I made from babysitting or working at my dad's restaurant. I would save and save until I found something I wanted and would spend my money on that, but always made sure that I had money left over. I remember that my mom would always say, "Chinese people don't talk about money. It is not a good thing." Maybe this is where I developed my thoughts.

Don't get me wrong, I like to look good and enjoy nice things, which takes money, but that was not a priority or motivating factor for me and though I was impressed with Jeffrey's acumen when we first met, I was more drawn to his unpredictability and bad boy tendencies. And even wealth can get old. So, when Jeffrey started to make a lot of money, I never paid too much attention to how much he was earning or how much money we had. I knew he was earning beaucoup money, but I didn't know how much he was stashing away. I just knew we had a lot. For me, as long as we could pay the bills and have some money in the bank, I felt safe and happy.

The whole time during my relationship with Jeffrey, I always maintained my own bank account, so I had a sense of having my own financial security. I called my account my "nest egg," which Jeffrey always thought was funny and ridiculous as he would say what I had was menial compared to what we had together. I never really felt all the money he made was my business and I was happy to continually add to my nest egg.

In Chinese culture, family is always first. This was instilled in me by watching how my parents brought us up. My mom's whole life has been about me and my siblings, then once we had children, her grandchildren became her priority. My mom was a classical pianist and a very good one. Like my dad, they both subordinated their gift to honor the ideals of a Chinese family. I believed my responsibility as a partner to Jeffrey was in raising and caring for our boys and our home life. Jeffrey's responsibility was to earn money to support our family. It's what I saw and it's what I knew. We both understood our positions and roles and didn't interfere in the other's duties. I had a basic understanding of Jeffrey's businesses and knew his different partners in the various companies he owned, but for the most part, I stayed out of the day-to-day business dealings.

Damien was the owner of a building where this hot nightclub in Fort Lauderdale was located. Jeffrey used to frequent his club, but it got into some pickle and was closing. Damien had met Jeffrey at the club and instead of closing the club, Jeffrey said he'd go in fifty-fifty and they could revive it. They created a restaurant/ nightclub called Christopher's which became quite successful. They soon became fast friends and Jeffrey, being Jeffrey, had an unusual admiration for Damien, who was conservative and boasted about managing his money well. Jeffrey would call Damien the cheapest rich man he knew. I was home with the boys, and though I knew of Damien, I had only met him a handful of times because he co-owned our Learjet. On the third or fourth day after the accident, Damien showed up in New York and told me he needed to talk to me.

He was sympathetic and seemed kind. I was overwhelmed, distraught, and trying to keep Jeffrey alive. Between that and constantly managing our Florida household from afar, not to talk about being emotionally available for my boys, when Damien told me he had the Power of Attorney over the businesses, I was relieved. I couldn't imagine having to think about overseeing Jeffrey's business dealings. There were people far more adept at it than me. Had I been in my right mind, since he was a lesser partner than most, I would have wondered why Jeffrey would entrust him with Power of Attorney instead of the partner in his major companies. I trusted him to have him handle everything relating to the companies because Jeffrey had given him Power of Attorney. *How could I not trust a man who carries a rosary in his pocket and is a devout Christian?*

Out of sorts, throughout the thirteen months Jeffrey was alive, Damien never failed to check in with me regularly to inform me of what was going on with the business and my trust in him felt justified. He'd simply ask me how much money I needed and whatever bills needed to be paid, he would transfer the money into my account and I would pay the bills. I never questioned him about how much money we had and he never asked me what the bills were for, so it was very similar to how Jeffrey and I had always worked.

About six weeks into Jeffrey's treatment, Damien came to New York and told me that Jeffrey hadn't filed any tax returns in several years and that the IRS was going to come after us. He told me we owed approximately eighteen million in taxes, fines, and penalties. He said because Jeffrey was "his brother" he would lend us the money and pay off the taxes immediately so the IRS wouldn't put me in jail. He felt it was far more important for me to be with Jeffrey and didn't want me to have to deal with the IRS problems. Damien said his accountant was a former IRS agent and could get the payment to an agent who would take care of everything so our issue would be gone. He assured me all would be okay and that he would take care of everything. He said he knew Jeffrey would pay him back when he got better. Again, I was grateful. At the time, Jeffrey was still in a coma and the last thing I wanted to deal with was an issue with the IRS, so I thanked Damien profusely for lending us the money and for getting us out of a potentially sticky and unpleasant problem. I thought he was an angel sent to guard and protect us.

As I said, I didn't know Damien very well. I knew he and Jeffrey were partners in a couple of nightclubs and that Jeffrey would take him along on his casino trips from time to time. Damien, as I understood it, was going to help Jeffrey with the new offshore sports betting business, which is why Jeffrey took him to Costa Rica with him.

In a lucid moment, I honored the nagging in my gut. I called Jeffrey's good friend Adam, whom I had known since I met Jeffrey. Adam strongly advised me to get an attorney and not just believe what Damien was saying. He said he couldn't understand why Jeffrey would give Damien, someone he briefly knew, all this power and responsibility not just over their business but all his businesses. Jeffrey loved and trusted Adam maybe because Adam had his own money, as he had several car dealerships, and did not "need" Jeffrey like everyone else. But I knew that Adam, who was single and had a house in South Beach where Jeffrey would stay, was an enabler of sorts to Jeffrey, so I didn't listen to his warnings. My suspicion of him as Jeffrey's enabler made me think that maybe he was just a little jealous and didn't recognize his concerns for me.

Damien had been diagnosed with a brain tumor a while before Jeffrey's accident, which led to them taking out Key Man Life Insurance policies on each other. This would cover buying one another out of the clubs, should anything ever happen to him. Given he was facing his mortality, the policies had to have been Damien's idea, as Jeffrey did not believe in life insurance. I once asked Jeffrey if we should have life insurance policies now that we had children and after the psychic Iris's frightening suggestion, which he told me was the "dumbest idea he'd ever heard." He felt it was throwing away money on something we would never need. "Don't worry. We have enough money. If anything, ever happens there will be plenty of money to take care of it, so we do not need life insurance," he said. I just could not imagine a dying man being duplicitous or unscrupulous.

Damien became my support and confidant during this period of trying to save Jeffrey's life. He was the only person I would see regularly, aside from my mom, Sam, and Jay. He always told me how much he respected my dedication and the love I was giving to Jeffrey. Though he claimed to have been diagnosed with Stage 4 cancer he told me he would forego any radical treatments until Jeffrey got better. I couldn't believe this selflessness. It was so out of human nature to not self-preserve. I insisted he needed to take care of himself and went as far as seeking out doctors and treatments for his brain cancer. As we got closer, Damien began telling me stories about all the goings on with Jeffrey's South Beach friends and "family," which confirmed my desire to keep everyone away and out of our lives. I was only about positivity and optimism and didn't want any negativity around me and Jeffrey.

During the first few months, Damien thought the best thing to do was to try and liquidate some assets and get rid of some of the companies. If he and Jeffrey, were both incapacitated, it was a good and sound idea. I certainly didn't need a fleet of luxury cars, or helicopters, so those could certainly go.

He told me that he would sell a couple of the companies to get some cash to pay all mine and Jeffrey's bills and of course the repayment of the eighteen million dollars he had loaned us. Apparently, Jeffrey's partner Erik at the Day Trading Firm, wanted to offer twenty-five million dollars to buy Jeffrey out of the business. Damien expressed this was essentially stealing from Jeffrey at a time when he was down. That if it weren't for Jeffrey, the business wouldn't be as profitable and successful as it was. He reminded me that there was an offer of three-hundred million dollars still on the table from E-Trade. Since the company had hired someone to shop the company to other potential buyers, an offer of twenty-five million when Jeffrey was the majority owner, was a slap in the face.

The partner at Broadway Trading, Erik, was a friend I'd known for years. He started trading options for Jeffrey on the floor of the American Stock Exchange years before and we were close to him and his family. I was surprised and hurt when Damien told me that Erik was trying to "screw" me. Then one day, Damien came to me and said Erik wanted to see me and make me an offer to my face. Damien told me that even though it wasn't my decision to make since he had Power of Attorney, he wanted me to see first-hand how Erik was scheming to cheat me and Jeffrey. Hesitatingly I went to meet Erik and Damien.

Honestly, I was already mad about the fact that the CFO had lost us our unlimited medical insurance and he was still employed with the company! What made it worse was that the CFO was another of Jeffrey's longtime friends, so it wasn't a stretch for me to think that Erik was out to get us too. Damien would tell me stories about how greedy everyone was becoming now Jeffrey was out of the loop and that nobody cared about Jeffery as he and I did. That Jeffrey made everyone very rich by giving them opportunities and nobody was loyal to him.

When I went to the meeting I already had a tainted point of view. I told Erik that I wouldn't accept any offer especially with Jeffrey just being a couple months into his recovery. That if I sold out for twenty-five million, Jeffrey would kill me. I told him I needed the company to pay for all the expenses incurred because we were not medically insured anymore. This should have been another red flag as Damien had promised to take care of this and had not. Erik agreed to this and asked me to re-consider his offer adding that when Jeffrey was better he would let him buy back in for the same amount. In hindsight, this could have been a real deal but with three hundred million still on the table I could not, under any circumstance consider such a deal. Jeffrey just had to get well as all this business stuff was driving me nuts.

After the meeting, Damien turned to me and said, "See what I mean? Erik knows the company is about to sell for three hundred million and all he wants to give Jeffrey is twenty-five million. That is stealing."

Throughout the following nine or so months, Damien would sell off the companies and our assets. Because we owed him the eighteen million for the taxes, he would keep the money to recoup his loan. I was still getting money from Broadway Trading to pay our bills, so I didn't think we'd ever have a financial problem.

When Jeffrey died, because Jeffrey had no Will, probate took over. I was shocked to learn that we were broke. When I questioned Damien as to how this could be, he told me that everything we had went to pay him back for the tax bill and that we were even now. He said that he had bought out Jeffrey's half of the clubs and put one million in a joint account. He explained that if Jeffrey died, he would get any other money due back when the Keyman—a life insurance policy was paid out. He told me he'd done this months before to protect me just in case Jeffrey did die. He seemed to always have my back.

As bad luck would have it, shortly after Jeffrey's death, Broadway Trading filed for Chapter 11 bankruptcy. Not only did the most profitable and successful of Jeffrey's companies go bankrupt—after Jeffrey's passing—Damien had me engage in a bitter lawsuit against the company and partners. Damien had had all the companies wire him the funds and as he told me they had stolen money and changed Jeffrey's percent of ownership to a higher distribution for themselves before the company went under. After spending hundreds of thousands of dollars on lawsuits between the medical insurance company and Broadway Trading, I told Damien that I couldn't keep spending all our money on lawyers and that I wanted out. I wanted to settle the lawsuit against his partners and keep things moving.

With all our business dealings done, Damien said that he needed to focus on his health. He was living between Arizona and Florida because he said he was receiving alternative treatments in Arizona, where he could get experimental medications from Mexico that he couldn't get in the U.S. and they were saving his life. Now that probate was taking over, his job was done.

He told me that the doctors didn't give him a long time to live, but it was important for him to take care of "his brother" as he knew that Jeffrey would have done the same for him. I felt terrible Damien had sacrificed his well-being to help us out and always told him so. I couldn't have been more grateful and appreciative of him. Not in my wildest dream would I have suspected what came to pass.

More removed from day-to-day vigilance a modicum of myself returned, my gut felt something was off. And indeed, sometimes things were just not as they seemed. I would learn a hard life-lesson when after going through years of probate issues and several attorneys, that while it was true that Jeffrey didn't file a couple of years of tax returns, he'd been making payments, and in fact, had made a $2.5 million payment a few months before his accident. So, while there were a few million still due at the time of the accident, it was over ten million off from Damien's eighteen million dollars claim. Damien turned out to be the best con artist and he got me good. Not only did he know how to play on my heartstrings with his claims of dying (as of now, 2024, twenty-three years later, he is still alive from Stage 4 brain cancer), but he exploited my vulnerability when caring for Jeffrey. Damien had created so many loopholes and weaved such an elaborate web of transactions and accounting nightmares that it took fourteen years to finally close out probate. He had struck pre-emptively, disparaging people who could get in the way of his scheme and he had been the most disloyal, unethical, and deceitful. Here it was, as I always knew and quoted from Oprah…all the people who drove in the limousine had no intention of riding the bus.

It never once dawned on me to question Damien's motives or why Jeffrey would have given him Power of Attorney only two months before he died. Had Jeffrey sensed his demise? No, he hadn't, because he had never given Damien Power of Attorney. The real kicker, as I came to find out was that Damien's "Power of Attorney" was fake, but because he'd had me sign papers alongside him, one being a real Power of Attorney naming him in charge, everything he did was "legal." I use the term loosely because I find being conned, lied to, and defrauded far from anything considered legal.

Does it make me sick that from the very beginning of Jeffrey's tragic accident, Damien set about concocting elaborate schemes to steal a fortune right out under us as he saw Jeffrey dying? Of course, it made me sick to my stomach, but I do not believe in carrying anger and such negativity. I truly believe that "what goes around comes around" and it was not my responsibility to seek retribution to make Damien's life terrible. Revenge is something I will not partake in. Was I gullible? I was but I am not going to beat myself for being a trusting person. Everything happens for a reason! Instead of revenge, anger, or bitterness, I chose to make the most of what I was blessed with, my family; let fate deal with Damien. This very situation proved the adage that only the good die young. Damien and Jeffrey's story was a zero-sum game.

Story Twenty-seven
HERE I GO AGAIN

When my mom called to tell me her mother (my PoPo) was not well and they were going to start hospice, I immediately packed up my boys and set off to Wisconsin.

It was the first time we'd flown commercial since Jeffrey passed. We had first-class tickets so were allowed on the plane first. We were seated when the other passengers started coming onboard and Sam blurted out, "Why are all these people coming on our plane?"

I loved my PoPo and we had a special bond. Maybe because I was sickly, she showed me a lot of attention. When my grandfather (YeYe) resigned from his post as Ambassador to Cyprus, he and PoPo settled in Wisconsin to be near their eldest son and his daughter-in-law. Growing up we would travel to see my grandparents, our uncles, aunts, and cousins every summer. We didn't live close by but our sojourn on the Ohio Turnpike was always an exciting time for us kids. Because PoPo didn't speak a lot of English, we didn't say a lot to each other, but the feeling of love and closeness was always there. PoPo was the only person who didn't criticize my Mandarin. She appreciated my attempts to speak our native language, which always made me happy, and made me want to try harder to speak more in Mandarin.

PoPo might not have spoken English but she was observant and keen. She never missed a beat. One summer with nothing to do, my instigating cousin Delilah suggested we should egg the neighbor's house. Now my cousin Rebecca and I were not rabble-rousers so we declined the offer but soon gave in to the prodding of Delilah. We each had an egg and when the countdown started both Rebecca and I dropped our eggs on the grass while Delilah threw her egg at the neighbor's house. The following morning the police arrived at the house. Delilah the culprit had gone back to her house but Rebecca and I were punished and sent to clean the neighbor's house. It was so unfair. When we got back PoPo told me she knew it was not me and that it was our trouble-making cousin, Delilah, and commended me for doing the right thing. That was my PoPo: quiet, observant, and loving.

Once my grandparents moved to the U.S. my mother would speak to her mother every day. Another trait I got from my PoPo is my mom and I speak daily, sometimes several times a day. Because of their daily interaction and my daily interaction with my mom even to this day, I always knew how my PoPo was failing as Mom would update me on her well-being. I had always felt close to PoPo but these daily updates made me feel even closer.

When I arrived at the house, PoPo was still coherent and lying in bed. We were both very happy to see one another and she was especially delighted to see Sam and Jay. Throughout the next twenty-four hours, family members began arriving to see PoPo. My cousin from Singapore, Jennifer, and I spent most of our time on the bed with PoPo. We would talk to PoPo during the moments she was awake. But as the hours went on, the moments became rarer and there were long stretches between her being asleep and her being conscious. Afternoons would turn to evenings and PoPo's eyes did not open.

One afternoon Jennifer was sitting in a chair on one side of PoPo, and I was on the bed on the other side when suddenly PoPo sat up with both arms outstretched and said, "No, go away. Turn out the lights," Then she fell back onto the bed with her eyes shut. Jennifer and I looked at each other and then in the direction of PoPo. We looked around but there was nothing there. There was a hallway light on, but nobody was in the hallway. As soon as she laid back down, I asked in my broken Mandarin, "Who's there?" When she didn't respond, I asked, "Is it Ye Ye?" No response.

"Is it your mom?" No response.

I was trying to think of those who had passed on so then I said, "Is it Jeffrey?" Immediately, PoPo started shaking her head with a disgusted look on her face like "Are you crazy?" Jennifer and I started to crack up laughing. It wasn't a disgusted look like she didn't like Jeffrey, but it was rather like saying to me, "Why the heck would he come to me?"

My grandparents didn't know Jeffrey well but they liked what they knew of him from our visits to see them. My PoPo thought he was funny and my YeYe was impressed with his business acumen. He was a real charmer. After that, PoPo stopped responding to any of our guesses, so we will never know for sure who she saw coming to take her home.

Jennifer and I both had the same thought…someone from the "other side" had come to take her into the light, but she was not ready to go. A few hours later, PoPo's sister called from Taiwan. They had a close relationship and called each other all the time. My mom explained to her aunt that PoPo wasn't responding but she could hear and so my mom put the headset by PoPo's ear and her sister spoke to her then said, "Goodbye."

Not long after the call, we could tell that PoPo was getting ready to take her last breath. The time between her breaths had grown further and further apart and was shallower. The family was in the room and I was still on the bed. The moment PoPo took her last breath and I said, "She's gone," the humidifier that had been in the room started making loud noises. All of a sudden the Chinese nurse jumped onto the bed next to me and opened the window above the bed, while I yelled to turn off the noise. As soon as the window opened, the noise stopped. The nurse was upset and said that PoPo's soul couldn't get out because the window was closed. Was it a coincidence that the humidifier was clicked off at the same time the window opened or did PoPo's soul find its way out? You already know what my answer would be.

Story Twenty-eight

DADDY'S GIRL

One of my most cherished photos is my dad giving me a piggy-back ride in our backyard while smoking a pipe. I had just turned seven years old and it was one of the rare times that I remember him being home and not working or cutting the lawn. It was probably a Monday, as that was Dad's only day off. Of all of us kids, my dad and I had a special bond because I spent more time with him going back and forth for allergy shots. I wish like with Jeffrey I knew what was inside my dad's heart and mind. Had his actual life versus his potential life been a disappointment? Had family altered his fate? Is that why he found joy in gambling? None of it I suppose matters because Dad was dad, a hard worker who loved his family.

My dad, as I said, was the hardest worker I have ever met and the most dedicated son. He never showed his emotions, showing his love for us by buying us whatever we needed. Alongside Dad, his parents both worked at the one restaurant, Sue Fong, until they were both very old. They too believed in hard work and worked hard. My dad had so many talents and in his time, he was a scratch golfer, a good basketball player, and a bodybuilder/weightlifter. He's vicariously lived out his love of sports through my brothers Alan and Brian who inherited his athleticism, and it was my dad's greatest joy to watch his sons play sports. My dad was also the biggest Philadelphia Sports fan…the Phillies, Flyers, and Eagles were his teams. In his bedroom, he had a few televisions so he could watch different games at one time. Growing up with Dad and sports was my training to become a mother of two athletic boys.

Being so sickly, I probably spent most of the time, out of all the kids, around my dad though all of us girls worked in the restaurant from a young age. From peeling onions and deveining pea pods to eventually taking and ringing orders, I learned how to work the family business. It was the time Anita and Betty got to spend time with Dad. My dad spoiled me by always buying me things and giving me money, and I could never do wrong in his eyes. He told me when I was young, terribly skinny, and not very attractive, that I was like the ugly duckling. Then he would say, "But you know, Tina, the ugly duckling turns into the beautiful Swan at the end of the story. So, you know one day, you'll be a beautiful Swan." He would also tease me about eating so slowly by saying, "You better learn to eat your food faster, because if you ever go to jail everyone will steal your food if you eat so slowly." I would laugh and tell him I didn't expect to go to jail.

My dad and Jeffrey were not only the same in their love for me, but they both loved to gamble, specifically playing blackjack. The difference between them was that Jeffrey had a much larger bankroll so could afford some losses here and there. My dad on the other hand never believed he couldn't win at the casinos, and he never stopped playing which eventually led to his losing the restaurant. Over the years my mom, Jeffrey, and I knew that my dad had a gambling problem, but I had insisted we stop bailing him out of his debts. Though it was a hard and heartbreaking decision on my part to make him sell the restaurant, I did. I never say this as mere disappointment for my father but rather as a tough love stance to get him to own his up to his mistakes. After he sold the restaurant he took a job as a cook at a nursing home. Here was a man who was a great artist and a great sportsman who'd given up his dreams for family; this karma was probably too much to bear.

While working at the nursing home wasn't what he'd ever imagined he would be doing in his sixties, it did take a lot of responsibility off his back, was much easier work and he had more time off. He'd come to Florida to visit and would spend time at the Jersey Beach with the family, where he loved to relax and fish.

In August of 2005, during our Jersey beach house vacation, my dad had a horrible cough. Everyone at the house was telling him that he had to get it checked out, but my dad didn't like to go to the doctor. Fortunately, he had always been very healthy, so never really needed to see the doctor. But towards the end of the vacation, he was complaining about his shoulder aching and not being able to sleep and agreed to go to the doctor the next week.

Sam, Jay, my mom, and I left the beach house to go to Hawaii to visit my mom's brother. Alan and his kids were staying on a few extra days in Philadelphia, so Alan said he'd take Dad to the doctor. I was sitting on the beach in Maui, watching the boys take a surf lesson when Alan called.

He said that the doctor did an x-ray and was concerned as there was a big gray area that didn't look like what we were expecting to be pneumonia, but rather a tumor. Then came the C-word…cancer.

Story Twenty-nine
THE "C" DIAGNOSIS

My dad would often tell stories of how when he was young and in China, he would walk miles to school or ride water buffalos. I am not sure if these were tales or the truth, but he also told how he would roll tobacco to make cigarettes and smoke them. So, he was smoking tobacco or cigarettes from a young age and continued to smoke until I was diagnosed with severe asthma and the doctors told my parents I could not be around cigarette smoke. So, my dad went from smoking cigarettes to smoking cigars and pipes until he eventually gave up smoking some years later. Another sacrifice, albeit a good one he made for his family.

When the oncologist told my dad he had Stage 4 Lung Cancer with an inoperable tumor and asked if he was a smoker, he responded, "No, I do not smoke."

When my dad told me how he responded, I asked him how he thought he wasn't a smoker and he said, "But I stopped smoking about forty-five years ago." He didn't account for the ten or so years he was a heavy smoker. While I can't be sure that Dad got lung cancer from smoking all those years before, no one in our family ever had lung cancer. A soul not at rest manifests as dis-ease and eventually as disease. If Dad couldn't live the truth of his life and instead swallowed his disappointment could that have been the cause of his illness? What did the cause matter, he had been given a death sentence any way you looked at it.

My cousin more like a sister, Sieu Fong, is nine years younger than me and grew up with us. Her mother is my dad's older sister, who had Sieu at forty years old. Since Sieu is an only child she spent a lot of time with my parents and was exceptionally close to my dad, as she was his "favorite" niece. Sieu is a nurturer and extremely giving of herself to others. So, naturally, when my dad found out about his cancer, Sieu volunteered to go to appointments with my mom and dad. Fortunately, she lives outside Philadelphia, so she didn't have to travel too far to the Hospital at UPenn.

While Sieu and my mom were the on-hand caregivers for my dad, my mom and dad asked if I would be the healthcare surrogate for him. What this meant was that along with my dad, I would make decisions regarding his health and be in communication with the doctors. One thing I learned from taking care of Jeffrey, was that somebody needs to take control, be an advocate, and manage the medical issues that arise. I was especially adept at asking the doctors questions, researching options, and pressing the doctors for answers. I was more than happy to be Dad's health proxy.

In the beginning months, we saw improvements with a shrinkage of the tumor, but the chemo and radiation were taking a toll on him. At first, he continued to work but eventually had to stop because he would get so tired, weak, and sick from the treatments. He lost his hair and lost a lot of weight. His appetite changed, as he said that things didn't taste the same anymore. I'd made a pact to myself when my dad was diagnosed, that I was going to call him every night to say "hi" and go up to see him monthly. I did this because I knew that while I wasn't sure how long my father would live, I knew that it wasn't going to be years and I wanted to take advantage of every day that I had left with him. I used to call my mom daily but didn't really speak to my dad, but now I called and made sure to speak to him first. I know that he enjoyed this and sometimes would revel in saying to my mom, "Oh, Tina called, but she only wanted to talk to me."

I told my dad that I was going to move back up to Philadelphia, so he could be close to Sam and Jay. The thought was that my dad would be able to go to Sam and Jay's sports games like he used to for Alan and Brian. One thing Dad always loved to do was hear about Sam and Jay's sports games. When I would tell him about Sam hitting a grand slam or that pitchers were intentionally walking Sam because they were afraid of his hitting home runs, my dad would say, "That's Slammin' Sammy for you!" He was also always amazed at how Jay, who was small for his age, was so dominant at basketball. So many of our daily conversations were centered on the boys and we tried not to talk too much about his cancer. I knew that he wasn't feeling good and getting sick, but he liked to talk about sports or the kids and not think about his disease.

The boys and I went up to Philadelphia at least every month to visit and check on my dad. It is funny, my siblings and I used to say that my dad was like "the Boy who cried Wolf," because my mom was always away taking care of one of the grandchildren, so to get attention, my dad would make up stories of how he was sick or hurt. But now when he was really sick, he really didn't complain, at least not to me.

He always tried to put up a good front for me and the boys but I could see as the months went on and winter set in, how thin and weak he was becoming. My mom wanted to believe that he was getting thin because he refused to eat her home cooking and at times felt upset and offended when in reality, his taste buds had changed and he couldn't eat a lot of things. Even with supplements such as Ensure he had a hard time keeping his weight up.

As winter turned to spring, Dad's health was unchanged. We would get good reports of the shrinkage of the tumor, but eventually, the shrinkage stopped. Dad spent most of his time in bed now, as he said that his walking was getting harder and harder. In late March, as my parents were heading out, my dad slipped and fell on the cold concrete patio of their house. As he was getting so weak, he couldn't get up and my mom wasn't strong enough to lift him. Luckily, since we lived next door to the police station, a policeman was pulling into the station and saw my parents and quickly came to help them. My dad refused to go to the hospital and his pride wouldn't let them call 911, so the policeman helped carry him into his bedroom. More and more, I would get sad stories like this from either my mom or dad.

On May 21st, I got a call in the middle of the day from my mom because my dad fell again going to the bathroom. She had to call 911, but once again, when the paramedics arrived, he refused to let them take him to the hospital so they just helped him into bed. My mom said, "Tina, you have to convince him that he needs to go to the hospital. Something is going on and he needs to be checked out." So, I told my mom that I would fly up to see him. The next morning the boys and I got a flight and headed to Philadelphia.

When we got to the house, I had a feeling that his cancer was spreading into his brain. I knew that this was always a possibility and with all his falls I figured that this could be the reason. I sat with my dad and told him that I needed him to go to the hospital. He told me that he didn't want to go to a hospital, as he was afraid he wouldn't come back home. I promised him that I would make sure he came home, but he kept refusing. Finally, Sam came in to say "hi" and heard me asking my dad to go to the hospital, so he said, "Grandpa Ben, you really need to go to the hospital. Would you please go for me?"

My dad looked at Sam for a long moment and then said, "Okay, for you I will."

After a grueling registration process at the hospital, which was infuriating because my dad was so weak and could barely sit in a wheelchair, we were admitted but the "process of admissions" took hours. Again, I thought of how unsympathetic the entire healthcare system had become. The next day my dad went through several medical tests, blood work, MRIs, etc. The doctor had the same thought as I did and when the results came back, it showed that the cancer had metastasized and was now in his brain. As I had the Power of Attorney over the medical decisions, the doctor gave me the option of starting chemotherapy, which would be administered through his skull, which was very invasive, and the prognosis wasn't so great. I was told that my dad could live a few months to a year, with or without the treatments it wasn't anything that would be a sure thing. What I did know was that if he were to do the chemo, he would be hospitalized and get even sicker and weaker. I thought about my dad's quality of life and how important it was for him to get home and out of the hospital. I knew that the reality either way was that my dad was not going to "get better" and had to recognize that we would be losing my dad sooner rather than later. I was not giving up, but I also wanted my dad to maintain his dignity and fulfill my promise to get him back home. So, I told the doctor that I would not authorize the invasive chemotherapy and I wanted to get my dad home as soon as possible. He told me that we could set up hospice at the house and keep Dad comfortable for as long as he needed. We figured that we had the summer and I could get him down to the beach house, a place he loved. The doctor told me that he would have made the same decision had it been his father and agreed that at this point, the best we could do was keep my dad pain-free and let him be happy at home.

I went into the hospital room, where Sieu, my mom, and my dad were all waiting to hear how my meeting with the doctor went. I walked over to my dad's side and told him that the cancer was now in his brain and that there were only two options, chemo to his brain or forego any more treatments and live the rest of his life as comfortably as possible with hospice at the house. I told him that I was against the chemo, but if he wanted to try it, I would go along with his wishes. I told him that it was uncertain how long he would live, with or without the chemo. I knew that I was delivering a death sentence to my dad, which is the hardest damn thing I have ever had to do in my life. So, I held in my emotions for his sake, knowing that if I fell apart, everyone including my dad would crumble. I had to be strong for him, even though my heart was in so much pain and I was screaming inside my head.

By now, Sieu was crying and my mom was in a state of shock. I looked at my dad who looked so incredibly sad. He had started to tear up, but then composed himself and said, "Tina, I agree with you. I don't want any more chemo, needles, or radiation. I just want to go home." And so that was it. We were going home.

On Friday, May 26th, my dad was discharged and I decided to ride in the ambulance back home from the hospital with him. As we were approaching the Chestnut Hill area, Dad said, "Tina, ask them if we can drive by the restaurant. I just want to see it again." As we did a drive-by, we sat my dad up so he could take one last look at all that was his life. My heart broke into a million little pieces watching my dad stare out the window with no expression on his face, but I knew his heart was breaking too. It's just that our Chinese pride wouldn't let us break down and cry.

When we arrived home, the hospice nurse had already set up the room with the medications and oxygen tank that would be needed. I sat next to my dad and we talked about how he felt badly that he never went back to China to see where he grew up and he retold stories I heard all my life of how he walked miles to school and rode water buffalos.

He told me that he knew that I would take care of my mother so he didn't worry and that he wanted me to be happy. I assured him that nothing made me happier than being with him. I shared a secret that I'd met a guy and was sort of dating him. I told my dad that the boys and I were going to have to leave for Florida so Sam and Jay could finish school, but we would return as soon as school was out for the summer. I explained that I rented a house in Avalon and that we would go there again and he could be by the ocean. Before I left for the airport on Saturday afternoon, I told my dad that I was leaving and he asked, "Will you come back?" I told him again and again that I would be coming back soon and that if he needed me, to call and I will come back. Then he said, "Okay Tina, thank you."

Story Thirty

THINGS HAPPEN IN THREES

When the boys and I landed in Florida, I turned on my phone and saw I had several messages. I called my voicemail and heard my mom telling me that my dad was unconscious. So, I immediately called and learned Alan had arrived shortly after I left. He'd spoken to Dad and then my dad said that he was going to take a nap, so Alan left his room. Anita arrived shortly after and she said when she went in to see him, he was unconscious. I was in a quandary with an upcoming settlement hearing I could not postpone so mom told me to go home and let the boys settle in and she'd let me know how things were progressing.

Nothing seemed to have changed after a few hours, with the hearing a few days away I decided to return to Philadelphia the following morning. The boys and I returned to Philadelphia to find my dad unresponsive as I was told. I couldn't believe it. Not 24 hours earlier, I was sitting by my dad's bedside having a conversation and now he was exactly like my grandmother was before she died. So, as I had done with Jeffrey, PoPo, and now my dad, I sat with him and just talked to him. At times it would appear he was listening as his breathing would change or he would sigh. Anita, Alan, and my mom would take turns being with and talking to my dad. The hospice nurse said she believed his body was shutting down and that he wouldn't live much longer. It was Memorial Day weekend and Betty and Sieu's family were down at the shore. After hearing about my dad's condition, Brian rushed to the airport but was still in Florida and waiting to get a flight up.

Throughout the night, just as I was about to try and get a little sleep, someone would come in and wake me up saying, "This is it. Dad is going to take his last breath." So, I'd jump up and go to Dad's bedside. The last time I was called, I sensed Dad was ready to leave us so I told him "Everything was going to be fine," and to "follow the light." "Go to the light," I kept repeating trying to gradually and lovingly persuade him to cross over. Each time, however just when we all thought it was the end, Dad would move and then start breathing the slow, shallow, and rhythmic pace he had been all day, all over again. This process went on three or four times.

The boys and I had a return flight home at ten fifty-five a.m. because I had this important settlement meeting the next day on Tuesday that couldn't be changed. It was a settlement hearing and there were no options for me to change it. Having been through this process a couple of times already, I was prepared for my dad to die. I wanted to and made good on my last promise to him that I would "come back." I shared with Dad how much I loved him and that I would make sure that my mom was well taken care of. I told him that the boys and I would be fine and that he could go in peace and know that we all loved him. It took a lot to keep my composure, but I didn't want to break down because it would have a snowball effect on everyone else and that was the last thing I wanted for my dad…to be surrounded by weeping and crying people. Sam and Jay also held back their tears as we said our goodbyes and left for the airport. By now my precious sons had been witness to too many people they loved… leaving. In just a few years after Jeffrey's passing, we'd lost PoPo and now Dad, and they were still so young.

When we arrived home and were about to walk into the house, my cell phone rang. My brother, Brian, called to tell me that my dad had just passed away. When I hung up the phone, I said a little prayer to myself and then proceeded into the house. Sam and Jay had run ahead and were in my bedroom. When I turned the corner to go tell the boys, I was stopped in my tracks by an amazing sight. My house had two sixteen feet etched glass front doors with etched glass panels on each side. Above the doors and panels was a huge glass window. When I approached the doors, I saw that the top of the door, the panels, and the window were covered with hundreds of bees. The bees were golden-colored, not flying, but rather hovering, not even moving all over the window and doors. I immediately called my housekeeper, Amy, who'd been in the house all day. "Amy," I asked, "Do you see all the bees? Did you know they were there?"

Amy was just as shocked as I was to see the bees everywhere.

"That's impossible! I was just at the front door checking to see if you were arriving and those bees were not there. The door was locked, and had not been opened all day."

Maybe they came in when the boys did. Immediately, we grabbed a newspaper and swatted at the bees. As we did this, the bees started to fall to the ground. They did not fly towards us, or around but instead dropped to the ground. This was so strange. My immediate thought was that it was a sign. I wasn't sure what the sign was about or who was sending it, but my instincts told me that it was a sign.

Feeling overwhelmed with emotions, I decided to sit outside by the pool to gather myself together and get some fresh air. Laying on a chaise lounge I was thinking about my crucial impending meeting and the death of my dad when I had a funny feeling someone was watching me. I sat up and looked around when suddenly, I saw three long black snakes slithering across the pavement heading towards the foot of my chaise. I have never been a fan of snakes and was feeling a bit uncomfortable, thinking *what should I do*? So, I just waited and watched as the three snakes made their way towards me. When they were about a foot from the end of my chaise, they split up in different directions and slithered away. I thought, *okay Dad, Po Po, and Jeffrey, I know that you are all together now. I know that you are with me.* With that thought, the sadness that I was feeling went away and I felt at peace. After I was sure the snakes were gone, I decided to go back inside the house.

I was walking through my living room towards my bedroom where the boys were playing Nintendo, when all of a sudden I heard the boys yell, "Mom, Mom, come quick! There's a snake in here!" I thought, *oh come on, I get it, Dad.*

Before I could get to the room, Amy ran in front of me with a broom. But when she got to the bedroom entrance and saw the snake, which had been facing the boys who had jumped on top of my bed, it made a turn, and started slithering towards her and the door. She moved back and then to the side and the snake started slithering out the bedroom door into the foyer and down the marble steps heading to the front door. Amy recognized that it was going towards the door, so she ran ahead and opened the door.

The snake slithered across the floor, where the bees had been cleaned up earlier, and made its way out the doors and out of the house. It was so incredible to witness; this snake, without being prompted, just turned, and made its departure. As soon as Amy shut the front door, Sam came out of the room. He looked up toward the sky and said, "Okay Grandpa Ben, we know you are okay. You can stop sending us signs now."

I was truly worn out and decided to have a massage. Later that night I was telling my massage therapist, Alex, about the snakes and bees. I told him I knew snakes symbolized transformation but didn't know what the bees symbolized. Alex said he would ask his wife, who is from Chile and has strong spiritual beliefs. Now here is another post-event knowledge, the snake is revered as a symbol of wisdom and transformation, of shedding the old and embracing the new—it was time they were telling me, for renewal and to move forward.

After Alex spoke to his wife Daniella, he told me she said, "When bees swarm an area inside your house it is a sign of protection. And if they swarmed the front door, it is a sign that your home is being protected." I liked that explanation and thought that was probably the truth. I had also read that in Ancient Egypt the bee was a symbol for the giver of life, birth, death, and resurrection, which made a lot of sense to me. I also read that the Chinese believe that bees are bringers of good luck and prosperity and that gold bees equal wealth. When I read this, I thought, *let's hope so!* I would later learn that in many traditions around the world, the bee is a sacred and divine symbol. They represent the natural order of a hardworking and industrious life. In Chinese feng shui, the literature on Chinese symbolisms says, "if a bee makes a hive in your house that place will be blessed with joy and great fortune."

The next day of meetings did bring me good luck, prosperity, and wealth as I settled a lawsuit that was years in the making. The settlement would provide for me and the boys forever. The case was closed.

Story Thirty-one

FOOL ME ONCE, SHAME ON YOU; FOOL ME TWICE, SHAME ON ME

Or so I thought. After Jeffrey died, I went back to dedicating all my time and energy to raising Sam and Jay. This is what gave me a sense of purpose and my life meaning. Had I not had the boys, after Jeffrey died facing every morning would have been difficult and honestly, I don't know if I would've gotten through that time as well as I had without them. Every day I woke up and put on a "happy" face to go out into the world. Though pained inside, I made it a habit to wake up with a smile and tell myself, "It is going to be a good day."

I was fortunate to have a therapist whom I could talk to whenever I needed, which helped my emotional and mental well-being. Even though the boys were seeing a therapist too, the kids had their own way of expressing their sadness. While Jay cried himself to sleep every night, Sam remained stalwart in his disposition. Fifteen months after Jeffrey died, one day, Sam said to me, "Mom I wish I had friends who understood what it felt like to not have a daddy." That statement broke my heart. Sam expressed how hard it was for him because none of his friends knew what he felt like every day.

Once again, my girlfriend Chris came through and told me she'd read about a Grief Support Group called Hearts and Hope in Palm Beach. To this day, I know that Hearts and Hope was a blessing to me and the boys. What I thought was something I was doing for the boys and that we would be done in a year, ended up being the best life-changing experience which lasted over three years. Hearts and Hope consisted of a group of other "only parents" with children the same ages as Sam and Jay. We met twice a month on Tuesday nights. I would sit in a group session with the other women (and occasionally a man) and the boys would go with their appropriate age group. I never knew what the kids were doing, but the first night we attended I noticed while walking to the car that both the boys had a lightness and happiness I hadn't seen since before Jeffrey's accident. By the time the next session was scheduled, the lightness was gone but a Hearts and Hope session always brought it back. Hearts and Hope allowed us to be happy without feeling guilty, we could laugh and be free to feel carefree.

Hearts and Hope changed our lives for the better. I found that when grieving, there is nothing better or more priceless than someone who can completely understand and empathize because they are walking the same path. It's a common bond like no other. One topic that would come up from time to time, would be the topic of dating again. For several years I couldn't even imagine dating. I would tell everyone I was going to wait until Sam and Jay went off to college. Only then would I start to live my own life, and I was sure that was the way it was going to be. I was now forty-one and Jeffrey had been gone for five years but I still felt I had plenty of time to date later in life. In all honesty, my relationship with Jeffrey was so exhausting and controlling, now I had my independence and complete freedom back I seriously questioned why I would want to meet someone and change everything again. The boys and I had developed a great life; we had our routines—school, sports, play dates, and travel to anywhere I chose. I had a lot of close girlfriends and from time to time would venture out on a girl's night out. My life lacked nothing as far as I was concerned and I had everything I needed to live my life with my boys for a long time.

So, when a friend Lucia invited me to her birthday party on a yacht in Palm Beach, I gave it some real thought. Lucia had mentioned there was a guy she wanted me to meet, named Chad, who was her boyfriend's good buddy. She waxed on about how great a guy he was and was sure I'd find him interesting and fun. I had no intention of dating, but to placate her I agreed to think about attending the party. Plus, what could it hurt to meet new people? I also knew that my close girlfriend, Amy, and her husband would be there, and that put my decision over the edge, so I decided to go.

When I arrived, I recognized a couple that had been friends with Jeffrey. Rob was a wealthy guy who gambled a lot and we would see each other in The Bahamas and Vegas. Rob and his wife attended our tenth anniversary Party Extravaganza. I was chatting with Diana, Rob's wife, and discovered she was a cousin to a childhood friend of mine, so we enjoyed talking about our high school days when Rob came up to say hello. With him was his friend who turned out to be the guy Lucia had mentioned, Chad Cheshire.

Big-boned, Chad reminded me a lot of Jeffrey. He had a commanding presence partly due to his huge stature of being 6'4." My initial impression was he exuded confidence, seemed charming, and had impeccable manners. I would soon find out Chad was a former Penn State football player who had a brief stint in the NFL before getting injured and retiring. I was ready to steer clear when I heard he worked on Wall Street. After 9/11 he'd left New York and opened a Hedge Fund in Palm Beach. I was gracious however and continued to talk to Chad. As it turned out, we'd frequented some of the same places in New York at the same times and knew the same people. I found it easy to talk to Chad after that and ended up enjoying the evening. As we were leaving, Chad told me that he was leaving for China the next day to visit his investors and hoped to meet again.

To my surprise, I thought, *I might enjoy that.* Two nights later, as I was relaxing with the boys asleep next to me, my phone rang and it was Chad. He said he was in China and had been thinking about me, so asked my friend for my number. We ended up talking for a short while and then a few times more that week. I was going up to Philadelphia for a doctor's appointment with my dad and then to New York the following week, so we continued to speak a lot on the phone. The day I was returning from New York, Chad invited me to a dinner he was having at his home for our mutual friends. I knew everyone who was going to be there and thought it would be a good opportunity to see how he lived, so I accepted the invitation.

When I pulled up to Chad's home, I was greeted by this beautiful, giant wood-carved Buddha by his front door. *This is a spiritual guy and maybe someone to whom I could relate.* Chad knew a lot about fine wines and was a culinary fan and had put together an incredible dinner that was catered by a local chef. The dinner was wonderful and Chad was the perfect host who told fascinating stories about his life. I found him to be suave, exciting, interesting, and gentlemanly. His height and physique were a bit intimidating, but I thought he was handsome. *Had I fallen back into my tall, handsome, blue-eyed, blond-haired pattern?* I don't think so, but Chad was a rebound and my first relationship since Jeffrey, so I was hopeful. That he treated me and the boys so well and was generous at first, made me fall into my comfort zone. My glasses were very rosy and heavily tinted.

I had always liked to escape the summer heat, humidity, and hurricane season of South Florida so when the school year ended in June, the boys and I would always leave Florida for vacation. Whether we started our vacation in the South of France or the mountains in Beaver Creek, CO, we always ended the summer by renting a beach house in New Jersey so we could be with my family. When Chad mentioned he wanted to come visit me and meet my family at the NJ beach house, I was a little apprehensive and hesitant as I hadn't told the boys yet that we were dating. But because I always had male friends vacation with us in the past, I didn't think it would be a big deal so I consented. Chad came for a weekend visit and got to spend time with my family and all my nieces and nephews. One undeniable aspect of being with my family is that we all are all about our family and families. A trait each of my siblings inherited from my mom and is ubiquitous amongst us is the underlying importance and love we all have for our family and children. This is not to say we don't have arguments or disagreements, but there is a unique bond that truly connects us to one another and transfers to our parenting. On several occasions, Chad spoke of how he admired the relationships my family shared and was especially touched by the bonds we have with our children. Alan did not like Chad and that intensified when he went to work for him. Betty and the rest of the family seemed to tolerate him fine. In fact, Betty would later say he had them fooled.

Since my father had passed away at the beginning of the summer (actually Memorial Day), my mom decided to come and stay with me and the boys in Florida. Ever since I had given birth to Sam, my mom spent a significant amount of time living and traveling with me so, it was natural that she'd come to Florida after the summer to stay for a while. I had also told my dad that I would make sure my mom was okay and wanted to make sure I upheld that promise. When Dad died, Mom was left without much money, but she was fine and was able to maintain her household. Still, I made sure she had whatever she needed.

Having my mom around to help out with the boys, freed me up a lot to see Chad more often. The more time that I spent with Chad, the more we got to learn about each other, and the more I started to let down the guard rails around my heart a little. I had been told in therapy in the past, that I had built an impenetrable wall around my heart because I was afraid to be hurt, and if I didn't let anyone in to love me, I would never find love again. So, slowly I let myself put my trust in Chad and allow myself to have feelings of love for him.

After I told the boys that Chad was "my boyfriend," it made the stones in the wall fall faster. Although Sam had some reservations and wasn't as quick to develop a closeness to Chad, he was happy that I was happy and didn't make it hard to have Chad around. A couple of weeks after I met Chad, I made the mistake of confiding in him about a lawsuit settlement that I knew was going to happen. I thought since he was a highly respected Financial Advisor and the head of his own Fund of Funds, he would be very knowledgeable about investments and finance. Because I always let Jeffrey take care of our finances and never wanted to be involved, I had no understanding of what to do with my and the boy's money.

In the fall, when my settlement was due to take place, in my mind Chad and I were in a pretty serious relationship. I had total trust in his advice and was open to any of his suggestions. Because the boys were minors, I was instructed by my attorneys to set up trust funds for them. Chad introduced me to his trust attorney in NJ, who drew up Delaware Trusts for each of us. I was told that a Delaware Trust is the best trust because it is very hard to litigate against and being that the boys were so young, it was the best security against someone trying to sue them or get to their money in the future.

The trust attorney and Chad then introduced me to Commonwealth Trust Company in Delaware to act as Trustee on our trusts and as explained to me was another layer of security for our money. Because I had complete trust in Chad and his capabilities, I assigned him as our Financial Advisor. The first investment the boys and I made was into Chad's Fund of Funds. His company had shown earnings of ten percent and had a "winning" record in the past compared to the market, so I decided to invest a significant chunk of money. Undereducated in the world of finance, I didn't see the red flag that said Ponzi scheme. A couple of months later, Chad mentioned he was "selling" percentages of the company to bring in new investors, "would I like the opportunity to buy in." I thought it a good idea, so I gave him money to acquire five percent of his company.

I told Joyce about my investments with Chad and she told me I was crazy.

From the first time Joyce met Chad, she didn't like him. Because she was so very close and loved Jeffrey, anyone I brought around I figured she would not take to easily, so I put no stock in her words. I accepted her feelings but didn't change mine. Many times, Joyce would tell me not to invest any more money with Chad and make sure I keep money in other investments outside of Chad's company. Kevin, Betty's husband who oversees my mother's money was more than concerned. But my hard-headedness kept me from listening and over the next year increased my investments by three hundred percent. I also loaned Chad four hundred and fifty thousand dollars in cash to pay off bills he had from attorneys, as he was in litigation against an old business partner who was trying to take money from him and his company.

Chad had become close with the boys and he became involved in their lives. The boys loved him. He'd stressed to them the importance of "being a good and honorable man" and would always stress manners. He taught the boys how to do things like tie a tie and other things being a female, I didn't know. The boys were always involved in athletics and because of Chad's former football career, the boys started to play flag football and then eventually tackle football.

When the boys started playing football for their school he never missed a game. It was fun to have "a man" who took a keen interest in our lives and wanted to be involved in everything with us. Because we lived forty-five minutes away from each other, we never spent any prolonged time together, which for me worked very well. I could still enjoy my time with my boys and do what I wanted to do, and then when Chad was available, we could do things together alone or with the boys and all was great.

Around wintertime, Chad invited me to his sister's wedding in Paris. I was excited to be going away on a vacation together and also I would get the chance to meet his mother and sisters. Chad had arranged and paid for everything. We flew first class, had a huge suite at one of the best hotels in Paris, Plaza Athenee, ate at the best restaurants, and spent time shopping on Avenue Montaigne at Chanel, Hermes, and Gucci. It was like the best of the old times with Jeffrey.

Chad's family was not mean, but not overly friendly. I got the feeling that they were surprised by my being Chinese and overheard his sisters saying to one another they were shocked that I wasn't blonde. Chad was not very close to his family and would tell me how his father left them when he was a teenager and he was left to provide for them. He provided them with money for education and living. He felt responsible because when he was a teenager he had a physical fight with his father which landed Chad in the hospital. When he returned home, he learned that his father had picked up and left the family. He hadn't had any contact with him since that fight. I always felt sympathy and hurt for Chad for that reason and the fact that he didn't have the loving, closeness, I shared with my family. I figured this was the reason why he had never married and had commitment issues. Like Jeffrey, he harbored family issues, but he was far more open than Jeffrey had ever been.

The rest of the year Chad and I would continue to see one another when we could. He was always busy with work and travels, and I was busy with the boys. At Christmastime, Chad joined me, Sam, and Jay on our trip to Park City for snowboarding but left on Christmas Day to spend the day with his mother and family. The times we spent together were easy and enjoyable, especially since he got along so well with the boys. It was nice to have a man around to teach them especially since they were getting older and needed a male to identify with sometimes.

Winter turned to Spring, then Spring to Summer. For the summer, like always the boys and I were getting out of the heat of Florida. They were enrolled in a summer camp in Boston for two weeks. I would stay in a nearby hotel and meet up with friends in the area. At the end of the two weeks, Chad said that he would fly to Boston and drive my new car, which was delivered to me in Boston, to New Jersey to our rental beach house. My sisters and their families, my mother, and my brother and his kids would be with us as usual. My family time was always the highlight of the summer for me and the boys. It is always a time filled with chaos and high activity but also so much love, laughter, and great times. It was wholesome family time at its best. I have never stopped appreciating how fortunate I am to have this unique bond with my family, where we all truly enjoy and cherish our times together.

Chad was again welcomed into my family and everyone made him feel comfortable. He only stayed a few days, but while there seemed carefree and happy. A real guy's guy, he regaled us with his football stories and could talk about sports with authority. My brothers, being sports aficionados found him entertaining, if a bit boastful, and to us women, he was a real charmer. With his sparkling blue eyes, his good manners, and constant compliments, he sucked us in too. By now, however, Alan and Kevin felt something iffy about Chad and Brian had never liked him. My mother's jury was also out.

Before he left, Chad mentioned that the house next door to his was being put up for sale. A friend of his had bought the house a couple of months before but decided that he didn't want to keep it. Chad thought it was a great investment and asked if I was interested in purchasing the house to renovate and flip. He thought that the boys and I could make a lot of money if we put a little bit of money into fixing it up and then reselling it. The idea sounded good and Chad said he would manage all the construction and renovations since he was right next door. Since he enjoyed designing and was very handy, he said a lot of the things he could do himself so costs could be contained. I proposed the idea to the trust managers for the boys and they approved the idea, so we went ahead with the purchase. Chad suggested I should form an LLC to purchase the house, as protection for me and the boys were there ever to be any issues. I hired an attorney at Chad's referral, who set up the company and represented the company at the closing, because I was in NJ at the time.

When I returned home, I was back to my busy schedule with the boys and seeing Chad whenever time permitted. Chad was very busy with the house renovations and took all the responsibilities of the project on by himself. I thought that it was so kind of him to do this so whenever he needed more money for the project, I didn't hesitate or think to question him about what the funds were going towards. I kept no log and quite honestly, I never paid attention to my financials, so statements went unopened. As long as I knew or felt I had plenty of money in the bank, I didn't take notice of any statements.

Months turned to more months turned to more months and after a year the house never seemed to get to completion. There was always an issue and Chad would complain about different sub-contractors he'd fired. He got rid of the general contractor and said that he was finishing the job himself. But the house became a "money pit" and the distance in our relationship showed up. We saw less and less of each other and could go several weeks without seeing each other which was becoming the norm. While we would speak to each other all the time, there was always a reason why Chad couldn't get together.

A few days before Christmas we met at a supply store to pick out the marble for the house. When we were leaving, Chad told me that he was going with his friend, Francois to The Bahamas to fish for a few days at Christmas. He needed time on his own to think about us because he was feeling conflicted. Chad said the times he spent with me and my family made him think he wanted a family of his own but I was so opposed. When we'd first met, I had told Chad there was no way I would think about remarrying let alone having any more children. I was content with dating and would in no way ever consider having children. Chad went into a bit of a tizzy. He was going to be unreachable because the reception in the area he would be in was bad. It would also give me time to think about our future. I wasn't happy with what he was saying and told him I thought it was wrong, but he'd made his decision and that was that. We'd already had plans to take Sam and Jay to see a college football championship game on New

Year's Day, so he tried to rationalize his Christmas trip further by saying he was taking time to be with us over the New Year's holiday.

So, we spent the holiday apart and didn't speak to one another. When he returned, he kept his word and drove us all to Tampa to spend the weekend and see the game. At the time, Beyonce's song, "Irreplaceable," was hot and we would always listen to it. Things were feeling unnatural between us. Since Chad's return, he seemed distant and aloof and I wasn't feeling all in either. Every time the song came on, I would turn the radio up and sing along. At one point Chad turned to me and asked sarcastically, "Are you singing this song with me in mind?" To which I replied in a serious manner, "Definitely."

In the past, we didn't fight. Given we didn't spend much time together, our times together were nice and he was always gentlemanly. He would always open the door for me, carry things for me, and was always very complimentary and generous. But since I'd purchased the house and he was putting a lot of time and physical energy into the renovation, it seemed there was a change in the relationship. Where we used to go out to lunch or dinner and talk about our childhoods, events in our past, family, friends, aspirations, etc., now all we spoke about was the house or his business. For a while, I had been putting together his monthly company performance letters, as he was busy with other things and he liked the way I fashioned the letters. Grateful for his support on the house, I enjoyed being helpful to him, while also liked being productive in a business sense. I'd helped Jeffrey out at the American Stock Exchange which had given me the same sense of competency once I stopped my career in New York.

Sam was in eighth grade and I had to decide where he was going to go to high school. Since the school he was in only went through the eighth grade and with high school years being so crucial to getting into college, it was my main priority to find the right high school. After Jeffrey died and before my father died, I was planning to move to Philadelphia so my dad could attend the boys' sports games, which was a favorite pastime for him. At the time I was thinking about different private schools and at the top was The Lawrenceville School in New Jersey.

The academics and sports were remarkable and they are recognized as one of the top college preparatory schools in the country. The only problem was that Jay being in middle school would not be able to attend since Lawrenceville didn't have a Middle School. Education to me is a difference-maker in the development of a child and it was my top priority for my boys. Fortunately, I was in the position to afford any private school for the boys and the boys had the intellect to be accepted. I was still in a quandary about my decision.

Since my father had died and my mother was spending most of her time with me and the boys, I didn't see any reason to uproot the boys and move to Philadelphia anymore. I had narrowed my search down to two schools. One was in Miami and the other was in Fort Lauderdale. I thought if the boys went to school in Miami, I would get an apartment down there. We would be able to do the same things we were used to doing for a few years already, except instead of being in Palm Beach Gardens, we would be in Miami. It would also be great for me as I would be close to my Miami girlfriends. My opinion on Pine Crest School was formed back when Sam was three years old. At the time, he was in a 3's class at our Temple. His teacher told me Sam's intelligence was way beyond that of a normal three years old. I had no idea. I took the teacher's advice and had his IQ tested. I always knew Sam was bright, but as my firstborn I had no one to compare. He started to read at three years old and that he could add and subtract didn't seem odd. In fact, it seemed very normal to me. Sam's test results came back, his scores were significantly high, and he was labeled as highly gifted.

I have never been impressed with "labels" and thought they were divisive or in some way negative for children so while I shared the results with Jeffrey, I'd told him not to tell anyone as it would only make things hard for us and Sam. I thought being labeled so young could lead to ridiculous expectations that would be very stressful for Sam and all I wanted for my boys was for them to be happy and normal.

Fool Me Once, Shame on You; Fool Me Twice, Shame on Me

The psychologist advised that I enroll Sam into a preparatory school so he could learn and excel at a high level. The only preparatory school I knew of that had that reputation nearby was Pine Crest in Boca Raton. I'd made an appointment for me and Jeffrey to meet with the Admissions Director at Pine Crest. When the Director reviewed Sam's IQ test results and psychologist's report, she very honestly told us that she didn't think the school would be able to help Sam. She said that he would be bored and unchallenged, which may eventually lead to his not learning to his potential.

Now ten years later, my options were again to look at Pine Crest in Fort Lauderdale for high school or another school in Miami. I decided to call both schools. I called the Admissions Office for the school in Miami and to my surprise, was completely turned off by the attitude and demeanor of the admissions staff. The manner in which they spoke to me was condescending and elitist. Maybe the woman was having a bad day, but that was no excuse. She went on to emphasize that the school was a very elite program and gaining admissions was very difficult. She said that they had very prominent families from South America who brought their children to Miami to attend the school and that would be a priority. The whole time she spoke, I thought to myself "There is no way I would send the boys to this school." Like the trauma doctor I first encountered when I arrived at the hospital for Jeffrey's accident, this woman made it clear to me that I needed to find another option.

My call to Pine Crest Admissions was the complete opposite. The admissions representative was kind, and informative and took time to ask questions about what I was looking for and needed in a school. I set up a meeting and in the end, made the decision for the boys to attend Pine Crest School in Fort Lauderdale. Because the school was located thirty minutes south of our home in Boca Raton, this meant we could continue to live in our home full time. It was nice for the boys not to have to live somewhere else during the week to attend school anymore.

After the boys were accepted, while out to lunch with Chad one day, I told him that the boys were accepted and would attend Pine Crest in the Fall.

Unexpectedly, Chad responded aggravatingly, "How come you didn't ask me first about where the boys would go to school?" I didn't expect this negative attitude or response! It was not that he was upset but rather quite mad. I thought to myself, why would I need to consult you on where my children are going to school? Instead, I asked, "Why are you upset that I decided on Sam and Jay's education?" I didn't understand at the time that it was about control. Here was a guy who at this time I was barely dating and he thought that he should make important decisions on my children's lives. No. This can't be.

He then went on to state that we were renovating the house next door to him so the boys and I could live there. That he was doing all this work to make a beautiful home for us but I didn't appreciate any of it. He said how he was tired of having to drive forty-five minutes to see me and that the house was meant for us to be together more. Had he been verbalizing all this in a hurt or sad manner I may have felt bad but he was angry. He was accusatory, and making up things that I had never, ever contemplated. He was trying to make me feel like a bad person and girlfriend.

In reality, I think he was looking for an excuse to say there was a problem with our relationship and I was ready to hear it. I should have felt sorry for him but instead, I felt the familiar madness that came with control. I'd purchased the house as an investment to renovate and flip and I never once thought about living in Palm Beach. All his squabbling about what I didn't do and how terrible a girlfriend I was, was absolute nonsense. Looking back, this is probably what opened my eyes to start seeing the relationship for real and not through rose-colored glasses. I had learned a few lessons in my short life and I was not about to get taken again either emotionally or otherwise and I was most certainly not going to be controlled by anyone.

With the Financial World in crisis in 2007 and 2008, life seemed to have become much more stressful for Chad and I thought I understood why. His company's success was contingent on the stock market's performance and with everything in a tailspin, he said he had to focus on his work. Then to add to his stress, his lawsuit against his former partner was coming up and I was on the slate to be deposed. He said that I was being deposed because I was in partnership with his company and also an investor. We rarely saw each other during these times because he was busy finishing up the house to put on the market and trying to keep his company above water. I didn't mind as the boys had started their new school and I was very busy with their sports and with volunteering at the school. Even on holidays or vacations, Chad always had an excuse for why he couldn't be with us. Alan who was working for Chad, as Chad had asked him to start up a day trading business at his firm, was becoming more suspicious of him and was in my ear, but too stubborn I didn't listen.

December 2008, I was called in for my deposition for his lawsuit. At one point the opposing attorney asked me if I knew that Chad went away with another woman for a Christmas vacation with his friends to the Cayman Islands. Before I could answer my attorney interrupted and said the question had no relevance. I didn't get time to think about the question or look at Chad who was in attendance, because the opposing attorney then asked another question. At the end of the deposition, Chad's ex-partner who had accused him of not honoring their partners split financially looked at me from across the table and said, "You seem nice and should watch out. He is not a good guy."

After the deposition, Chad was visibly upset and mad. His face was red and with squinted eyes, he said to me, "You just lost me my case."

I was appalled. The truth is, there was nothing relevant I said in the deposition that could have been used negatively. My attorney confirmed that the deposition was useless as I didn't have any information for them. I didn't know Chad when the alleged incident took place, so it was meaningless to have me deposed, to begin with. I was so stunned and hurt by Chad's reaction. I hadn't even remembered the information regarding Chad and another woman for a bit. He'd even lied about the location he was going to as The Bahamas is not the Cayman Islands and as a world citizen, I should have known that every crevice of The Bahamas would have connectivity. For goodness' sake, it's like being on mainland USA. Still, I being too trusting and with not a duplicitous bone in my body, believed him. Later, when I finally spoke to him on the phone, he claimed that the attorney made it up to upset me and hopefully get me to tell them some information against him. What malarky.

The house was ready to be sold in the Spring of 2009. We listed it but unfortunately, this was the worst time to try to sell due to the Financial and Mortgage Crisis. Chad said I would need to price the house higher than I had thought because so much money had been sunk into the house. Since he was managing the renovations and bills for the house, I had no idea how much money was spent.

In the beginning, he would send me bills and I would write checks, but then he suggested that I just sign some blank checks and leave them with him so he could pay things as they came along. When he told me that he'd spent a couple of million dollars on the renovations I nearly fainted. Of course, when I seemed shocked, he went into a rant about how he had to do everything, that the cost to renovate was expensive, that I didn't care about the house, and on and on and on. I kept my thoughts to myself.

About a month later, I was sitting at home when I received a call from a Palm Beach number. Sam had answered the phone and I figured it had something to do with the house, so I took the call. After I said "hello," a woman on the line asked me, "How do you know Chad Cheshire?"

"Excuse me?" I responded and she said, "How do you know Chad Cheshire? Are you his client?"

I said, "I'm not sure why you are asking but it isn't any of your business."

Then the woman said, "It is my business because he is my boyfriend and I see calls from you on his phone."

I had had enough drama in my days with Jeffrey and his bimbos but since being on my own had come to appreciate and love not having the chaos or drama of my life with him. I do not like confrontation, so even when Chad would get argumentative and mad, I would usually just keep my thoughts to myself and not stir the pot. The way I would get my thoughts out was by writing a letter or email. I could say what I was feeling and not be disturbed or debated. That is why when I heard the woman say that she was Chad's "girlfriend," I almost laughed, but remained calm and said, "That's funny because I have been with Chad for three years now."

When she heard my statement, she started crying and telling me that she had been with him for more than a year, that he took her on a vacation and bought her things, but she thought it was strange that he always had to be somewhere else or traveling someplace. She said that he'd been abusive and would get mad when she questioned his whereabouts. She said she had a feeling that there was someone else and since she heard my name come up before, she thought she would call.

I listened to her go on and as she did, while I was angry I was not sad. I felt like f-him. After I hung up with the woman, I dialed Chad. When he answered I said, "Hi Chad, I just got a call from Lilith, your girlfriend. She was very interesting. Anyhow, I don't want to see you anymore. I am going away for a week and when I return, we should meet and discuss how we will proceed with the sale of my house. As soon as the house sells, we can discuss my investments in your company and how I can get my money out. The personal loans are Promissory Notes, I will leave those as is. Thanks, I will be in touch." Then I hung up and didn't answer his calls or texts for the entire week I was away.

While we were away, I explained to Sam and Jay what had happened between me and Chad. I have always held honesty as a critical character trait and have preached to my boys about not lying or cheating. I wanted them to understand how wrong Chad was for lying and cheating and that I would not put up with these actions. The boys were more concerned that I would be sad, but I told them that I know from experience that the heart heals from pain and that love regrows in time. I was going to be okay. That I knew for sure. As I always said, "Things happen for a reason."

The boys had liked Chad a lot so it was hard in that way. It was about the same time too that my therapist had told me not to keep Jeffrey on a pedestal for the boys so I had the honest conversation with Sam about his father, which to this day I believe was too early. Being Sam, all he said was, "Don't tell Jay."

After a couple of weeks, I figured that I had to tie up loose ends with Chad, so when he called and asked to meet to talk, I agreed. We decided to meet at my renovated house, so we could discuss the sale of the house among other things. The renovations were completed and the house fully furnished was beautiful and modern.

Since I had rented it all the years in between…it recouped some of the money I'd spent fixing it up. Chad was very remorseful and apologetic. He said that he would be willing to try couples counseling if I would give him another chance. In my past relationships, I had been told that I was too strong and not sympathetic to my partner's feelings. So, when Chad said he would go to couples therapy, I thought that maybe I shouldn't be so tough and give the relationship another chance with help from a professional. For the next couple of months, we saw a therapist and tried to work through our issues but in the end, the sessions just highlighted the differences in what we wanted and who we were as individuals. Finally, at the last session, Chad got so frustrated and upset with what the therapist was saying, he got up and stormed out.

A day or two after he left the session, we both decided that we were better apart than together. The fact that he claimed he wanted children and I wasn't going to have anymore was a big factor. We decided that we would remain good friends and I would keep him as my financial advisor and stay invested in his Funds and that he would continue to maintain and take care of my house until it was sold. In addition, he would be welcome to take part in the happenings in the boys' lives. It was a very amicable split.

After surviving my tumultuous relationship with Jeffrey and the loss of my husband thereafter, a break-up with Chad was not so bad. My life remained the same, except for having a date to go out with every so often. Then one day I arrived home and our housekeeper, Amy told me that a policeman was looking for me and left his card for me to call. When I looked at the card, it was not the police, but rather an FBI agent. Rather than call the agent, I immediately called my attorney, Jourdain. Jourdain spoke to the FBI on my behalf. We learned that the company that I had started, which owned the house in Palm Beach Chad built on my behalf was being investigated for fraud. They told Jourdain they believed that I was a co-conspirator with Chad, who was being indicted in South Carolina for running a Ponzi scheme, wire fraud, and other financial crimes. They claimed that the money stolen was run through my company, making me a co-conspirator.

I was shocked and skeptical at the accusation at the same time. I thought there was no way that Chad was stealing and lying, two of the three traits I deplored in people. Then, I thought about how he cheated with the other woman, making him a cheater and liar, so maybe he was now a thief too. Three for three on the traits I detested. Jourdain asked if I had statements for the company's account, which I didn't. Since Chad was managing the construction of the house, he had me send the LLC's statements to the house and he'd picked up the mail there. I had completely trusted him as my financial advisor and never thought having my company bank statements going to him would be a problem.

Since I was the owner of the company and the only signer on the account, I figured nothing could go wrong. Jourdain, who had always been doubtful about Chad, looked at me sympathetically and said, "You need to go across the street to Wells Fargo and close the account immediately. Also, request copies of all the bank statements since inception so we can see the activity in the account."

I went to the Wells Fargo branch and told the agent I wanted to close the account. When he asked why, I told him that there may have been fraud committed on the account. He said if that is the case, they would freeze the account and do an internal investigation. The agent pulled up the account and asked if I knew how much was in the account. I told him that I knew that a transfer of sixty thousand dollars had been made recently because while waiting to sell the house, I had renters living there and they had just sent in a deposit. The agent looked at me and said, "I see the sixty thousand was received but debited right away, leaving about three thousand in the account as of today."

"Debited? How was the money debited? I didn't take the money out! Where did it go?" I was in shock. "How is that possible?"

The agent then asked if I had a debit card or if any other signers were on the account. I told him that I never request debit cards, so "no to the debit card" and that I was the only signer on the account. The agent asked if I was sure about not having a debit card because he said that he could see a lot of withdrawals using a debit card. When I assured him that I never requested a debit card, he told me he would freeze the account immediately and start a case of fraud on the account. In the meantime, he helped me set up online access to the accounts so I could review and print out any previous bank statements from home.

On my way home, I called Jourdain to tell him what had happened at the bank. He told me from this moment on I was to have no communication with Chad and to go home and print out every statement back to when I opened the account. To say I was thunderstruck when I looked at the statements would be an understatement. Millions of dollars had been transferred in and out of my account all funneling to and from Chad's business accounts. I found he paid his American

Express bill with the money from my account along with his household bills. As infuriated as I was, I was clueless about how this happened. How was Chad able to wire, transfer, withdraw, or make any transactions in my account? It didn't make sense as I never gave him authority to do so and he never mentioned anything!

I immediately got all the statements to Jourdain and expressed my concern, anger, and bewilderment. He said to sit tight and he would look into the matter. At the same time, he told me that I may need a criminal attorney to help me with the FBI matter. The best criminal attorney I knew was the attorney Jeffrey had to hire to depose me back in 2000.

As I credit him for connecting us to M. Gary Neuman, who'd saved our marriage, I immediately reached out to him and retained him. He set up a call with me, Jourdain, himself, and the FBI. I did hire very good attorneys who set up a call with the FBI. For hours I was deposed by the FBI and SEC regarding my relationship with Chad, my bank accounts, my investments, and the property I purchased to renovate and sell. Finally, after several hours of questioning it was determined that I was a victim and not a conspirator, as they had assumed. One of the only major disagreements I had ever had with my mom was over Chad. I wished I had listened to the family who had forever been in my corner but I think I was once again hoping against hope that what I believed was what was real. I was justified in everything and I was dead wrong.

A couple of years later, in 2011, the FBI won its case against Chad in South Carolina, but it did not include the case against the several million he had stolen from me and my boys. Chad was sentenced to sixty-three months in federal prison. One of the crimes Chad had committed, which enabled him to have access to my bank account, was that he had a fake signature card on my account which allowed him to transfer funds in and out of the account without my knowledge. The fact that I trusted Chad to receive the bank statements as the manager of my LLC that owned my property allowed him to use the account to funnel funds from my account to his accounts. Until the FBI showed me this evidence, I never would have believed it.

Unfortunately, I could not get any funds back from a lawsuit against Wachovia Bank/Wells Fargo for aiding Chad in having a false signature card on file for my account. Why? The banking laws state that any issues with an account must be brought up in the first sixty days after a statement is produced. All I was able to recover was a small amount that Chad had withdrawn, possibly to test the fraudulent act. When he saw that I was oblivious and his scheme was working, Chad went on to steal all the money I had including the funds I had in Trust for the boys. This left me in a horrible situation financially. For the first time in my life, I had to worry about how I was going to live. I had bills and private school tuitions to pay. I felt devastated that my terrible choice in a man had put me and my boys in a destitute situation.

Fortunately, my years of purchasing jewelry from Cartier and all my Chanel clothing and bags enabled me to sell some jewelry and items to get funds to live on and pay tuition. Once that dried up, a friend gave me access to his hundred-thousand-dollar line of credit with the condition that I would sell my last solid asset, our family home. I sold my townhouse in Palm Beach Gardens very quickly, which provided me with some funds, and then very significantly dropped the price on the house that I had renovated with Chad. Even though I knew that it would be at a loss as Chad had almost two million in mortgages taken out on the house. The house sold in March 2012 for two and a half million which was basically a fire sale. I put the leftover money into the boys' trust so I knew they had funds for their education. When I had to pay off the line of credit after a year and my house had not been sold, I was forced to take out a hard money loan of three hundred thousand dollars at ten percent interest. Chad put me in a horrible situation where I was in debt for the first time in my life and had two kids to provide for.

Story Thirty-two

AT LAST, MY PRINCE CHARMING

Chad dealt me a blow. I came face-to-face with my own strength and was determined to move forward. For my birthday, in July I would go to see a psychic, astrologer, or medium for advice or to see what they say my next year will bring. On my forty-sixth birthday, I went to see Leslie, a clairaudient. This is someone who can communicate and hear messages from the "other side." She told me I had to get Chad out of my heart to make room for someone who would come into my life around August. That if I didn't, I would miss out on my chance to meet the man I am supposed to love. She said that this man would be completely different from anyone else I have ever dated. This was in 2010 after Chad and I had broken up, but still friends and his criminal acts were not yet privy to me.

A couple of days later I met with my girlfriends, Chris Golden, Mara Reuben, and Tisha Hallett for a birthday lunch. I told them what Leslie had told me and that I honestly thought that I was over Chad, but I absolutely wasn't looking to meet anyone yet. After Jeffrey and Chad, I'd had enough of men. My track record on crazy was two for two and I had batted a zero on everlasting relationships. Being alone wasn't bad at all and I didn't want another man and his issues to deal with again.

Tisha, my therapist and dear friend, suggested that I make a list of the traits that I wanted in a man, not the things that I didn't want. This is a "man plan." Usually, she said, people focus on what they don't want in a man but that I should focus and put out into the universe what I wanted so I can recognize it when I see it. Since Tisha had always steered me in all the right directions, and I credit her for changing me from a weak girl into a strong and confident woman, I went home that night and started writing down things that I would want in a man. After I had my list, I added a little creativity of my own. I got a piece of paper and drew a big pink heart. Then I wrote all the traits I wanted down inside the heart, folded up the paper, and put it in my wallet so it would be with me all the time. After a couple of weeks, I forgot about the list, though it was always with me in my wallet.

About a month later on Saturday night, August 21, 2010, my Hearts and Hope girlfriends met up for a reunion of sorts. Getting together with them was always uplifting. Having a group of women who'd lived and experienced tragic lives and who were still in, or recovering from the grieving process, and were the only parent, lends itself to a unique and resolute bond like no other. With most of us having lost our husbands almost nine years prior, a couple of women were dating, in a relationship, or re-married but most of us were still single. We were all pretty content with our situations and preoccupied with raising our children who were now teenagers.

The conversation at our get-together somehow veered to dating options. I shared that my therapist had told me to put myself "out there" to meet someone because my Prince Charming wasn't going to come knocking on my door. I was happy to wait until my boys went off to college before thinking about meeting someone. In the meantime, I was happy with the way things were and grateful for how far we'd come in our new lives—our new normal. I was coming into my own. I left our dinner with my heart feeling refilled and full. We had come together in sadness, heartbreak, and loss, but now we were each other's source of hope, love, strength, and positivity. I knew

At Last, My Prince Charming

I would once again embrace a new path, but at the moment, I had enormous contentment.

The next day I promised my good friend Gina I would attend a meeting with her in Miami. Gina is a marketing agent with clients like Usain Bolt and she was meeting someone regarding a potential book deal. She didn't want to go alone as there would be two men in the meeting so she asked me to go along to give the air of a more casual meeting. Because I was out late with my Hearts and Hope girls I'd planned on canceling the brunch meeting. When I woke up I called Gina to tell her I wasn't up to going. Gina, the consummate negotiator, refused to let me back out of the brunch so I got myself together and drove down to the Mandarin Hotel in Miami for brunch. I arrived first, so I sat in the lobby and texted Sam and Jay. I was reading a text when the sliding doors opened. I looked up to see if it was Gina. The bright sunlight that came bursting through the opened doors momentarily blinded me. When my eyes adjusted it was not Gina but a very muscular and athletically built man in a tight short-sleeved white shirt. I immediately thought to myself, *Oh, that must be Jason Taylor.* I caught myself staring at the man, so quickly looked down and went back to texting as I didn't want to be caught staring. I then heard a man saying in a questioning tone, "Christina?" I looked up when I heard the voice and saw two men, one being the man I thought was Jason Taylor. Because I tend to smile when I am nervous or embarrassed, I had a big smile on my face. The voice calling my name belonged to a man I now recognized as one of Gina's acquaintances whom I'd met before, Anthony Liggins, a Miami-based artist. He greeted me warmly and introduced me to his friend, who was not Jason Taylor but instead, Harold Dawson, Jr.; Harold was there to discuss a book deal for his father.

For the brunch, I sat with Gina on one side of the table and Harold and Anthony sat on the other side. Harold and I hit it off immediately and we really connected when we started to talk about our children and high-school football. When Sam started playing football in high school, I became one of the football moms. This job entailed helping the Head Coach with fund-raising events, parties, and team dinners, and taking the uniforms to get washed. Harold found my participation and love of football intriguing. His son played football, too. I guess I learned my love of sports from my dad, who was the most devoted Philadelphia sports fan ever. As I said, he had a few televisions in his bedroom, so he could watch different games at the same time.

Before we started lunch, both Harold and I pulled out some Purell at the same time. It was very funny to us that we both had the same idiosyncrasy. Ever since being in the hospital with Jeffrey, I'd become a self-described germophobe. All Sam and Jay's friends knew this so as soon as they got in my car for after-school pick-up they would get in the car and put their hands out for a Purell squirt. Thus, we were many years ahead of the pandemic protocol of washing hands. For almost four hours, Harold and I spoke to one another and from time to time included Gina and Anthony, but we'd been more preoccupied with one another than I'd realized. When we got ready to leave, Harold looked at me and said, "If you are ever in Atlanta, I would love to show you around."

My immediate response was, "Oh, I never go to Atlanta," then I caught myself and thought that was rude, so I added that if he came back to Miami, I could show him around, or something silly to that effect. We all got in our cars and left the Mandarin.

As a habit, Gina who lives in Miami, and I speak to each other on our drives home whenever I visit Miami. We have done this for many years. So, Gina called and we began talking about the brunch. She asked what I thought about Harold. I said I thought he was nice and good-looking, then said, "I don't know. It is strange, I think I could see myself with him."

Gina who is always animated, laughed, and proclaimed, "Whatttt?" I had never shown interest in a Black man. Gina is a half-Chinese Jamaican who was married to a prominent African American actor. She was right, I hadn't dated a Black man not because of prejudice but because I was always in a social circle of mostly Caucasians and Jews. Jeffrey was also the first Jewish person I had dated. We laughed and then she said she was getting a call from Anthony and to hold on. After a few minutes, Gina came back on the line and said, "Well, Anthony was calling because Harold wanted to know if he could get your number."

I was surprised at that request as I didn't think that Harold had any interest in me even though we had connected so well throughout the day.

Gina asked if it would be okay to give out my number and I said that it was fine. When I got home, I got busy with the boys, so didn't think about the brunch or Harold. But after the boys went to bed, I thought I should send Harold a note to thank him for the brunch for which he had generously paid. I found his email on his company website and sent him a note of thanks. A few minutes later he responded with an incredibly moving and heartfelt text along with his cell number. I have always been a bit old-fashioned and usually hesitated when it came to calling men. Still, it would be the right thing to at least thank him, so I called his cell phone. To my relief, it went to the answering message, so I left a message saying it was nice to meet him and thanks for the lovely brunch. I had done the courteous thing.

I was getting ready for bed when my phone rang. It was Harold. I was surprised he was calling so late since he'd told me he had a six a.m. flight back to Atlanta. For him too, it was the first day of school for his kids so he wanted to be there with them. That night we ended up talking until it was time for him to leave for the airport. I would never believe a man could be so comfortable in his skin that he could openly talk about every aspect of his life. We freely spoke about everything: our families, growing up, our prior marriages, our dreams and hopes, and more. I felt something different about this guy. I have never spoken of my dreams before and had this kind of relationship with a man before. The conversation never got boring, or tedious and the time just passed so easily and quickly. I don't recall ever having such an easy and interesting conversation with anyone else and certainly not one so intimate.

After that call, we started texting throughout the day and then would spend hours on end on the phone in the evenings after the kids went to bed. We were like teenagers. This went on for four nights, where we would talk until early morning and only get two or three hours of sleep. I have never done this with any man. This was a soul-to-soul connection but before I went down the man rabbit hole I needed to know a lot more about him. So far I hadn't batted a perfect home run in any of my relationships and I was adamant not to lose myself in anyone anymore. After a couple more nights of all-night talking, I called Gina and said I needed to find out more information about Harold, "He seemed too good to be true." After my disastrous track record and my wipe-out relationship with Chad, I was more than cautious. My duplicitous man antenna was on high alert and one thing was for sure, I was never going to be taken for a fool again.

Yes, we went sleuthing. Not only Gina and I but several close friends too. We spoke to friends in Atlanta who knew Harold and everyone came back with great reports. One friend did comment that Harold dated a lot of women and was always with different women at various functions but he was a consummate gentleman, a real stand-up guy, and always the best dressed. On Thursday, four days after we met, I received a beautiful bouquet of Calla Lilies and a note from Harold that said, "Out on a Limb." I had to laugh. That is the very title of Shirley MacLaine's book on metaphysics. If he believed in psychics and metaphysics, well…Bingo.

When I called him to thank him for the gorgeous flowers, he explained he felt that I needed reassurance that he wasn't a "player" and that if I wanted, he would commit to telling the women he had been dating he'd met someone and wasn't available anymore. He said that he believed in being transparent, after being duped in his marriage, where his wife cheated on him with his friend and stole funds he had put away in trust for his taxes and children, he too, was cautious. While our circumstances were different, we had both been victims of partners who lied, cheated, and stole from us; that was another interesting coincidence. Another thing we had in common was that Harold had remained on good terms with his ex-wife to ensure his children's emotional stability. We had too been single for over five years. It was then that I felt that the walls around my heart were starting to crack. Had my Prince Charming simply walked right through the doors of the Mandarin in a haze of sunlight and right into my heart? Could it be that easy?

Harold, who said he knew I was the one from day one, was different than anyone I had ever dated. He was disciplined, forthright and open. I allowed myself to take the next step. *Christina was going to allow her belief in faith to guide her to where she was meant to be.*

Story Thirty-three
LIFE WITH MY BLENDED FAMILY

Harold was the real deal. The glass slipper fit perfectly. It was hard not to wait for the other slipper not to fit, but it never didn't fit. Harold and I enjoyed a blissful, romantic, sensuous, and adventurous first few months, and feeling it was right, we agreed our kids should meet. We never considered or thought too much about whether the kids would get along, because we were so in love, and everything was so perfect. I kept looking for cracks and wrinkles, but none ever appeared. Harold was impeccable. And he had the qualities I admired in a man…intelligence, leadership, and honesty. A Princeton and Harvard Business School grad, Harold had followed in his father's footsteps and was the CEO of The Dawson Companies founded by his father. There was no bravado or ostentatiousness, no need to be the center of attention; in fact, his humility and quiet strength, given his pedigree, was a breath of fresh air. He had an ego, but it was healthy self-assuredness. I was in awe over our compatibility and that I had found someone I could share all of me with. Had my steps been ordered to be right where I was?

Had I not known Jeffrey, I would not have known Gina. Had I not known Jeffrey or Chad, I would not have been able to distinguish a healthy self-assuredness without the chaos. I didn't hold back any part of me from Harold. Being with him was like sitting in an easy chair, snug and comfortable. After a month of dating Harold, I went up to Atlanta to meet his parents. I had heard a lot about his parents from our daily conversations and was excited to meet the Dawsons. Harold's father was a force in Atlanta who claimed many firsts as an African American.

A Morehouse Man turned real estate tycoon, Mr. Dawson was a civil rights leader in his own rights who started his career selling real estate in Atlanta, GA. at a time when there was still a lot of racial segregation in the South. Redlining, a practice of segregating neighborhoods was common. Redline area loans were harder to come by and housing discrimination was common practice. Throughout his career, Mr. Dawson worked hard to get his fellow African American peers, known at the time as Realtists, access to the same tools and resources as their white counterparts or Realtors. In 1970, he became the president of the Empire Real Estate Board, then in 1977 was named the president of the National Association of Real Estate Brokers.

During this time, he worked on implementing what is now the Fair Housing Laws. In 1972, Georgia Governor Jimmy Carter appointed Mr. Dawson to the GA Real Estate Commission & Appraisers Board. He was the first African American president of the Real Estate Commission in the South. In 1985, Harold Dawson Sr. became the first African American president of the National Association of Real Estate License Law Officials. He was a change agent of significant gravitas.

At first, Mr. Dawson was a bit apprehensive and seemed to be checking me out and sizing me up, but after a short time he got comfortable with me and we connected. He told me how Harold had called him and said, "I am in love."

Where normally Mr. Dawson would have told Harold he was being irrational or silly, he said that he could hear Harold's smile through the phone and he knew this was real. That comment caught me by surprise, but then when I was getting up to leave, Harold's mother,

Rose, hugged me and whispered in my ear, "Thank you for healing my son's heart." The emotion was so pure and beautiful that it instantly connected me and Rose forever. We had the same heart and loved in the same way. I should have said, "I too thank Harold for healing my tattered heart." I was so touched that I didn't say anything but hugged her even longer. No words were needed to express what we both felt.

Rose Dawson was a career woman, who spent thirty-five years in the Atlanta Public School system. Her heart was evident and my connection with her lasted. After graduating from Morris Brown College, Mrs. Dawson applied to the University of GA for her Master's in Speech Pathology. At the time, the University of GA was not accepting African Americans for their program, so instead of admitting Mrs. Dawson into their program, the State paid for her to go to Columbia University. She and I would remain close until her passing.

The next step in our relationship was to meet each other's kids. In October, I went to Atlanta to meet Harold's three kids, Brianna, Allen, and Katrina. Our connection was easy and organic. Both girls were taking Mandarin in High School and the eldest, Brianna, had just returned from a study abroad program in China, so their knowledge of the language was already better than mine. Allen was especially easy to connect with because I was only accustomed to dealing with boys and he too played football. I was especially careful not to try to be their Mom but someone in their life. Harold would later be able to help me become more comfortable in my role as a second mom to his children and it has been extremely rewarding to be a Mom of five beautiful children.

When Harold came to meet Sam and Jay, the moment he walked into the sitting area our dog Monchi ran to the sliding glass doors and started barking. We went over to the door and saw a blue snake that seemed to be trying to get inside. I thought, how appropriate. I already had the snake experience and believe that snakes indeed symbolize transformation and rebirth. Was I being reminded that my transformation and rebirth were still ahead of me? It was in 2006 when the three snakes approached my pool chair and another one entered the house. I had always wondered why the extra snake. The three in my mind represented PoPo, Dad, and Jeffrey. The one in the bedroom that had just willingly slithered out the door was a mystery. Did the snake that graciously left know it would be back? But this one was blue. The blue color of the Blue Jay bird I always associated with Jeffrey. I think you know what I believe. Yes, I took it as a sign that Jeffrey was coming to acknowledge and bless the magnitude of the meeting. Finally, I was where I was supposed to be.

Sam as usual was reserved, but Jay was happy to meet Harold. When I had mentioned to Sam that Harold is Black, simply because I thought the kids should know beforehand, he looked at me crossed-eyed as if to say what century was I living in. Our own family was a mix of everything and it was a complete non-issue. It wasn't long before the boys came to adore, admire, and love Harold and Sam would go on to say his new family should have come into his life sooner.

Since the meeting of our children went so well, we decided the kids should meet each other, especially since they had been asking to do so for some time and so the Dawson kids would come to Florida for Thanksgiving. It turned out that Allen's football team had a post-season championship game, so Harold and Allen couldn't come to Florida until the Friday after Thanksgiving. Instead, Brianna and Katrina came on Wednesday and this enabled Sam and Jay to get to know the girls first. Katrina and Sam bonded over Wiz Khalifa. They both loved the rapper and their music taste was the same.

For Thanksgiving, my girlfriend Tracy Mourning, invited us to have Thanksgiving with her and her family whom I had known for several years. I knew that Tracy would make the girls feel comfortable and help me with connecting with teenage girls. Like my boys, the Dawson children had Asian blood as their mother is half-Filipino. The children instantly bonded over music and similar interests and it was like they had always known each other. Everyone got along well and then when Allen arrived it was as if they all had been childhood friends.

Everything went so well, we decided to spend Christmas together in Atlanta.

Shortly after Christmas, the three boys came to me and Harold and said they needed to speak with us. The boys had decided that Allen needed to move to Florida to be with his "brothers." They told us that Florida had better high school football and that Allen would have better opportunities playing in Florida. Allen was in tenth grade and planned to play Division One football in college. Within a couple of months and with his mother's blessing, Allen was applying to high schools in Florida and it was decided he would move in with me, Sam, and Jay. They were amazing together. Allen and Sam being only one month different in age had a special relationship, and like true siblings, they would fight and carry on like my own brothers used to do when we were young.

Nine months after Harold and I met, Harold's son moved into my home in Florida and attended the same school as Sam and Jay. By the time school started, Allen was referred to as Sam and Jay's brother and my son. At first, it seemed odd that people would say son rather than stepson, but in hindsight, Harold and I were the ones to set that precedent in motion. We didn't want to differentiate between the kids and thus did not assign the normal "step" to our children when we spoke about our kids. To this day, our kids act and co-exist as one family unit. While there is always something going on with one of the kids, we always act as one strong and undivided unit and as we say, we always have each other's back. We are a "ride or die" family. Growing up my favorite television show was *The Brady Bunch*. I have seen every episode several times. I call our family "The Blasian Bunch" or Modern-Day Brady Bunch.

Story Thirty-four

SIGNS, SIGNS, EVERYWHERE THERE ARE SIGNS

My belief in a life beyond this life is something I have shared with very few people. Only those I am close to. And even then, I don't say much until I feel a connection or someone asks me to, "Tell us your story about…."

The first time I spent the night with Harold, we'd shared our life stories and of course, part of my story was all the stories I have regarding "signs." After I was finished, Harold, who is extremely practical, levelheaded, intelligent, and brought up in a Presbyterian Church, looked at me and said, "My Big Mama used to tell me stories like you just did." This gave me confidence and a sense of validation. Sometimes I sense people are more fascinated by, more than in believing my stories. I told Harold, "I think the more you believe, the more you receive." Me, I am always receiving signs, which make me feel happy and hopeful.

One night Harold and I were sleeping in at my house when Harold woke up because he said he felt someone sitting on his legs.

He opened his eyes but did not see anyone but could feel the weight of someone. He immediately thought it was Jeffrey. He said the feeling he got was that Jeffrey was sending him a message; *Harold you are where you should be and should stay put.* A sort of passing of the torch, one could think. The funny story Harold tells is that when we first started dating and he came to my house everything belonging to Jeffrey was where it had always been. Instead of being upset that I hadn't yet let go of the past, he simply informed Jeffrey that he'd have my back from now on, right there in Jeffrey's closet.

A couple of years after we met, Harold's father passed away from the cancer he had been fighting for years. His funeral was a beautiful tribute to a man of strength and courage. At his funeral which was held at the Martin Luther King Jr. International Chapel at Morehouse College, filled with dignitaries, associates, men whom Harold Sr. had throughout his career mentored, and family and friends from near and far. There were speeches from The Reverend Dr. Joseph E. Lowry and the Honorable Congressman John R. Lewis. The eulogy was presented by Ambassador Andrew Young. It was an affair that Harold Dawson Sr. would have been very proud of, especially the heartfelt words expressed by his children, Cari and Harold Jr.

Not long after Mr. Dawson's funeral, Harold and I were sitting in our kitchen when a Blue Jay with a red Cardinal appeared outside the window. From my understanding, Blue Jays are very territorial birds, so when it arrived with a Cardinal, both Harold and I thought, "Oh my God, it's Jeffrey and Dad. How incredible is it that both birds would come to us. They both sat on a branch outside the window we were sitting so I acknowledged them by saying, "Hi Jeffrey and Mr. Dawson" and after a few minutes they flew away. Ever since then, we have seen the two of them together wherever we go. We have even seen them together in other cities when we travel. It became a common occurrence for us. The spiritual symbolism of a red Cardinal is a sign that those we have lost live on forever as long as we keep their memories in our hearts.

One day, I was with Harold's helper Mr. Willoughby, buying a gift for Mrs. Dawson. Mrs. Dawson had advanced Alzheimer's and eventually had to live in a memory care unit in Atlanta. I was going to buy an insulated cup with a pretty butterfly on it when Mr. Willoughby looked at the cup behind the one I'd picked up and said, "This is the cup you need to buy." The cup had a big red Cardinal on it. While I thought he was exactly correct, because of my experiences with the Cardinals, I was wondering why Mr. Willoughby said what he did. When I asked why he had insisted on the cup with the Cardinal, he said, "Because Mr. D. always said he would come back as a Cardinal." And so, it is….

A few years after Mr. Dawson, Mrs. Dawson passed away. Unlike the pomp and circumstance of Mr. Dawson's funeral, Mrs. Dawson's funeral was intimate and all about love. At her funeral, different students spoke about how she had changed their lives for the better.

Harold had lost his rock when his mother died and he was going through some transitions himself. His hard-charging life was not going the way he wanted, and he missed his parents dearly. He was in a bit of a funk. He would wonder how I could wake up every morning and be so happy. At times it would annoy him, but when he realized that this was truly who I was, he too started to lean into some of my spiritual beliefs. Likewise, he was the person who empowered me to begin to understand financial wisdom and he always encouraged me to step into the light. Being a nurturing person by nature, I prefer to be in a supporting role but I have been learning to claim my spotlight. Harold and I are a perfect fit. It was scary at first, but we brought and still bring out the best of each other's gifts.

Not long after the funeral, Harold and I were again in the kitchen when along came the Blue Jay, the male Cardinal, and this time a female Cardinal was with them. The three birds sat together on a branch outside our window until we acknowledged them and this time included Mrs. Dawson. To this day, even though we have moved homes, we still see the Blue Jay with the male and female Cardinal all the time. I always say, "hi" to them by name as I feel that is what I should do if they are visiting me. It's gotten to be so commonplace with us, even the kids when they are with us and see the birds, know who they are. They too acknowledge their presence, and it is a beautiful thing.

Story Thirty-five

I DO, I DO

For my birthday, I decided to see Leslie, the audio-voyant again. Leslie looked at me with a big smile and said, "Well Christina, you are getting married again." I told Leslie there was no way I was getting married. Harold and I were perfectly happy with our relationship and did not feel we needed to get married.

Ignoring my response she said, "It is interesting. It looks like there are two perfect times for you to get married. The first looks to be more administrative or something and will be in September. The second is definitely the best and will be at Thanksgiving."

I laughed at Leslie's prediction and said, "First of all, who gets married at Thanksgiving? That's crazy."

Like I usually do, I kept what was said at the reading to myself. I consider the information to be interesting and somewhat entertaining but do not make changes to my life according to what I am told or change any plans on anything that is said. I loved my life with Harold but like with Jeffrey I didn't want to marry but for completely different reasons. We were mature, had our children, were content, and were both relatively independent.

The kids were swell and got along great. What would marriage change? One afternoon, while walking into a movie theater, Harold turned to me and said, "I think we should get married."

Honestly, I never thought that I would marry again. Sam and Jay were in their late teens and our blended family situation was working very well. Even our relationship with Anisa, Harold's ex-wife, was very good. When Allen moved in with me and the boys, he missed his mom. We would fly Anisa down on the weekends to see some of his football games and she'd stay with us at the house. When we had school meetings, Anisa was always included. Everything in our life was so civilized, devoid of chaos and so real.

To others outside our family, the relationship may have seemed strange, but my feelings were that Anisa is and always will be the mother to Brianna, Allen, and Katrina, and as a mother I respect and honor that position. Also, whatever happened between Anisa and Harold was between them and happened years before we met, so why would I have a problem with her? Anisa and Harold had a good parenting alliance, I wouldn't want to disturb that, and I admired how they decided to go on with their lives separately yet maintain a cordial co-parenting relationship. I respected them and being who I am, have the capacity for emotional tolerance and egalitarianism. There was never contention around this matter. Besides, I knew where Harold's heart belonged and where mine was meant to be. Right where it was.

Even though everything seemed to be perfect, there was still a little part of me that was skeptical, given all that I had been through with my previous relationships and as a result while driving one day, I asked out loud for a sign from my angels to let me know if this relationship was right.

A few days later, I was on my way home, when I saw people looking at the lake in our community. I slowed down trying to see what the attraction was when I saw a beautiful white Swan in the middle of the lake. I had never seen a Swan before and knew that this was not normal, which is why people had stopped to take photos. I thought *that's so cool* then continued on my way home.

Three days later, as I was driving by and getting used to seeing the Swan, the thought popped up in my mind. *Oh my God, my sign!*

I immediately thought of my dad saying I would be a beautiful Swan and how this must be his sign. He was telling me that Harold was the one.

I slowed my car down, looked at the Swan, and thanked my dad for sending me this sign. Later, that afternoon, when I drove back towards my home, I noticed that the Swan was gone.

Get married again? Why rock the boat?

Harold and my relationship were diametrically opposite from what mine and Jeffrey's had been. We were true partners in every way. Knowing how practical and logical Harold is, I thought if he thinks we should get married, then we probably should. So, I looked at him and said, "Okay" and that was that.

Earlier in the year, Chad had been sentenced and incarcerated, but I did not get any of my money back. I was still in debt on the three hundred thousand dollars hard money loan and Harold was rebuilding from the fallout in the real estate industry. After a few offers on my house fell through, I decided to just sell it for just about what Jeffrey had paid for it in 1995. Even though we had put in a million dollars of renovations, I knew that I had to sell to get out of debt. So, I accepted the low offer and we had a closing date in December. The sale of the house would be the last piece of something I shared with Jeffrey and I felt the time was right. This would allow me to move forward with Harold on a clean slate.

The week after Harold's "practical proposal of marriage," he and I were at our attorney's office preparing our Estate Plan, when Harold told Jourdain we would get married sometime. Jourdain was so overjoyed and when he saw that we hadn't made any plans yet, he said, "What better time than now? I can legally marry you two here, right now."

So, once again, I got married on the spot, without any prior preparations. The date was September 18, 2013. Both Harold and I thought, what an auspicious date 9/18. The significance of the number nine in Chinese Culture means long-lasting, maximum level of mortal happiness, and luck whereas the number eighteen in Judaism is Chai or life.

While driving home, we were excited, but Harold said, "We can't tell the kids. They would be unhappy if we got married without them."

With Sam and Allen up in Connecticut at post-graduate boarding schools, Brianna at the University of Southern California, Katrina in Atlanta, and Jay with us in Boca Raton, the only time the family would be together to have a ceremony was Thanksgiving. So, on November 30th, Harold and I were married by Ambassador Andrew Young at our home in Boca Raton. Each of the kids read a letter they prepared for us and Harold and I read the vows we made not only to each other but to our kids, too.

It was a beautiful ceremony that exuded pure, unconditional love. We only had people whom we had both known and who meant the most to us in attendance. That evening we invited friends to celebrate, for the last time, in the home Jeffrey and I had bought. The next day, we packed up in preparation for closing on the sale of the house. We were moving out to start a new life together in our new home as the Wilson Dawson Family. It was only right to leave the past behind.

As Ambassador Young said in his wedding speech, we were creating what Martin Luther King coined as a Beloved Community with our multi-ethnic and multi-cultural family. It is as if the whole planet was coming together in our union as a family.

My life had been transformed and renewed and life was predictable, serene, exciting, and comforting, with our commitment and emotional togetherness, I knew, without a doubt, that my Prince had arrived. Harold and I have been together for over thirteen years and, pardon the cliché, we only get better with age.

Story Thirty-six

A DECADE AND MORE OF WEDDED BLISS

My steps had indeed been ordered. I had found the man who I could give my heart to for safekeeping. I now understood what love was supposed to feel like and I thanked my infinite source for leading me to Harold, the only man I have genuinely loved.

Ten years later, after putting all five kids through college: Brianna to the University of Southern California, Allen to Boston College, Sam to Williams College, Katrina to New York University, and Jay to Boston College, Harold and I are happily living a peaceful and transparent life together. We travel, love, and love some more.

For our tenth anniversary, Harold and I decided to take the five kids and their significant others to Italy to celebrate our Wilson Dawson union. Harold and I had to stop up in NYC for a wedding on Saturday, September 16th, and then fly out to Milan to meet our kids, who arrived a day earlier, in Tuscany. When our car service picked us up at LaGuardia Airport, the driver greeted us on the sidewalk with a smile and said, "Wilson." I thought he was confirming my last name being Wilson (the reservation was in my name), so I responded, "Yes,

Wilson." I expected him to turn around to open the car door for me, but he stood there with a smile and once again said, "Wilson." Confused a bit, I looked at him, repeated myself, and said, "Yes, Wilson."

Once again, the driver looked at me with a smile and said, "Wilson." Before I repeated myself, Harold said, "I think he is saying his name is Wilson," so I said, "Oh, okay, hi," and then he turned around and opened the back door for me to get in.

When I got into the car I looked at Harold and giggled at what had transpired. I asked Harold if he could read the driver's name tag that was on the front dashboard and he said, "Looks like his name is Millson" and we laughed. As the driver pulled up to the hotel where the wedding party was staying, I looked out the car window and thought *wow, this brings back memories.* We were driving up past the Wall Street area and pulling up to the now-closed American Stock Exchange, where Jeffrey made his start as an Options Trader. I had not been back to that area in over twenty years, so all my New York memories came flooding back. To my surprise, the car stopped right on the corner, where the hotel we were booked at happened to be.

When we went to check in to the hotel, I walked up to the front desk and gave my name to the receptionist. The receptionist looked at me and said, "Wilson?" I assumed she was asking if that was the name on the reservation, so I said yes, "Wilson. Christina Wilson." The woman smiled and again asked "Wilson?' I thought to myself, *what the heck is it with everyone saying Wilson today,* then clarified, "Yes, I am Christina Wilson."

"I have a reservation." Harold and I looked at each other a little dumbfounded.

The woman laughed and said, "Oh, I thought you were asking for Wilson. My associate, who just left the desk, is named Wilson." I thought *this is so strange.* We were back where it started but we were just passing through.

Unbeknownst to me, our trip to Italy was actually a 4-day long Surprise Anniversary celebration that Harold had orchestrated. He invited about twenty special friends and family members and swore them all to secrecy about the trip because I once told him that I could never be surprised, as I am always the person doing the organizing. With my financial acumen, and I was really good at it, I was handling all of our accounting and financing for the business. I had even become a tax pro! But with help from our cousin, Jennifer, our friend, and Harold's business partner, Dennis, Harold was able to pull off the greatest surprise I have ever witnessed.

I thought we were meeting the kids and their significant others for dinner, but instead, I walked out of the hotel to find all our friends, my Uncle John, cousin Jennifer and her husband Brandon, and my brother Alan with his fiancée, Dina, waiting for us. It took several minutes for me to put it all together. I was overwhelmed with emotions that everyone was in Tuscany as a surprise celebration for me. I am usually the person who does things for others. I get so much joy out of making others happy and really do not like to celebrate myself. Maybe from having a summer birthday, where I wouldn't have birthday parties like the kids who had school-year months birthdays, I rarely make a big deal when it comes to my birthday. So, when I realized that everyone came all the way to Tuscany, it was extremely humbling and touching.

Before the dinner started, Harold suggested that we go around and introduce each guest and how they were a part of our lives. When I got to my girlfriend Gina, whose insistence was the reason I had met Harold, I started telling a story, and just as I said, "When Jeffrey..." and all of a sudden, one of the legs on my brother Alan's table broke, but he quickly caught it before everything crashed down. Everyone was silent and then our cousin Jennifer yelled out, "It's Jeffrey!"

Right then I realized the signs that Jeffrey had been sending...the driver saying Wilson, the receptionist at the hotel which happened to be next to the American Stock Exchange saying Wilson, and then the table breaking just as I said his name aloud. I knew that Jeffrey was letting me, and Harold know that he was present and celebrating our marriage with us. Jeffrey, after all, had led me to Harold.

The next night, Harold and I had a spectacular private dinner at Villa Garzoni Garden in the Tuscan town of Collodi, the birthplace of Pinnochio. After taking family photos at the top of the Villa, we descended to the garden to join our guests. When I arrived at the bottom of the long flight of stairs, I noticed a beautiful fountain in the middle of the garden. When I looked closer, I couldn't believe my eyes. Swimming in the water fountain were a pair of big white Swans. I had been so overwhelmed and moved by the outpouring of love from all our guests and family, and especially finally fully accepting the true love Harold had for me was real and pure and grateful for the comfort I had felt with him all these years…I could finally let go of the last shard coving my heart and it shattered. When I saw the Swans, it was the final validation that this marriage was meant to be…*beshart* (destiny in Yiddish), and I had arrived at my point of destination. My father and Jeffrey were with us, blessing and celebrating our ten years together, and telling us that, like Swans who chose a mate for life, we are meant to be mates for life. My search had ended. My life had been perfectly ordered and my Prince Charming was and will forever be by my side, I hope, until death do us part.

Story Thirty-seven
HINDSIGHT IS TWENTY-TWENTY

With life changes, you can lose and gain so much: friends, love, and even yourself. Selves you didn't even know you had to lose…and then a new dawn…a new love; the right love comes and then you understand the journey. Like a diamond, I have withstood the pressures of living and I can truly say I feel like a brilliant yellow diamond. I have walked in my path without judgment or criticism, giving what I had to give…love.

As I sit here now at almost sixty years old, I can look back over my life and say, this life has been quite a journey. One can never appreciate the moment until looking back. I never knew how strong I was until it was my only choice. My choices too have impacted people in ways I am yet to understand. It's the Butterfly Effect.

As much as I have given the best of me to my kids and loved them with all my heart, their journey is not mine. The impact of my life choices on them will be their journey and I hope my love has paved the way for them to embrace and live their lives as is needed for their own spiritual attainment.

Of one thing I am certain…for *my* life everything, that has happened to me, happened for me, and for a reason. My steps were perfectly ordered. I have arrived at a place of true understanding of who I am and am not. It is only then that I came to realize that one cannot love another until they love themselves. I believe the sacred bond I made with our universal source when I inhabited my physical bodies from lifetimes forgotten was to love. I have "loved" with rose-colored glasses, I have loved with sacrifice and I have loved because…

This life has acquainted me with all the lessons I needed to learn to attain bliss and claim my joy. In this earthly lifetime, the lessons I had to learn came in the form of challenges and obstacles to overcome along the way.

Each of us is on a journey and every journey is as different as each of our fingerprints. Of the seven billion people on earth, no two fingerprints are alike. That is why we cannot judge another. Each journey is singular and if we don't learn the lesson the first time around, we will be presented the same lesson in another fashion until we learn the lesson. Most significantly, because my mom had come to dislike Chad, this led to a rift between us and my asking my mom to leave our home in Boca Raton. What might have appeared harsh turned out to be the catalyst for my mom to have her own independent life for the first time in *her* life. At eighty-five, she calls this her "selfish time" but I see it as being her well-deserved reward time for all the sacrifices she'd made for all her children and grandchildren. My mom continues to inspire me and I cherish the ability to talk with her every day.

If you ask me now why I was paired with Jeffrey, I might venture to say Jeffrey might have been a young spiritual soul completely given over to an ego-bound world, who needed paring with an older soul who needed confirmation of the distance it had come on its own spiritual journey. I know that I am still evolving and life is constantly teaching me, but I also recognize how far I have come and how I have gotten here and I couldn't feel any more blessed. There is no doubt in my mind that there is something or someone greater than us. The something or someone I believe is what some people call God. I believe this to be true, but not in a conventional religious way. I believe that God, Allah, Yahweh, Buddha, and Source are with and for everyone, no matter what religion one claims because God is simply LOVE and there is nothing greater than Love. And love, neither Eros nor Philia but Agape, is the full recognition of the Love inside yourself.

Initially when finding out about Jeffrey's accident, I had responded similarly to how my mom had responded when I was in a coma. From her actions and experience, I learned to listen to my gut instincts. Something told my mom to get me out of the first hospital and that same thing told me to find Jeffrey another doctor. In the thirteen months of keeping Jefferey alive, I believe he might have finally grasped the concept of unconditional love. That's why the situation unfolded the way it did. To have been able to get the treatment he did, money was necessary, and he had made that money just for those moments. My struggles with Jeffrey taught me to be a stronger woman but also affirmed the strength I possessed that allowed him to grow on this path. It also showed me how far along my path of acceptance and nonjudgement I had come and what I needed to work on in this lifetime. My childhood of being sickly and being the "Ugly Duckling" with Prince Charming dreams might have set me on a path of acquiescence because who would be able to love me? It also set me up to accept obsession as love. Yet that love/obsession had given me two of the most amazing children, made me a citizen of the world, and opened me up to the love that was intended for me.

Today I am a woman who stands up for herself and is not afraid to be alone. A woman who is not controlled by money and is no longer naive. A woman who will not be bullied or abused into being who she is not. A woman who knows and can give love is all I have learned and I am truly thankful for every experience I went through—the good, the bad, and the downright ugly. If I hadn't learned to be the strong woman I became, I never would have had the courage, integrity, or determination to keep Jeffrey alive in his last thirteen months. Those months, I believe, showed Jeffrey he could receive love and taught him one of the lessons he might have been here for. It might also have given him the blessings he needed to step into his new life of fulfillment when he was ready. By showing him that all the money in the world could not save his life but all the love he deserved tried; I pray his new incarnation brings him the goodness his heart always knew.

While I was conned by the unscrupulous Damien because my naivëte and single-minded focus on Jeffrey allowed him to steal all the money Jeffrey made, I basked in the simplicity and beauty of a life in moderation. Still with my head in the sand however, not wanting to believe I could let this happen again, I was once again conned by Chad, in a different but just as or even more unscrupulous and impactful way. I did eventually learn my lesson to be more careful with my finances and to appreciate that money itself is but a neutral tender that responds to its director's command.

The thing is, that money was never mine but Jeffrey's. The outcome of the money reiterated the adage, that what goes up must come down. Still, as Jeffrey's partner, I should have understood the value of a dollar and respected the work it took to make it and not just take it for granted as I always had in the past. Jeffrey's hard work was for his money and that deserved respect. But most importantly, I have learned that it isn't money that makes you happy. Money can pay for the comforts of life, but it does not make you happy nor does it make you better than anyone else. The lengths to which people will go for money are frightening. The things the love of money will make people do, even worse. When Jeffrey and I were together we had the most money I have ever had, yet I was the most unhappy in my life. There is no correlation between money and happiness.

While Chad was a liar, cheat, and thief, the traits I most detest, I do believe he came into my and my boys' lives for some positive and negative reasons. Because of Chad, both Sam and Jay decided to play football. The game of football was instrumental in teaching the boys the lessons of being a part of a team, working and sacrificing hard to achieve a goal, to toughen up mentally and physically (being raised by a mom and Nana couldn't teach this), and so many other character-building attributes. It also allowed Sam to express his suppressed anger, because to this day he finds it hard to forgive Chad for his betrayal. My interlude and rebound experience with Chad compelled me to stop being so trusting, presumptuous, and naïve about my life and my finances.

The tragedy of losing Jeffrey also taught me a tremendous amount about advocating for my health and the health of those I care for and how important it is not to just take one doctor's diagnosis as certitude. It is always best to get more than one medical opinion and research on your own to learn all you can about your health. I always say, "Without your health, you have nothing."

Most of all, this journey has affirmed the distance I have come and that I can get through life's greatest adversity and come out stronger. But likewise, to believe that fairytales can indeed come true. They may not appear or present like a Disney story, but I am a believer in making a wish as eventually, it will come true. My Prince Charming didn't ride in on a white horse, quite the contrary. He walked through the glass doors, bathed in sunlight, into my life, and changed it forever.

Harold has been the catalyst of the greatest growth and change for me, Sam, and Jay. He is always there, dependable, generous, honest, compassionate, intelligent, hard-working, and the loving man I had always wished for; my life has never been better. After we met, I took out the list I had made and kept it in my wallet and if I could have created a man from the traits I wrote down, that man would be Harold. Harold is truly my "Ride or Die." With Harold, I know true love. I know that love doesn't ask permission, it just moves boldly and with certainty through the heart, caring very little about what tomorrow brings. Together we have traveled a road where love has revealed itself—as truly unconditional.

My time at the Hearts and Hope group taught me to be vulnerable and trust others with my deepest fears and feelings. The connection and sisterhood that came out of our group therapy changed my life. A couple of years ago, with so many people losing their loved ones from the Pandemic, I got together with five of the women from my group and we started a Grief Support Podcast. Initially, we thought we might be able to help a few people, who didn't have a support group to attend, by telling our stories and sharing our experiences. Now, we have created a successful tool that many people around the world are listening to and finding hope and healing from our podcast, Sisterhood Through Grief. To be able to give back and help others has been an incredibly humbling and rewarding experience.

There is a poem that expresses how friends come into your life in three ways: a reason, a season, or a lifetime.

I truly understand and believe that this is the case. I have been so fortunate to have so many great friends. Some who came into my life for a specific reason; some who have been friends for a short but important time; and then the lifetime friends and family-like friends, who have been my support system, my guidance, my protection, my teachers, and my always there by my side crew. It is said that "it takes a village" and I have been blessed with a wonderful one.

Family is and always has been my superpower. The support and unconditional love that I receive from my mother and siblings have enabled me always to forge forward in life without feeling lonely or alone. Now, I am the mother of five children, and we have the same unique and incredible bond. My family fills me with purpose, strength, and enormous love.

Looking back through the rear-view mirror of my life, I can honestly say that I have zero regrets. My life up to now has been sensational. I have learned the life lessons that I have been challenged with thus far, which have contributed to the person I am now. I am an accumulation of my past events; things that happened for me, not to me. I know that I will be given more to learn, but due to my strong sense of beliefs, I am optimistic about my future and continued evolution. Undeniably, I know I have come this far because I believed.

This is my memoir of stories and life lessons. Life can be messy and complex. People can be messy and complex. But each person's journey could be leading them to the place they truly belong—to discover the diamond waiting to be polished to brilliance. My life has been mine and mine alone to experience and here is what I know: Life is held up as a mirror to the soul, all we need to do is look. Life is not something to regret. It is something to experience. Every experience is a step along the path to the full realization of who you are at your core. There should be neither judgment, explanation nor expectation about your life because it is just what it is—a lesson in self-discovery. I believe I have withstood and I have been made to gleam. There are more lessons I have yet to learn and I welcome them because I know I'm a Believer.

ACKNOWLEDGEMENTS

Marva Allen—I believe that it is our destiny to have met and completed this book, as I knew in my heart that you saw me, maybe even more than I see myself. I am grateful for your magical editing. Taking something black and white and making it come to life in illuminating brilliant color. Thank you for making this a reality.

Patrice Samara—Thank you for giving me the courage to be vulnerable and convincing me that my stories need to be told. Your just-do-it coaxing made this endeavor come to being.

My mom—I am, because of you. Your unconditional love has taught me how to love and give love unconditionally. I am forever grateful for your presence and support throughout every moment of my life.

Sam and Jay—Truly my heartbeats. I live and breathe every day for you both. I wrote down these stories with the hope that you can always understand my life and who I am. You are my greatest blessings.

My husband, Harold—You absolutely love me for who I am, which fills my heart daily. Your wisdom and intellect have taught and continue to teach me to be a wiser and better person. I now know what true love is with you. Thank you for making my fairytale come true.

Brianna and Katrina—I am blessed to have been given two daughters. You both are a big reason why I finished this book. I hope my life lessons will teach you the importance of inner strength, self-love, and healthy love.

Allen—From the day that you came into my, Sam's, and Jay's lives, it was a perfect fit. You are my bonus-son. I cherish our deep and honest conversations and appreciate your enthusiastic listening.

My heavenly husband, Jeffrey—My time with you made me become the strong and independent woman that I am. I have had the most incredible experiences with you, which provided me with beautiful memories that are always on the top of my mind. I am most grateful for the gifts of our sons, who would not exist without you.

My heavenly Dad—whose hard work, sacrifices, and dedication to me and my siblings have never gone unnoticed. I wish that I had more time with him but know that he is always with me.

My siblings—Anita, Betty, Alan, Brian, and Sieu Fong too. The unique bond I share with my siblings is rare and beautiful. The support and love that is always there have enabled me to be who I am and survive all I have been through. I hope that my five children will share this same special bond that we possess.

My family—My aunts, uncles, cousins, nieces, nephews, Cari, and John. My greatest joys come from being with family. I am blessed with a very large family and this is what makes my life so fun and interesting.

Fran, Herb, and Nicole Wilson—Thank you for your unwavering support and love. You are one of the Jeffrey's greatest gifts to me and my family.

Joyce Silverman—From the moment we met, you have been my greatest support system. Your friendship knows no bounds. I don't know how I could have made it through the darkest of days without your love and support.

Anthony Liggins—I am grateful for your friendship. You have been the conduit to some of my most life-changing events.

Amy Gao—Thank you for giving all of yourself to take care of me and my family. You so happily made my life so much easier.

My sisterhood of strong women who have been there for me at different times of my life.

My New Yorkers—Helen Herssens, Annie Hausman, Bridgette Gottlieb, Karen Krieger, Minh Oishi

My Miami Sisters – Gina Ford, Tracy Mourning.

My Boca Ladies – Chris Golden, Rona Goldberg, Robyn Chwatt, Johanna DeKama, Amy Cavayero, Robin Rubin, Brooke Porter, Mara Reuben, Roxane Lipton, Sheila Fuente.

My Yackity Yaks – Marsha Eisenberg, Wendy Zoberman and heavenly Kim Lindsey and Eliette Otero-Romano.

My Hood Girls – Jane Martinez, Betsy Reed, Stacey Baum, Jennifer Matts, Alex Mores.

Families who have taken care of and supported me, Sam, and Jay through our lives: Gonzalez, Eisenberg/Krieg, Lindsey/Lambert, Goldberg, Herssen, Silverman, Ford, Mourning.

The doctors, nurses, aides, and therapists—who came into my life at the worst of moments and who provided me with strength and hope to get through the most traumatic of times.

The other men in my life who have been there when the boys or I needed some male support—Joe Hood, Andy Friis, Ezra Krieg, Joe Goldberg, Alexis Somoano.

My Hearts and Hope Family—Patrice Austin, Ami Reece, Brenda Firestone, Kris McNeal, Melanie Perkins, Patti Karoussos, Nisa Birnbaum, Lillian Fennell. I can't imagine how I could have gotten through my grief without the love, understanding, and support I received from you special women. We walked a tough journey and got to the end of the last bridge together with each other's strength and support.

My secret readers: Kaeli Subberwal, George Allison, Juliana Cavallaro, Mara Reuben. Thank you for reading through and helping me edit the manuscript draft. I appreciate the time you spent, the suggestions you made, and the edits you marked to help create this book.

Tisha Hallet—Thank you for creating the greatest changes in me in my most dire time of need. Your confidence in me provided me with the inner strength and self-love I now possess. Your friendship, advice, and help have been invaluable. I highly recommend your therapy services to anyone looking to find peace in their life. (directyourmind@yahoo.com)

M. Gary Neuman & Moshe Winograd—Thank you for your compassionate advice and life-changing family therapy. You both are experts at creating a cohesive and strong family centered on love.

My Guardian Angels—Dad, PoPo, Jeffrey, Kim, Willis, Mr. and Mrs. Dawson. I get the signs and feel your presence all the time, which fills me with hope and provides me with a sense of protection and incredible love. Thank you for always watching out over me.

Last, but definitely not least—To me, God is Love. Every day I thank God for blessing me and keeping me safe, protected, healthy, and prosperous.

www.ingramcontent.com/pod-product-compliance
Lightning Source LLC
Chambersburg PA
CBHW051615010526
44107CB00037B/1434/J